ARTS
AWARENESS

A FIELDBOOK FOR AWAKENING CREATIVE CONSCIOUSNESS
IN EVERYDAY LIFE

PATRICIA HOY

"Patricia Hoy invites the reader to apply insights distilled from her long career as a performing musician and conductor to the art of living, working and leading with vitality, joy and meaningful achievement. But take your time. This is a thought-provoking Zen-like stroll. Hoy's insights and the stories she uses to illustrate them stem from a powerful little-examined source. They form the foundation that supports the 'creativity and possibility thinking' of successful artists. These proprietary truths cannot help but shift your perspective and elevate the quality of your life. As you make your way through Hoy's compelling *Arts Awareness Fieldbook*, don't be surprised if you find yourself becoming more effective, and at the same time, more playful. Such is the magic (and wisdom) of art."

— Margaret Martin, DrPH, MPH
Harmony Project Founder & National Director

"*Arts Awareness* brings to life the principles that artists of all kinds use in their creative process. Dr. Hoy's stories and examples make it easy for readers to employ these principles in their own art. The questions for reflection help readers take a step further, reflecting on how to live a creative, fulfilling life by using the lessons learned in making art of any kind. Collaboration is an integral part of my artistic practice and I found Dr. Hoy's ideas on working with others creative and inspirational. Even seasoned artists will find inspiration to carry their craft to new levels."

— Anne Patterson
installation and theater artist

"In her book, *Arts Awareness*, Patricia Hoy reveals herself as both creative-scientist and arts practice-sociologist. Acutely aware of the human experience, she translates how the nature of inquiry, curiosity, and self-journey, when married to arts and creative practices, can become a road map for a more dimensional awareness, a more dimensional world. For those who argue that the arts and creativity are inconsequential, Ms. Hoy provides a strong argument that life beyond prescribed technical demands can create a wondrous and effective world."

— Peter DiMuro
choreographer/director/teacher
Creative Director, Peter DiMuro/Public Displays of Motion
Executive Director, The Dance Complex, Cambridge, MA

"I have had the great good fortune to attend many of Dr. Hoy's dynamic face-to-face trainings over the years, but now to have her creative and profoundly moving ideas and systems compiled together in one place is remarkable resource. The concepts in this book are nothing short of transformative. A must-read for anyone involved in the arts, anyone who wants to better understand the arts and/or anyone who is striving to find their place, or potential place, as an artist."

— Richard A. McEnaney, EdD
Coordinator, Secondary Fine Arts
Clark County School District, Las Vegas, NV

"Dr. Patricia Hoy, having lived the creative life herself, examines in fascinating detail the artistic life and discusses how educators, administrators, artists and students can transform themselves from highly competent technicians to fearless, inspired risk takers and become transformational artists and leaders."

— Nanci Lee Woody
author, *Tears and Trombones*
Winner of the (IPPY) Independent Publishers Award
for "Best Fiction in The Western Pacific Region."

ARTS
AWARENESS
A Fieldbook for Awakening Creative Consciousness in Everyday Life

PATRICIA HOY

Foreword by Benjamin K. Roe

GIA Publications, Inc.
Chicago

Cover and book design by Martha Chlipala

G-9072

ISBN: 978-1-62277-168-4

Copyright © 2015 GIA Publications, Inc.
7404 S. Mason Ave.
Chicago, IL 60638

GIA Publications, Inc.
www.giamusic.com

GRATITUDES

*A*rts *Awareness* came about from the opportunities to observe and meet and work with countless performers, artists, educators, and community members in diverse settings across the country. My life and work have been deeply touched by so many. The influences and support of all of the students, colleagues, and arts supporters in Flagstaff, Memphis, and Boston are particularly meaningful. I have been blessed with the opportunity to conduct and clinic students from all around the country, engage as a collaborative artist in performance in professional, educational, and semi-professional settings, and interact with true masters in professional associations and organizations. I offer my sincere appreciation and gratitude to all the kindred spirits who have inspired me along the way.

I am particularly indebted to friend and colleague Joseph Edwards for his continuous support, weekly proofreading, and flawless integrity. His wonderfully dry sense of humor and "comma sense" carried me through even the most trying times.

I am especially grateful, too, for paper collage artist and intuitive Chris Donovan for her kindness and patient listening, for sharing her artistic sensibilities, and helping me find my true inner creative voice. For her insight and association, I am profoundly grateful.

Book writing coach Lisa Tener has helped me bring my book to life. She read every word I wrote with care, and I am grateful for the invaluable guidance and editing skills she provided, while encouraging me to evoke my own voice.

For his full support and endless commitment to spreading the word about my work, I offer special thanks to Jake Messier. He continues to promote my *Arts Awareness* concepts, expand opportunities for my speaking and consulting, and build a following through social media and traditional media outlets. I am grateful, too, for Benjamin Roe and his generous and thoughtful words in the Foreword.

Thanks, as well, to Sophie whose wise and independent nature supports everything I do. She walked in my open door one day and, after drinking a little milk from a saucer, decided to stay. Her friendship and intuition cannot be matched.

Finally, I offer thanks to Alec Harris at GIA Publications for his interest in my book, along with the valuable work of Kirin Nielsen and Martha Chlipala. I am deeply appreciative of his support and belief in my *Arts Awareness* concepts.

TABLE OF CONTENTS

FOREWORD

BY BENJAMIN K. ROE

In the mid-twentieth century, *The Age of Anxiety* was, in the words of composer Leonard Bernstein, "the record of our difficult and problematical search for faith." In the first decades of the twenty-first century, the title of W. H. Auden's epic poem (and Bernstein's subsequent symphony) could well serve to describe the anxious state of American education. But this era of STEM, Common Core, and No Child Left Behind has all too frequently left our nation's artistic and cultural literacy behind.

Into this vacuum steps Dr. Patricia Hoy and her unique worldview, forged in her varied and impressive career as an educator, administrator, and performing artist. Just as a great conductor simultaneously leads an orchestra in the moment and prepares them for what's next, Dr. Hoy has produced a timely and indispensable manifesto that offers both practical day-to-day concepts for "creative living," as well as a compelling vision for how understanding and applying an artistic mindset can become a powerful organizing principle for our daily lives. Creativity and flexibility, yes, but not foregoing, as Dr. Hoy puts it, "a will of mental and physical grit."

Whether you draw stick figures or restrict your singing to the shower, with this important *Fieldbook* Dr. Hoy has written a guide about the arts that is designed to unlock the hidden artist in all of us, and with it, a method to tamp down those anxieties of our age, suggesting, "new answers to old problems…new career opportunities, improved living conditions…and new ways to lead."

NPR and WGBH veteran Benjamin K. Roe is a Grammy- and Peabody-award winning producer, broadcaster, speaker, writer, and arts administrator. He currently serves as Executive Director of the Heifetz International Music Institute.

BEGINNINGS

LIFE AS A STAGE

ACTING THE PART

My friends joked about my shiny hair as we traveled to the Music Recital Hall at Sacramento State. You see, my mother had heard the mayonnaise trick! To get the most beautiful and shiniest hair you have ever seen, put mayonnaise on and let it sit for five minutes before washing. In the name of vanity and beauty and in preparation for this important scholarship audition performance, she slathered Hellmann's on my hair. Well, it certainly became soft and shiny—I looked like an extra from *Grease,* and while at first it smelled something like a ham sandwich, as the day wore on it became more like grandma's potato salad. I imagined walking out on stage as the hot lights turned my mayo hair rancid.

Whether from lunacy or courage, I walked out into the lights, acknowledged the applause, positioned my flute, and began to play. Something truly remarkable happened. I discovered that while a distraction might seem overwhelming in a performance, with a little mental agility and focus it can actually become something unbelievably special. As I sensed the amusement of my friends in the third row, the distraction of the mayonnaise in my hair inspired me to be carried higher rather than diverting me from my purpose. Although I wasn't fully aware of the nature of my learning that day, it grew clearer at deeper and deeper levels as I continued my education and began my career in the arts.

Experiences in the artistic process can teach you to rise above doubt and distraction.

There is so much to be learned from a journey of lessons in the arts that it is truly astonishing when you take a moment to seriously consider the transformations possible as a result of the obvious—but often unexpected—experiences you encounter along the way. This experience of distraction and focus, and many other lessons that followed, completely opened the artistic process for examination, ultimately revealing its value for thriving amidst the changes and upheaval of the twenty-first century. The knowledge is open to anyone who takes the opportunity to reap the benefits of learning through the arts.

SHARING THE GIFTS

For instance, lessons in the arts helped a former student to extend the success he enjoyed in his individual saxophone practice to ordinary details of his daily life. In the practice room, John dealt with the same problems over and over again on an ever rising level and with corresponding rising success. With this knowledge, he extended the success he enjoyed in his individual saxophone practice to work on a recurring problem in a close family relationship. He learned to use his previous experiences to practice and view the same problem with a new perspective in order to improve his understanding and skill and to successfully deal with the situation. In *Arts Awareness* you can learn new ways to solve problems in your own personal life.

In another instance, several departments in a college had been operating for many years with a "silo mentality." They were unable to see the value of opening up their processes and policies as part of a cohesive institutional initiative, fearful they would lose control and weaken their department, diminishing what they considered to be a position of importance. They learned to use a process that could connect their deep knowledge of how the individual components of a work of art add meaning to the whole—whether theater, dance, music, painting, or poetry—and extend that knowing to the dynamic relationship between the bigger picture and the viewpoints and expression of every part of

The artistic process can help you learn to view everyday challenges with a new perspective.

the organization. They grew to understand that the greater the number of parts, materials and/or people involved in collaborative work, the greater the complexity—but the artistic principles are the same. They thrived as they discovered how the big picture added meaning to their individual departments and how their destiny was beneficially affected by this larger perspective. It allowed them to experience support they hadn't previously experienced and a coherent problem solving mechanism that expanded their options. In *Arts Awareness*, you will discover opportunities to apply insight in leadership, relationships, and community building.

The processes of creating art can help you learn the benefits of a larger perspective.

Kathleen was experiencing a challenging situation as the director of a large children's dance program. She learned to successfully assume this new leadership role through the knowledge she had gained as a dancer. She developed confidence using the same skills of taking risks, being willing to make mistakes, adjusting, and trying again, just as she did in the studio. The self-reflection necessary for high-level dance performance was a fundamental element in her ability to move forward in difficult circumstances. It gave her the ability to live inside the spaces—the rests or silences in music, if you will—giving her the flexibility to handle the unexpected. These experiences helped her handle the mental challenges of maintaining her integrity while in the midst of leading change. *Arts Awareness* will help you gain confidence by learning the value of taking risks, self-reflection, stillness, and flexibility through the many changes in your own life.

Learning experiences in the arts can help you gain confidence and open up new possibilities in everyday life.

THE NEXT ACT

At a time when parents are testing ways to help their children succeed in a world that is unlike anything they experienced and when leaders in our organizations, institutions, schools, communities, family units, and churches are searching for ways to succeed in this dramatically shifting environment, *Arts Awareness* offers a fresh perspective.

There are many challenges in today's world—our education communities, organizations, government, businesses, and family structures seem to always be stumbling forward, constantly judged by others who believe they know what's best. There are endless conflicts over who should make the decisions and what exactly—if anything—needs to be changed or improved. While the solutions are not easy, our private, work, and organizational communities are buffeted around by the continually shifting cure-alls that seem to come forward only to break down time after time, often at the mercy of those in power. This situation creates an environment that does not necessarily serve our best interests—particularly those of our children who deserve quality educational experiences.

Arts educators can make a big impact on the creative consciousness needed in the world today, but they often become frustrated with the idea that they are forced to justify arts education with assessment techniques that disregard the creativity and possibility thinking that come from learning in their disciplines, or to simply validate the way in which it can help learning in math and science or other disciplines. They are often placed in a position to defend the arts from those who look on it as something extra that can easily be reduced or removed in a budget crisis. When they attempt to speak of the values the arts can provide, they often try to use qualities learned such as teamwork, work ethic, responsibility, sense of achievement, and other behaviors that come from the practice or performance of art. These arguments often place the arts in an extremely weak position, and they may be told that sports or other activities can provide the same learning.

All of the arts are vital in our twenty-first century world. There is embedded within the arts disciplines a natural, beautiful, and deep body of knowledge that we haven't even begun to tap. Contemporary thinkers say that the world is experiencing another major paradigm shift. Many of them suggest the need for new ways of being and thinking. It is of great consequence now for artists, arts educators, and creative souls to seriously consider the full depth and breadth of what can be learned

There is a natural, beautiful, and deep body of knowledge embedded in the artistic process that we haven't even begun to tap.

through deep exploration of the principles of artistic expression. People everywhere are looking for new ways to reach out, to interact, and to share their inner spirit with the world. The basic principles of artistic expression can provide the synthesis of creating art with guiding others—teaching, coaching, training—leading, succeeding, and living a more fulfilling life. The imaginative competence and meaningful insight that comes from a deep understanding of the arts and the artistic process offers awareness critical to learning and thriving in contemporary society.

The term artistic process as used in this *Fieldbook* refers to the imaginative, flexible, and dynamic way artists apply their individual concept to the medium they choose. While the basic aspects of the process include certain steps that one must take in making art, the lines between those steps are not distinct— often shared and overlapping from one to another. Each step is in essence a process itself. The general term artistic process is used to refer to these collective processes of creating art.

Is Arts Awareness for You?

Arts Awareness is for everyone—educators, artists, parents, leaders, families, communities, organizations, and businesses. *Arts Awareness* is for educators who want to succeed and help their students thrive in an increasingly complex world. It is for educators, administrators, and leaders at all levels who would consider using the basic principles of artistic expression in the arts in a way that serves as a foundation for their work in guiding others, while at the same time developing their own personal mastery and expressing themselves more fully as human beings. It is for artists who want to reconnect with the love of what they do. It is for parents, arts advocacy groups, and lobbyists. And it is for those in businesses and organizations who face the difficult task of decision-making in a rapidly changing world. It is for anyone who is seeking a dynamic way forward.

Arts Awareness will give you a way to discover, inspire, and promote the learning that comes from the arts. The thoughts

Through the basic principles of the artistic process, you can learn to make informed decisions that move you forward in a dynamic way.

and experiences expressed here can lead to fresh and imaginative experiments with curriculum and advocacy in the arts, personal satisfaction and success in life, as well as useful ways to realize your goals in organizations, communities, families, and businesses. *Arts Awareness* focuses on what is at the heart of a meaningful experience in the arts. Moving forward in this way, you can create new models that will enhance the experiences of those you lead—employees, students, and children—and enhance your own personal expression and experience of life. Regardless of your career, this more expansive view of artistic expression— the value of the arts and its enhanced role in education and our world at large—will lead to more focused efforts, more open hearts and minds, and the ability for everyone involved to enjoy greater success and satisfaction in the increasingly abstract world of twenty-first century society.

Here are some questions to consider:

- How can we integrate the overall patterns of life with new learning that focuses on the expansiveness of creating or performing a work of art?
- What steps can we take to awaken our own enthusiasm, and that of our students, children, friends, and those we lead?
- How can we begin to design a more meaningful curriculum in our schools that maintains a learning environment steeped in the basic principles of artistic expression?
- How do we find a way past typical views of others regarding the purpose and value of the arts?
- What steps can we take to develop forward-thinking business and organizational cultures?
- How can we help employees in businesses and organizations see the bigger picture and develop new broad-based methods of working together?
- Where do we start?

Exploring the arts with an expanded view can lead to greater success and satisfaction in an increasingly complex twenty-first century world.

While this *Fieldbook* is a book of ideas—a body of knowledge—rather than a list of steps that must be followed, it uses the natural dynamic qualities of artistic expression to suggest a new way forward.

Interestingly, in the process of artistic expression there is not one correct path—different people can perform the same piece of music, create a painting, write a story based on the same theme, or teach the same material in different ways, and each path can be fresh, imaginative, and inspired. The only requirement is that each person must use the creative elements in a meaningful fashion, working within, and looking deeply into the principles of artistic expression.

Educators might ask, "But what do I do in my class tomorrow morning?" Parents may say, "But how can I begin to use these concepts immediately to guide my children and strengthen my family?" Leaders could question, "But how do I improve my organization or business right now?" The basic concepts presented here are universal and allow for deep reflection aimed at helping you productively change the way you approach everything in your life. They allow you to enhance and sharpen your skills; they encourage you to imagine the possibilities, build momentum, and create "your own art" in a meaningful way. Each of us, to the extent of our abilities, can adopt the attitudes of artistic process thinking and learning.

My goal is that *Arts Awareness* will not only inspire you personally, but that it will also inspire an ever-increasing and motivated group of arts educators, leaders, lobbyists, and advocacy groups committed to viewing the value of the arts from this more expansive viewpoint. The seven creative concepts presented in this book will serve as a catalyst for experiments and initiatives that foster a stronger position for the value of arts in twenty-first century education.

CHAPTER 1
CREATIVE CONSCIOUSNESS: GOING BEYOND TECHNIQUE

OVERVIEW

An artistic masterpiece is an expression that arises from the authentic inner world of an artist. The expressions are imaginative with multifaceted layers of meaning that make significant connections, often between disparate things, to create a unified whole. The possibilities for this kind of expression come from openness:

- A flexible mindset, open to change, risk, and mistakes
- A will of mental and physical grit to work through chaos until the tension reveals a new way forward
- The energy to tear apart recognized patterns and relationships and put them together in new ways
- The focus to truly get inside and explore your thoughts and beliefs

Creative work arises with desire and courage from the depth of your innermost self. It manifests itself through the artistic process in a way that allows you to share it with others. Although it takes practice, everyone can learn to tap into this imaginative power.

THE SEVEN CONCEPTS

The strategies and tools outlined in this *Fieldbook* are presented as seven concepts designed to stimulate your imagination and help you tap into your creative power. Although it might at first feel a little scary, diving deeply into these concepts can fuel your desire to share and expand the process with your colleagues, students, business partners, or families. Your new inner knowing deepens as you share it with others. Everyone in the shared experience enjoys enhanced communication, greater understanding, more informed decision-making, and the powerful impact of creating together. The seven concepts in *Arts Awareness* are:

- **Back to Basics: Expanding the Building Blocks.** Use the patterns that come from your unique array of internal and external experiences to build and sustain momentum in your life and work.
- **Artistic Expression: Exploring the Wholes and Parts.** Manage the challenge or expressivity of each moment and achieve greater success by maintaining a balanced perspective in relation to the bigger picture.
- **Passion: Critical Partner to Meaningful Action.** Unlock the power of pull by getting inside whatever it is you do with openness and curiosity.
- **Potential: The Power of Possibility.** Manage tension points and releases, and move more easily beyond difficult circumstances while fully enjoying the easier moments.
- **Planning and Momentum: An Unfolding and Evolving Path.** Produce meaningful results and achievements through the stark beauty and freedom of structure.
- **Act, Measure, Adapt: Building a Sense of Commitment.** Take the risk of a first step to reveal new possibilities, new adventures, and new connections that are always within your reach.
- **Fill Your Cup: The Practice and Discipline of Lifelong Learning.** Open from the inside out and allow imaginative ideas to come forward with a constant process of learning and letting go to make way for new understanding and beliefs.

WHY THE SEVEN CONCEPTS?

These concepts represent the core components of the book and flowed naturally out of my experiences as an artist, educator, and administrator. Taking apart each new experience and examining it in relation to the panoramic view of the whole revealed a clear picture of the value and resourcefulness of the artistic process and its ability to transform all of our experiences. From this bigger picture vantage point, the importance of veering from a well-trodden path—of daring to be different and going into the unknown—is essential to access the powerful gifts that come from your own unique set of inner and outer experiences. Any opportunity to connect your deeper understandings from these explorations with others can become a powerful transformative force. This kind of connection is increasingly important in today's rapidly changing, globally interconnected world.

Artists explore their work with much more than their intellect. Delving into the seven concepts with an artist's approach will help you find new answers to old problems, develop new career opportunities, improve your living conditions, understand the arts more deeply, and find new ways to lead or teach others.

EMPOWERING FIELDBOOK FORMAT

Each chapter begins with an overview of the concept, followed by motivational stories, lessons you can apply to your life, and deepening perspectives that come from "the field." Chapters also include Concept Practice, a Summary, questions to stimulate further thought, Artistic Insights, Consciousness Queries, Quick Tips, and Continue the Quest—ways to further explore the topic. The pages are filled with quotes, readings, and examples.

Explore the chapters and, once you have a basic understanding of the contents, if one concept has more appeal for you, go back and pursue it, moving on to others as you see connections. The stories are deeply reflective, aimed at helping you change the way you think and interact. Play with the ideas, reflect on your own stories, and make notes in the margins about your experiments and the results. Study your notes and reflect on where to go next.

You may say I'm a dreamer, but I'm not the only one. I hope someday you'll join us. And the world will live as one.

~ John Lennon
   "Imagine"

The term "artist" as used in this *Fieldbook* is meant to describe people who engage in creating a widely inclusive range of fine and performing art.

Extraordinary changes are taking place in the world today, and there is an important role for the arts and the artistic process in this new environment. If you wonder if you can learn something new here, reflect on your life and work with genuine truthfulness, and ask yourself the following questions:

- How do these ideas show up in the way I create art or live my life?
- In what ways do I—or can I—use these concepts to guide or teach others?
- By what manner do I use these processes in leading or managing others in my community, organization, or business?

Determine your approach making your way through the book based on what you discover from this questioning and reflection.

In artistic work, it is necessary to first master the techniques of the art form so you can use them automatically as a natural means of expression. The effortless use of your creative voice along with the language of the artistic medium is essential to realize your full expressive power. This means that while you do have to use the techniques, you have to go beyond them. Not only does artistic expression suffer, but good teaching or leading or managing cannot be reduced to mere technique either. When you step beyond a technical focus, you become an artist, fully involved in what you are doing, moving with a more playful mindset, and being vulnerable. Your perspective changes completely. The seven concepts are designed to help you go beyond technique.

BEYOND TECHNIQUE

Early in my career at a large public university, our faculty grappled with an important change that would ultimately have an impact on all of us and the students in our department. We could see that a change was needed and that it would open up a whole new world of opportunities for everyone involved. But at the time, there was a general complacency with the way things

Technique, wonderful sound…all of this is sometimes astonishing—but it is not enough.

~ Pablo Casals
  Casals and the Art of Interpretation

were. While we were experiencing some successes, the results were short-lived and becoming less and less meaningful. But the purpose and process for moving in another direction did not seem clear. There seemed no real opportunity to connect the thoughts of everyone who might be affected by changes. We struggled to create a positive urgency that could inspire thinking that would lead to a more expansive vision for the future.

This was on my mind as I went to the studio to coach a student clarinetist on the performance of a solo cadenza he was preparing—part of the first movement of a four-movement work. If you are not familiar with the term "cadenza," it is essentially an ornamental passage placed in a movement of a musical work, like a concerto. It usually allows a great deal of rhythmic freedom for the performer to display virtuosic technique. As I listened to Paul perform the cadenza, it occurred to me that, while the technical aspect of his playing was outstanding and his performance showed some expressive elements, it lacked a general sense of the cadenza as a whole and how it fit with the surrounding parts of the piece. As a result, his playing felt disconnected and lacked direction. It appeared he was confused about the way the notes and rhythms in the cadenza worked together. Paul's playing revealed that, in his mind, the notes and rhythms did not appear to have any organization. They seemed completely separate from the main body of the piece. Because of the lack of unity in his mind, every time he made a mistake, he stopped. In fact, the lack of understanding created mistakes that would not have been there otherwise.

We discussed the solution and spent the rest of the lesson taking it apart, keeping the order of the notes intact but exploring various sections of the cadenza more deeply in terms of their placement and musical function. Next, we worked together to piece it back together again in a way that made more sense. First, we analyzed the basic rhythmic and harmonic structure created by the sequence of notes and grouped them according to their relationship with one another. We placed appropriate pauses, emphasis, dynamic, and tempo variations to fit that underlying structure. The momentum we achieved led beautifully away

The moment a man begins to talk about technique that's proof that he is fresh out of ideas.

~ Raymond Chandler
Selected Letters of Raymond Chandler

We shall have no better conditions in the future if we are satisfied with all those which we have at present.

~ Thomas Edison

from—and back to—the main body of the piece and the cadenza itself felt complete, like a cohesive statement within the overall structure. The result was fantastic. At the end of the hour, Paul performed the cadenza again, but this time it fit together in a way that led to its conclusion with ease and a deep quality of beauty and meaning.

After leaving the room, it struck me that this process was the answer to crafting a plan for change in our university department. Going beyond technique could help us move beyond complacency toward a new vision. The faculty got together with a new mindset and started to explore the issues facing our department with the same analytical skills of working on the cadenza. As we took the various aspects of our operational methods apart and pieced them back together, we experimented with emphasis and focus in an effort to create the momentum we sought. In much the same way as the work on the cadenza, we found the connecting elements and the underlying structure of what we were doing. As we examined it, we discovered the moments that called for pause and reflection and those that required more emphasis. We determined how quickly we should consider certain aspects of the plan and what should be spread out over a longer period of time.

The changes began and we all experienced renewed excitement, clarity, and purpose. The little successes we previously experienced had hindered our growth until we learned to move beyond complacency and create momentum to sustain us well into the future.

The cadenza experience led to my further exploration of compositional unity, the relationship of elements, and the role of momentum. It helped create an image of how the world shapes everyone through events that take place in their personal experiences. The extent to which you are able to expand your awareness and pay attention to all the ways of sensing things can significantly influence your understanding of what happens around you. Taking things apart and putting them back together in a new way can help you create a clear sense of purpose and forge a new path with a different kind of momentum. The result is a deeper awareness that comes from a somewhat complex but natural movement forward.

LANGUAGE OF UNITY

While the contrast of dynamic, rhythmic fluctuation, and emphasis in the cadenza created variety, the unity came from the sense of harmony of the elements in a relationship that brought them all together as a whole expression. Similarly, unity in the department planning process took us beyond technique to bring everyone together as a unified whole. In the cadenza, the unifying aspects of grouped rhythms and notes created a sense of connection and direction. In the department planning exercise, the structure we found from the array of the issues we faced created unity.

A sense of unity was a key compositional factor in my appreciation for one of the works— the *Glagolitic Mass* by Leos Janáček—I heard at a recent concert. Janáček's music is deeply influenced and inspired by Moravian and other Slavic folk music. From early in his career, he committed his energies to folkloristic research that informed his work throughout his life. He ultimately developed a highly original style using the fundamentals of folk music—without being stylistically imitative. Janáček developed a particular sensitivity to the melodies and rhythms of speech and used the essence of the inflections, cadences, and emphases of Slavic spoken language in his works. In many ways, the *Mass* brought together his research and lifetime of experiences.

What is perhaps most interesting is the way the basic form of the traditional Catholic Mass, along with the ninth-century Slavonic language of his countrymen, was used to give voice to his expression of faith in the certainty of survival of the nation. He said he was not only expressing faith on a religious basis but on the basis of moral strength. Janáček set the *Mass* in Old Church Slavonic, which uses a distinctive alphabet called "Glagolitic," the first written form of the Slavonic language, to celebrate and unite the Slavonic people as they spread across Europe. Listening gave me a sense that the principle of unity in musical composition

What I find interesting about folklore is the dialogue it gives us with storytellers from centuries past.

~ Terri Windling
The Long and Wind(l)ing Road—An Interview with Terri Windling

was mirrored in Janáček's desire to celebrate the common ties, or cultural roots, they shared.

ARTISTIC INSIGHT

Artists give you a sense of unity in their works by creating the feeling of familiarity. Here are some basic characteristics of unity in a work of art:

- Unity is the result of how all elements work together.
- All of the parts must have some relation to each other.
- Everything must fit together in a way that creates an overall momentum and resulting meaningful message.

While unity means that nothing detracts from the whole, too much sameness is boring, and it is critical to add just the right amount of variety to stimulate and maintain interest. In the earlier cadenza story, we avoided monotony in performance, adding relevant emphasis and varying dynamics to shape the music. The reflection of this principle in both Janáček's compositional elements and the message fascinated me. The lilts of the language and the basic Mass structure gave a sense of familiarity to the work. Janáček expressed a sense of unity among Slavic nations along with the concept of pantheism. The variety came from aspects such as the scoring, the manner in which he used instruments like the timpani, and the use of the Mass from more than just a religious basis. Janáček used the principle of unity to go beyond technique and express the profound spiritual bonds underlying the disparate cultural traditions of the Slavic nations.

ELEMENTS IN RELATIONSHIP

Both the cadenza and the department planning process required the ability to skillfully place various elements in relationship with each other. In the mid-nineteenth century, composer Richard Wagner sought to synthesize the poetic, visual, musical, and dramatic aspects of his compositions in an effort to engage all the senses. He felt that the various art forms had become too disparate. He strived, particularly in his later operas, to engage and awaken all senses so the audience could be led through a more profound appreciation and experience. Wagner even wrote a manifesto, *The Artwork of the Future*, which detailed his vision for the arts. While his philosophy focused on how the arts should be integrated in a single work, this concept of experiencing with all the senses can be expanded well beyond his initial vision. Artists of all kinds now bring various elements and disparate disciplines together into a single artistic expression.

Auguste Rodin, Frank Lloyd Wright, Wassily Kandinsky, Gustav Mahler, John Cage, and Merce Cunningham are a few of the artists who expanded upon Wagner's inspiration. They created great works as they too searched for ways to reach across disciplines, placing them in relationship to create a more expansive sensory experience that fully expressed their ideas. Today, the digital world dramatically expands the relationship and synthesis possibilities of artistic expression. Broadening and deepening your understanding of relationship can help you go beyond technique and make the most of the seven concepts.

MOMENTUM

The concept of momentum—the breadth and depth as used in this *Fieldbook*—represents various aspects of a full cycle of creative effort as well as those of an ongoing series of cycles over time. From the point of beginning—then building, maintaining, then to the point of release and sending it back to stillness with a certain kind of energy, and to the motivation to begin again— momentum is central to the principles of creative consciousness explored in *Arts Awareness*.

The cadenza work with Paul, and the faculty departmental planning process that followed, allowed things to flow and speak with an expressive essence that would not have been possible otherwise. Momentum generates the emotional content of art. It may sound simple, but moving forward and creating momentum demands movement. Placing elements in relationship and creating a unifying connection between them led to a clear sense of

Nothing is more revealing than movement.

~ Martha Graham
The Modern Dance

purpose. In both the student and faculty group examples, a new and meaningful path was revealed by going beyond technique. Once you understand the importance of creating momentum, you gain perspective as you learn to sustain it.

My experience as a conductor was transformative in this way. It may seem obvious, but while you are responsible for the totality of the sound as a conductor, you cannot produce any sound without the musicians you lead. With the knowledge of guiding the entire piece to its full expression, the conductor has to simultaneously be ahead of the music and with it, experiencing it in the moment and looking ahead at the same time. A mistake made in the process of performing a piece of music is only momentary in relation to the entire composition. If you stop or get preoccupied with a particular moment, you are not able to grasp the entire piece as a whole musical expression and confidently set a pace that allows the music to say something meaningful. While you reach the end of the performance, if you are overly involved in a single moment, the whole experience is lifeless—there is no cohesive statement. At the same time, guiding the pacing does not mean controlling every aspect. There are relationship elements that are critical to consider in a combined group experience.

A performance is full of life when the musicians have a certain amount of freedom within the structure. A conductor is responsible for always keeping in mind the entire composition, guiding the musicians to do the same regardless of circumstances, and reaching a meaningful conclusion. Each performance leads to an opportunity to begin anew with the next one through an ongoing expansion of your skill and understanding that allows you to move beyond technique. It is a process of creating momentum and building relationship—with the musicians, the elements of the music, and within yourself—forming a unified whole to move forward artistically.

CONSCIOUSNESS QUERIES

Consider your relationship with momentum.

- Have you ever driven a familiar route, certain you knew what to expect, when you were suddenly surprised by a new stop light that had been installed?
- Have you experienced recurring discussions with someone only to end up in the same place as before, never solving the disagreement?
- Have you considered reflecting critically on a conversation, reordering and expanding your own ideas before your next conversation?
- How can you structure an important event or purposeful dialogue that allows for freedom of expression for all involved?

OPEN NEW DOORS

As you work your way through the seven concepts, keep in mind that your enthusiasm and willingness to experiment will carry you through and help you go beyond mere technique. While focus is important in order to get going, in order to keep moving, it is also beneficial to experiment with a playful mindset. Use the seven concepts to understand the skills of the artistic process and go beyond technique to enjoy increasing success and satisfaction in today's dynamic environment. Then the real treasure in arts learning comes from sharing your new awareness and using it to serve others.

Around here we don't look backwards for very long. We keep moving forward, opening up new doors and doing new things…

~ Walt Disney
Meet the Robinsons
film credits

Chapter 2

Back to Basics:
Expanding the Building Blocks

Overview

Patterns and Momentum

One of my most vivid memories is observing Kathy, a former student, prepare for an audition. She practiced her routines day after day. Her warm-up always included scale and interval patterns before she moved on to rehearse written exercises and pieces of music. She loved the sound and ease of playing scales, except for one: B major. Something about B major caused her to tense up in the same place every time. She knew from previous sessions that when she got to B major, struggle ensued. She had practiced it the same way so many times that she tensed up in anticipation before she even got to the trouble spot.

One day, she decided to spend most of her time on that frustrating scale. She found the place where she experienced difficulty, isolated it, and tried it over and over again in different ways:

- Playing it slowly
- Gradually speeding up, adding one note at a time from beginning to end
- Starting at the end and working backwards one note at a time, gradually adding more notes until the entire section was included
- Using different rhythmic patterns
- Playing at different dynamic levels
- Emphasizing a different note each time through the section

After all this focus, she cautiously played the entire scale. To her absolute delight, the problem had lessened. After repeated practice sessions like this, she finally mastered the scale. Kathy later went to her audition and when she walked in the room, the first thing the adjudicator said was, "Please begin with a two octave B major scale." She was stunned! At the same time she felt extremely grateful she had noticed the recurring problem and made the effort to overcome it; she played it flawlessly. After that experience, she saw that she could use this same awareness to understand patterns in her personal life, possibly providing insights that could lead to accomplishment, success, and happiness.

For example, after her college years, she noticed that every time she faced a stressful situation, she became nervous, upset, and uncommunicative. As she reflected on the situations that caused this angst, she realized that she didn't have to accept those feelings or react in that way, and just like the B major scale, it was her choice to practice moving through those tension points in a different way. She practiced these situations in her mind, going over them again and again in different ways just as she did in scale practice. She noticed where the tension started, how it built, and how she reacted—where her body tightened physically and where her mind went emotionally.

Knowing she wanted to create a different feeling and experience greater ease, she deliberately set out to change the kind of momentum she was experiencing. Kathy took this practice to actual situations and became more conscious of her responses and where the tension caused difficulty. Without saying anything to anyone, she chose to move with greater awareness through the tension points that arose, adjusting along the way. After many "practice sessions" like this, she began to respond naturally with a newfound strength. At times, she still noticed the previous angst begin to grab hold, just as she did with the scale experience, but because she had practiced, she knew that it was in fact all under her control—not determined by the situation or other people. She experienced the ease she sought and created a much different kind of momentum moving into and out of the experience. Discovering the impact of creating the tension, release, and momentum she desired powerfully influenced all areas of her life and work.

Each individual decision made in the process of creating or performing art involves various decisions and groupings of elements that form patterns, similar to the specific grouping of notes in the B major scale that had become such a struggle for Kathy. Artists shape these wide-ranging elements into patterns that set up tension and release effects. Ultimately, the work with its points of tension and releases create varied intensities of momentum. A work of art begins to take shape as artists use various techniques to organize and manipulate these elements. Each decision serves as a building block, creating momentum that ultimately leads to the full realization of the work as a whole.

ARTISTIC INSIGHTS

Combinations of basic elements artists use to build and create patterns lead to various ways of moving forward with momentum, and include:

- Aural and tonal factors—This includes influences of pitch, melody, harmonic structures, rhythm, tempo, timbre, tone of voice, and dynamics.
- Physical aspects—For example, body movement, gesture, and facial expression
- Visual qualities—The treatment of elements such as line, shape, texture, color, use of space, value, and rhythm
- Descriptive features—Using words imaginatively to describe the *way* someone or something moves, the *way* someone or something feels, the *way* someone or something sounds, or the *way* someone or something looks.

Numerous methods are used to create momentum. Depending on the art form, the motion generated through the patterns using these basic elements evokes emotional responses in the hearts and minds of the artists, viewers, or listeners. We

It's all in how you arrange the thing...the careful balance of the design is the motion.

~ Andrew Wyeth

The implicit motion of aesthetic form evokes implicit motion at the heart of affect. Implicit motion comprises both tension and release of virtual motion inherent in visual art and music, and the tension and release of actual bodily responsiveness to the arts in the form of affect.

~ Gilbert J. Rose
American Imago

all have the ability to perceive motion, whether simply implied or actual physical movement. It's that perception that triggers the emotional response. Think for a minute about a time when you were sitting at a stop light and felt as if you were moving forward or backward, but it was actually the car next to you causing that sensation.

You may have seen films in an IMAX theater and had the sensation of moving, although all of the movement was actually taking place on the screen. Maybe you viewed a movie and experienced the anticipation and emotional build of the music to a dramatic moment and you felt suddenly consumed by fear, grief, or anger. Or you may have seen a painting that moved you deeply because of the way the artist used color, shape, and textures to create a sense of tremendous joy. This basic tension-release-momentum principle of artistic expression has a profound effect on the brain and body. Momentum leads the eye and ear through space or time, and each specific combination creates a pattern that generates motion and emotion. The empowering aspect of these individual moments for the artist is that there are many ways to choose to move forward, each with a unique quality of tension and ensuing release and resultant momentum. While the time aspect of some art forms might assist you to more easily sense movement, the perception is possible in all artistic endeavors. If you allow yourself to fully engage with the tension, you can experiment and physically and emotionally *feel* the release and movement.

ROLE OF TENSION AND RELEASE

Tension is the perceived need for release or relaxation created by the viewer's or listener's expectations. You experience this sensation every day in your personal life—whether standing in a long line at the grocery store, having a difficult conversation, stretching a tight-fitting slipcover over a chair, managing an argument between your children, or when you hear an unusual noise in your house at night. The wide array of tension nuance possibilities is important to consider in the artistic process. You would certainly experience different degrees of momentum depending on the stress, anxiety, or pressure in the personal situations you might encounter throughout the day. Artists use a dynamic process to imagine the possibilities that intentionally lead the viewer or listener through a particular sort of experience.

ARTISTIC INSIGHTS

Artists create varying degrees of tension to produce momentum of different types.

The tension may be:
- A gentle, guarded, or wary balance maintained between opposing forces or elements
- A situation or condition of hostility, suspense, or uneasiness
- The interplay of light hearted or weighty conflicting elements
- An act or course of action that stretches, expands, draws out, or yields to some degree
- A sense of force that significantly lengthens, increases, extends, or shrinks
- A sensation of physical or mental strain or stress

ACOUSTIC

Artists use sound variations to create tension in many ways. The most basic is to pair certain contrasting aspects of the elements together. For instance, in music, a rising melodic line creates tension and one that descends has the effect of release. The same is true for an actor's speaking voice when the pitch rises or falls. You may be able to think about people in your life—even your own voice—and the impact as the pitch rises or falls. A large interval leap in music creates tension and a smaller one repose. The same sensation is created when you suddenly speak with a higher or lower voice. Dissonance creates tension and consonance resolves it.

A harsh or unpleasant sound—whether vocal or mechanical—often accompanies a sense of tension and, when it becomes more harmonious, it feels like a relief and becomes calming. More divisions per beat in music create tension and fewer, release. Acceleration in tempo increases tension and deceleration relieves it. This same experience can come from walking or driving faster or slower. Similar experiences come from sound with greater density versus sparseness in the texture or the anxiety of an increasing or suddenly loud sound contrasted with the release of a contrasting diminishing volume or softer sound. Musicians and actors take full advantage of the widely varied imaginative possibilities for momentum using these kinds of contrasting elements.

Visual

Visually, the dynamic interplay of directed tensions can be as simple as the juxtaposition of two very different elements on a canvas or a subject on stage in an unusual or unfamiliar context. Elements that please the eye create feelings of calm while contrasting elements create tension. More complex shapes *feel* heavier than more simple shapes and darker color values *feel* heavier than lighter. Brighter things come forward and duller ones recede. Objects, actors, or dancers that are closer together create tension while those that are further apart create calm. When and where actors or dancers move on stage can add to tension or cause the audience to shift their attention to a new part of the stage. Things or people that touch, overlap, or interlock create spatial tension while space allows for greater ease. Quick, harsh motion is a contrast with more flowing gesture. Rhythms in stage movement are manipulated according to focus, situation, characters, and dramatic tension which all impact the audience perception.

You personally experience many of these sensations on a daily basis, possibly without ever realizing it—the feeling of standing in a crowded line at airport security and the feeling of momentum of finally getting to the front and gaining the freedom to move toward your gate. You might experience a contrast like this when sitting alone in a park as a large person dressed in dark tones comes up from behind you, moves closer, and sits near you on the bench. Maybe someone you don't know is standing in the doorway you are trying to pass through.

DRAMATIC

Drama with plots filled with irony and with characters facing dilemmas can lead audiences through conflict to an unexpected and satisfying ending. Conflict can be unspoken or addressed as a dispute between something as simple as truth and lies. Tension in written works can include actual danger or psychological danger involving something of importance to the character. The words crafted artistically lean into a situation with perfect pacing, then lead you to a new understanding and release. Tension is often created by shortening words and sentences while longer sentences create a more relaxed mood. And short, choppy sentences make a scene more suspenseful. Everyone personally experiences drama like this in daily life. If you think about it, you may be able to identify times when you have previously faced the tension of short, blunt statements as well as encountered lengthy, less pointed assertions that are more laid-back.

LAYERED PAIRINGS

Some pairings of tension and release are more complex and may be explored in layers, some even conflicting, as different elements used together may have different levels of tension—and thus solutions—for release and momentum. For example, the musical elements of harmony may have different levels of tension than melody and rhythm. Imagine for a moment that you are trying to understand a conversation in a room with several people—maybe it's your family. A cloud suddenly casts a dark shadow in the room on an otherwise sunny day, and one person standing close to you speaks softly. At the same time, a rather large person speaks insistently in a harsh, loud voice; one person sits in the corner crying; and everyone else dances happily around the room. Depending on the specific situation, many factors may need your attention. As you search for the best way forward through this complicated circumstance, you weigh and balance the options, ultimately choosing a resolution. The solution you choose determines the momentum you experience and the understanding you hoped to gain all along.

REPETITION

When using these basic building blocks of momentum, the tension and release principle of artistic expression can be further enhanced by using other techniques such as repetition, emphasis, various types of beginnings and endings of sounds in music and speaking, and visual designs on canvas or stage that use a mixture of angular or softer edged shapes. While repetition means doing the same thing over and over again, repetition can be regular or irregular, even or uneven, or spread out visually from a central point. Repeated elements have different effects as they become smaller or larger or louder and softer at different rates. The patterns they create establish a rhythm and mood that can be calm and restful or unsettled and anxious. Each art form uses repetition in its own way and, while an artist may focus on one form more than another, learning to explore the patterns and principles in all will add depth to understanding this aspect of creating art. The imaginative and ever-changing use of repetition in artistic expression will help you discover new ways to recognize the harmonies and qualities that bring about various events and experiences in your work and personal lives. If a situation keeps arising, whether the outcomes are favorable or uncomfortable, you may be able to stop and look at the series of events, identify patterns, and ultimately enhance or change the end result.

A former student came to me frustrated with the band he led at a local high school. He regularly received adjudicator comments at festivals—where bands and orchestras perform and are graded for their performance—that the music was lacking because there was no dynamic contrast. Everything was loud.

At his request, I went to observe his work in a rehearsal. He spoke very loudly all the time when giving instructions to the students. In fact, several times during the rehearsal he became frustrated with the volume and yelled, "SOFTER," while motioning with very large conducting movements.

After the rehearsal we discussed the experience. As an outstanding, sensitive musician, he felt embarrassed. He was so caught up in communicating to such a large group, that he wasn't able to see that his loud voice and large motions were the problem all along. It took quite a while for him to overcome this behavior, but he practiced every day. As he gradually learned to vary the volume of his voice and make motions more closely aligned with the desired musical result, the performance level improved, the students felt inspired because of their success, and negative adjudicator comments about performance dynamics stopped altogether.

EMPHASIS

Emphasis creates weight and gives a focal point to a particular aspect of the tension-release pattern. Artists use this technique through the creative use of aspects such as duration, extremes, or unexpected changes. The longer something lasts or the bigger or more contrasting it is, the greater importance it assumes and the more emphatic it is. Examples such as extreme changes in speed, texture, dynamic, timbre, or pitch in music might be used to emphasize a pattern or element. A shape that contrasts with its surroundings, a point formed by converging lines, a darker or lighter color value, or an isolated object or person could bring out something visually. An exaggerated move on stage or a move that is held longer or made bigger can provide emphasis. Pausing when speaking will emphasize a transition or repeating something several times will highlight a particular phrase or point. Being alert to emphases in your life and in your work— how they are created and what they signal—helps you recognize significant events. Emphasis is important in communication.

It helps to establish what is of primary importance versus what may be supporting or of secondary significance.

BEGINNINGS AND ENDINGS

Artists explore beginnings and endings and make choices that can significantly impact momentum. For instance, there can be variations of tension or ease in the way a note, or phrase, or musical composition begins or ends, giving the sense of struggle, constraint, freedom, or uninhibitedness. The same qualities are present in visual aspects of art—the *kinds* of shapes, colors, textures, body movement, and other elements used to lead your eye emotionally. While this was most apparent for me as a conductor, those experiences soon led to an awareness of how beginnings and endings are used in other arts forms, how they connected to other experiences in music, and ultimately how they added depth of understanding about relationships and experiences in everyday work and private life. How you choose to begin or end a relationship impacts the way you move forward either through the experience or on to the next.

This can show up in repeated personal, romantic, or professional relationships where one might move on. Everyone grows and changes over time, and the reason you initially engaged in a relationship might be completely different from where you are at the moment. You may have even started the relationship for a reason that wasn't sustainable. You might find it difficult to move on even if you know it's time. If you experienced a series of personal or professional relationships that ended suddenly, or that felt like you were struggling to hold onto, or dragged on seemingly endlessly, or felt devastating when they ended, this "beginnings and endings" aspect of momentum will help you experience ease and grace in these situations. It will not only help you with endings, but will assist you in having greater clarity in new beginnings.

One of the ways Jim, a friend and colleague, experienced this was through a series of professional relationships. Because he chose to continually move forward in his career, he necessarily had to leave close relationships with some people and organizations that had been instrumental to his work and success to that point. He began to understand how the beginnings and endings aspect of momentum in artistic expression can be used in moving on. While he continued to practice this aspect of expression as an individual, he became more and more skilled at choosing the type of ending he wanted to achieve and how to begin the next so he could chose the most effective relationship beginning and/ or ending.

In one instance, particularly, this was very difficult. In order to move forward, he chose to stop his active participation in an organization that was central to his success to that point. Jim's career was changing direction, his interests were broadening, and he could not dedicate energy and time to the organization any longer. In fact, his focus and energy had been seriously falling off for some time and he had been giving over responsibilities to others without ever checking in on them. The lessened interest wasn't from lack of respect for the tremendous opportunities he gained from his experiences with the organization or from lack of interest in the mission. It was a result of his own growth as a professional and human being. As Jim started his next project, he knew his deepened understanding of previous experiences would benefit him when he chose to move on.

CONSCIOUSNESS QUERIES

Consider your own beginnings and endings:

- Are there situations in your life that could benefit from this sort of practice and thinking?
- Are you clear about the reasons you begin a relationship or situation?
- Each time you move on from a romantic, personal, or professional relationship, do you consider the best way to end or reconfigure that particular relationship in order to move forward?

The more you practice beginnings and endings, the better you become. It takes the same focus, practice, and conscious awareness as your creative work.

BUILDING BLOCKS OF BEING IN THE WORLD

Ultimately, your greatest expressive act is the way you live your daily life—how you express yourself as a human being. In the practice of artistic expression in your daily life, you use your gifts, opinions, perceptions, natural talents, strengths, beliefs, and the character traits you value to build momentum toward full expression. You can build innovative ways of being in the world by taking action, learning, and moving forward through the creative tensions of your life in much the same way artists create these moments in their art forms. Creative tension moves you forward from situation to situation, and there are unlimited choices and ways of doing that. While these individual decisions can help you achieve your immediate desires, when you view a momentary decision from the entirety of your life, it can take on major significance. The consistent practice of artistic expression with an expanded point of view will lead you to a path of discovery and help you develop creative ways of being in the world.

As you explore the paths you have taken in your own life, you can become more and more aware of how the decisions you make take on greater significance when viewed from a bigger picture perspective. For instance, after seventeen years in one place, I moved fourteen hundred miles to a new job in order to explore and expand my career. While you may not know what a move will bring, or the exact details of the expansion, you might have a sense that it's important to grow and evolve no matter what the experience brings about. You simply feel drawn to the possibility of growth. In my move, everything about the new environment was new to me—the landscape, the weather, the architectural spaces, the culture—and while this did seem important at the time, it wasn't until I moved on that I realized how fortunate I was to have made this decision in the first place. This kind of experience can completely reshape your career, opening up opportunities you couldn't have imagined at the outset.

As my administrative role developed and became the focus of my career, I noticed I could practice artistic expression in my work using what I refer to as environmental elements to creatively build momentum. Business people, educators, community or church group leaders, and even parents in family settings can use similar environmental elements to creatively build momentum and guide any age group using a wide array of artistic options such as:

- Their rapport with their employees, students, children, or those they lead
- The learning they plan for those under their influence
- The discussion and exchange of ideas they would like to promote
- The knowledge and comprehension they want to develop
- The physical aspects and arrangement of the spaces in which they work

Experimenting with various aspects of these and other elements will lead to new ways of approaching and managing your own learning and the learning of others through a variety of creative tension-release experiences. Ultimately, learning is a collaborative endeavor, and the greatest benefit comes when everyone involved has the opportunity to grow together through diverse ideas and patterns in creative tension.

A musician friend who managed a local business told me he was concerned because of what appeared to be indifference of his staff in office meetings. While he had a plan, was well organized, and had a good rapport with his employees, they seemed unresponsive and aloof. As we talked about it, it became clear that a simple reconfiguring of the meeting space might help. At the next meeting, when people walked into the room, they saw the room transformed: the rectangular table was moved aside and the chairs formed a circle. The room was clear of clutter and it was apparent to everyone that this meeting would be different from any they had experienced so far. The change created a tension of anticipation that hadn't been there previously. At the same time, there was a real sense of excitement and interest that something very different was about to occur. Everyone engaged and participated in the discussion. It transformed everyone's expectations of what the meetings were about, ultimately creating momentum for the business that had not previously been possible.

LEADERS, MANAGERS, AND ADMINISTRATORS

Leaders, managers, and administrators are constantly engaged in a dynamic interplay of tension-release components that have critical functions in relation to what they want and feel they can achieve. As in the arts, the awareness of the overall goal—the bigger picture in the long term—is critical in the action and movement created through tension-release moments. At the highest level, quality artistic leadership is not manipulation of others or simply taking care of menial tasks as some might think; it is creating an environment and taking actions through the creative tensions of day-to-day organizational life that lead all involved to a level of appreciation and achievement that they would not have enjoyed otherwise. Leadership involves community—a collaborative effort among a variety of people—and is similar to the guidance provided by a conductor, choreographer, or director.

One of my former conducting students created a successful business using techniques he learned conducting an orchestra. Great performing organizations, just like great performing companies, are great because they hire people who can perform at a high level and there is a structured system to perform within. He set expectations for those who worked in the business, but structured an environment in which they each knew the expectations and were able to take ownership of decisions, actions, and ideas within the overall goals of the company. He guided and managed the day-to-day tensions of a growing business, moving the company forward from the larger perspective. This viewpoint was just like his work in achieving a convincing performance of a four-movement symphony, moving through each moment with the larger structure in mind. Everyone he employed had an investment in the outcome and that structure allowed them the freedom to take ownership and feel like they were truly part of contributing to something special.

Dancers, musicians, and actors take part in this sort of interaction and expression on a regular basis. Those involved in the highest level of artistic performance experiences in these art forms know that they are touched by the guidance of the leader; they are transformed into something that is greater than what they can each create individually. While many of these individual artists perform high level work alone as well, they don't engage with the same kind of intellectual and emotional sense as they do through this more multifaceted performing community. Quality leaders provide meaning and context in a complex setting using environmental and relationship elements. While the route you take as the head of an organization, community group, or family may not always be the easiest, thoughtful consideration of working together as a community will add value to the experience of everyone involved.

While this chapter explores the basic elements and patterns used to create art, concepts truly come alive and offer powerful life tools when you examine the larger design. When you look at the work of creating your art, your life, your leadership, or your teaching or training of others from a larger perspective, you can see how the individual decisions fit into the whole. While you can use each individual element or pattern to create a certain momentum, it may be that the most effective choice is something you haven't yet considered. Your choice of direction is often more effective with a viewpoint that encompasses a much larger perspective—the entire composition or canvas of your life.

While this larger picture may have several components, what truly matters is how those individual components fit into the overall span of time, and from that perspective, the way forward may not necessarily be the easiest solution, but one that serves a larger purpose overall. If the focus is too much on an individual element or tension-release pattern or an immediate desire at the

One danger for the performing musician is the search for easy technical solutions, inevitably at the expense of musical expression. I am sure that the line of least resistance inevitably leads to least expression. Having done something in a certain way, repeating it brings tranquility, the comfort of the familiar. However, real tranquility can only come from understanding what was done and how it was achieved, and then trying to better it. The only real assurance—having absorbed past experiences—is to start again from scratch. To look for the easy, physical, mechanical, or technical solution is an indulgence.

~ Daniel Barenboim
Life in Music

expense of the larger design, you get stuck there and are only able to focus on the moment–to-moment details, losing the bigger picture.

Whether as an artist, educator, leader, head of a family, or an individual, you must fit the sequence of the moments together in a sensible and functioning whole. While a whole work of art often possesses a main focal point, the work was created through several moments or points of creative tension and release. The overall structure is superimposed over those individual moments, holding them together with meaning and context. The next chapter explores how you can fit these series of decisions into a whole.

MOTIVATIONAL STORY— GETTING BACK TO NATURE

When I first started to conduct, I was nervous about being observed by my peers. It's easy to become fearful of making mistakes and looking inadequate under the watchful eye of others. Despite feeling very comfortable with the musicians in the groups and performing before thousands of people, the tension of a colleague walking in the room was tremendous.

Even when it is difficult, you can strengthen your resolve in a way that helps you get past moments of angst. It's important to persist in your work and keep stepping up to the plate under these circumstances. Part of my discomfort at the beginning was the strange sensation of guiding the music, but not being personally responsible for producing any of the sound—using a combination of words, gesture, and facial expression to influence the flow of the music. Reviewing hour after hour of videotaped rehearsals, then evaluating and adjusting for the next day, became a regular practice.

After years of this practice, in a rehearsal as guest conductor of a wonderful orchestra, the regular conductor—a gifted musician whom I respected greatly, but a rather ruthless man—stood at the back of the stage with his arms crossed and feet planted widely apart. The stance was a challenging one. Without consciously thinking about it, I closed my eyes and continued conducting. Moments later when I opened my eyes, he had gone. At that moment, I realized the fear of being observed had disappeared!

An important part of the artistic process is getting past the tensions of the moment to achieve the bigger picture. Without fully realizing it, the artistic process guided me all along to go beyond fear—doing what was needed to do to get past the tense moments of observation, finally moving forward, opening doors, and doing new things. Although you may know that some things are working and others are not, the tension and stress can help you grow and create something quite beautiful. Many opportunities present themselves when your effort becomes more natural. You can choose to participate fully in your experiences and practice, making use of deep reflection and meaningful action, and focusing on growth rather than fear. Each persistent moment led me to an experience of conducting joyously in any situation, no matter whether another conductor was observing or not.

This kind of perspective can lead you to notice similar efforts in the world around you— how nature innately remains connected to struggle but grows from it, blossoming into something new and magnificent. When I lived in Sedona, Arizona, my windows offered a 280-degree view of the red rocks—a stunning array of red sandstone formations. The formations appeared to glow in brilliant orange and red when illuminated by the rising or setting sun. They formed a breathtaking backdrop for everything that took place in the area. Each day when driving into the neighborhood, it felt as if you were climbing up into a majestic tower as the car ascended the hill. The large, 2000-foot-high red rock cliffs appeared as if they were right in front of you— almost as if you could reach out and touch them. It's the sort of environment that can help you see and understand artistic expression in greater depth than might be possible otherwise.

The red rocks held a special beauty, but their impact also stemmed from the similarity of their evolution to the tension-release-momentum aspect of the artistic process. Years of water and wind created these inspiring sculptures that rose out of the ground. They became more and more beautiful as they were worn away by the strong forces of nature. Each year, each millennium, they took on different shapes and colors, emerging as the strong and impressive art they are today.

It was natural to imagine that the rocks fought hard to maintain their integrity—they are, after all, rocks. If they were to give way completely, they would lose their splendor. Imagination could take you even further to consider the easiest route might have been to collapse completely under such pressure. But instead of complete collapse, they changed and were reshaped to become more beautiful. Year after year, the water and wind worked against these beautiful structures, sometimes moving around and other times appearing to fight hard against the resistance of the rock formations. The strong resistance and the influence continued over many years but, in the end, the rocks are likely much more beautiful than if they gave in completely in the beginning. In the end, the rocks took on a new form that expanded their magnificence. Just like the successful artist, these elements of nature bring their beauty to light, defined by the persistence and movement that was created even in difficult circumstances.

LESSONS LEARNED

While at first you may not recognize the learning that can take place in such an incredible environment, it becomes clearer when combined with arts experiences and reflection on other influences. Two instances in particular helped me further understand the beauty of the red rocks and the momentum it could create toward the future. One morning, while working in the office area of my house, unknown to me at the time, my neighbors were watching an incredible sight taking place right at my front door. They watched a mountain lion walk up our street in broad daylight, turn up my driveway to lie down and rest on my front porch for the morning, leaning against my front door!

They called later, and we searched the neighborhood to see if it was hiding somewhere after it left my front door. We never saw it again. After this occurred, a friend shared a book about mountain lions and their natural instincts. The study of animals, how they survive, and the qualities they embody is an important element of understanding for the native people of the Sedona area. The reading strengthened my understanding that the natural instincts of animals were closely aligned with observations of the red rock formations. It also added depth to a growing awareness about the importance of nature and its ability to break down old or outworn perceptions, much like creating momentum beyond the moment in a work of art. The insights you gain from this sort of reflection can help you expand your understanding of the importance of integrity, strength, and a broader perspective. It can serve as a reinforcement of the strength you gain in overcoming a challenge, such as conducting in rehearsal in front of fellow conductors. While I truly love the outdoors, and have never been one for camping, I wondered if this learning is what other people mean subconsciously when they speak of "getting back to nature."

A day or so after the mountain lion took a nap leaning against my front door, a strong monsoon rain, common to that area, left a foggy haze in the early morning. Just before dawn I opened the blinds of my bedroom, and there in the mist stood the most elegant and beautiful deer, less than five feet from my sliding glass door. It stood there with its head held high, incredibly regal, still, and quiet. By the time I blinked to see it more clearly, it had disappeared into the brush without a sound, almost as if it had appeared to help me further expand my thinking. At first I was alarmed, startled from the unexpected closeness of such a large animal—as tall as an adult with a massive two hundred pound body. Later, it appeared it was a gift—the graceful fluidity of the deer who was as startled as I was, moving forward nimbly, just as a conductor moves through the tension-release points in conducting a musical composition.

A series of moving experiences such as this can help you learn many things about artistic expression not only as an artist, but how it can also occur naturally in your life. The depth of knowledge I gained in the Sedona environment greatly enhanced my understanding of how the individual points and patterns of creative tension in artistic expression work together to make the whole work of art. Through further study and reading, I came to appreciate the tendencies of the red rocks, the wind and water, and the natural instincts of the mountain lion and the deer. The learning had to do with the complex yet simple balancing of personal power, intention, and strength. It involved the expression of self-confidence, using leadership wisely, and freedom from guilt. At the same time, the contrasting natural instincts of gentleness, of listening deeply, of understanding the power of gratitude and giving, and of alternative paths to a goal came forth in persistent whispers.

In such a beautiful and abundant natural environment, it's easier to find the value of many possibilities, of solidness, stability, and sturdiness as points from which you can gain a new perspective. Many people love to climb on the red rocks and observe the animals in that area, me included. It is hard to resist. I realized when climbing that it is this vantage point that allows you to gain a view of the surrounding terrain, much like seeing the bigger picture in the artistic process.

DEEPENING PERSPECTIVES OF THE BUILDING BLOCKS

USING THIS CONCEPT IN YOUR LIFE

When you create your art at the highest level, you use tension-release techniques all the time. It is easy to assume that tension means that something is hard to do or that something is bad. While the opposing forces or elements of tension often do cause anxiety, there is also a tension of excitement you can experience as something moves from interesting to utterly sublime.

You can shift the intensity or focus of the tension and the decisions you make to move forward just by changing your mind.

This shift allows you to experience greater freedom in the range of choices you are able to select from as you make decisions.

The tension of pairing and shading of opposites in a work of art ultimately creates its beauty. Your own life is filled with opposites and striving to get from one place to the next. You might describe the tensions that get you from one point to the next as good and bad or as easy and difficult. Words such as "happy" and "sad," "frightened" and "calm," "angry" and "passionate," "sobbing" and "smiling," or "hating" and "loving" might be used to describe your emotions.

Art brings us these same contradictions, often in extremes. You can learn about the beauty of these contrasting emotions—ways of moving forward—if you allow yourself to truly feel the tension, the sense of release, and the momentum through a deepening awareness and understanding of the artistic process. Part of the process is the understanding that you can choose how you move through the individual moments and how you view the relationship of that instant from a larger structural viewpoint. This helps you experience each moment, rather than resisting, and that's what makes us fully alive—allowing us to reach higher states of consciousness.

CONSCIOUSNESS QUERIES

- What are the creative elements you have available to allow your own art to speak?
- What are the individual points and patterns of creative tension in your life and work?
- How do these points and patterns fit together to create your overall experience?
- How can you energize your life, filling it with vital energy?

It isn't a single decision or even several decisions that have the greatest significance. The greatest value is in each particular decision with respect to the entire series of driving forces that create your life as a whole. When you participate in any process as an artist, you learn to enjoy the practice of moving forward toward your vision.

Michael loved to discover and solve problems in his performance. He practiced hour after hour, playfully working through the tensions he discovered—not only those inherent within the structure of the music itself, but the technical challenges that he personally experienced. He delighted in discovering the impact of a change in emphasis in the sequence of notes, the beginning of the sound and where it could lead, or the repetition of a phrase to gain complete expressive control. The result of that joyful effort was great success and the opportunity to travel extensively and perform in places he could never have imagined when he started his career.

QUICK TIPS

Essential elements in creating your life:
- Natural talents, gifts, and strengths
- Powerful and complex set of elements that come from life experiences—perceptions, opinions, beliefs, and character traits you value
- Willingness to celebrate past successes
- Doing what you truly love to do
- Using the full power of your gifts as the base for meaning and joy in your life

NATURAL TALENTS AND GIFTS

The creative elements that impact the way you move forward toward your personal goals are quite possibly influences you're afraid to consider. This powerful and complex set of elements comes from your life experiences up until this moment. When you can change your perspective and basic view of this particular life learning, you gain a new, wider perspective. The point of creative tension, of crafting things artistically and turning them into something new—of experimentation and transformation— is to find a way forward. When you find where the tension is and

Discovery holds meaning only for the one whose mind is prepared to draw an inference, the one who has applied himself most perseveringly to the subject.

~ Charles Goodyear
Trials of an Inventor: Life and Discoveries o Charles Goodyear

It is a happy talent to know how to play.

~ Ralph Waldo Emerson

make decisions that create just the right momentum, you become an innovator—an artist—in expressing yourself in life. Creative tension is natural; it is a state where disagreement or discord ultimately gives rise to innovation, better ideas, or outcomes. The most important characteristics you possess as a human being are your unique individual natural talents. These talents are the aptitudes you use to make the decisions that give you the amount and kind of motion to move forward in any given moment or situation.

One of my former students, a trumpet player, always found himself in the middle of the section. He felt disappointed in never achieving the position of "first chair." His physical characteristics and ear were well suited to another brass instrument—the French horn. One day I suggested he consider moving to this instrument. At first he was not inclined to do it. He was heartbroken. He felt as if he wasn't "good enough" because he had in his mind an image of importance and power as a trumpet player—it sounds in the highest register in the brass family of instruments and stands out to lead the others. After some thought, he switched instruments, and in a very short time, grew well beyond his level of achievement as a trumpet player. He found that his personal power meant much more than being the highest pitched, the loudest, or the most forceful. This type of power moved him toward self-realization, a state of mind, and larger goals in life— the full use of his personal talents and strengths.

Everyone has such talents, but you may take them for granted. Your talents are innate and similar to the natural instincts of the mountain lion or deer, or the tendencies of rocks, water, or wind in the earlier story. Ask yourself what you do that comes naturally and that you probably think is no big deal. Others might admire something about you that you ignore or make light of as insignificant.

Why is it important to know and identify your natural talents? In order to create great art, you must know and value the elements of the art form. Similarly, your natural talents are an important part of who you are and one of the most vital tools you must use and honor to create your life.

All life demands struggle. Those who have everything given to them become lazy, selfish, and insensitive to the real values of life. The very striving and hard work that we so constantly try to avoid is the major building block in the person we are today.

~ Ralph Ransom
Steps on the Stairway

If you need assistance or wondered about your strengths, these resources may help:

Strengths Finder 2.0 by Tom Rath (2007, New York: Gallup Press).

Now, Discover Your Strengths by Marcus Buckingham (2001, New York: The Free Press, Simon & Schuster).

Experiment without judgment. It is powerful once you discover your own strengths, use the principles of artistic expression, and manage your work and relationships based on an understanding of those findings. You can begin to enjoy personal happiness and success you might not have known otherwise.

Your life experiences may have made you feel that these natural talents aren't important or worthwhile, but they are indeed critical to creating art in your life. It takes willpower to move forward, even when using your natural gifts. As in creating art, just because you use the natural elements of the art form, it doesn't mean that artistic expression comes automatically without using the tension-release principle. Before you can honor anything, you have to know something about it. You have to see the evidence that it is worth honoring. You have something that can be honored that is yours to use in creating your life.

CONSCIOUSNESS QUERIES

- What are your natural talents or gifts?
- Do you appreciate them and use them to their fullest potential?
- If you don't know what your talents are, do you want to find them?

You might notice a co-worker, family member, or student who possesses a strong work ethic or a friend who is conscientious or well-organized. Maybe your own gift is generosity, confidence, or motivating others. A special talent might be sensitivity, perceptiveness, or curiosity. Other possibilities may be the talent of being loyal, persistent, or of being a team player or a quick thinker. It might be that you naturally take initiative, you can synthesize ideas easily, or that you are a natural leader, a good mediator, or are innately charismatic. Whatever talents you have, it is important to develop and use them to their fullest and to honor each step you take when you observe them at work in creating your progress in life. They are the building blocks that help you succeed and find the greatest satisfaction and happiness.

CELEBRATING PAST SUCCESSES

Celebrating past successes helps you to honor your natural talents and gifts. This is a simple and powerful tool in any artistic endeavor. When you acknowledge and celebrate your past successes, it is easier to address challenges—the tension-release points—as you create your life. If your tendency is to always view the glass as half empty, it can be defeating and disempowering. When you don't celebrate forward movement, tension points may make you lose hope that you can continue to move forward toward the bigger picture of your life. Inspiration gets lost. When you celebrate successes—and release or move through tension points in your experience—the pieces and patterns fit together as a series of successes that motivate you and build your confidence and your strength.

TALENTS REMAIN—STRENGTHS EVOLVE

As you gain confidence and your strengths evolve, your talents remain with you all along the way. This is because they are inherent in who you are as an individual. Your strengths come from further developing your talents, from gaining knowledge and skill. Your talents are like the foundations of a beautiful building. The use of these gifts and the acceptance and recognition of their power support the breadth of your learning. Your spirit will soar when you use your talents to take risks and to learn. Your talents are the structure upon which you can build your life. As your strengths evolve and grow out of your innate gifts and capacities, you gain courage and excitement in the process. This speaks about the excitement of life in its entirety, which is an important marker of success.

LIKING WHAT YOU DO AND DOING WHAT YOU LIKE

When you weigh and balance the decisions you make over time, you find that each point of change helped to create a stronger vision for the overall direction of your life. In your daily interactions with others, you may realize that many people have worked for a lifetime trying to get to do what they think they really like, yet as they experience more of life each day and each year, they realize that although they might do what they like, it isn't something that truly makes their heart sing—it may not be something they truly like to do.

> The person born with a talent they are meant to use will find their greatest happiness in using it.
>
> ~ Johann Wolfgang von Goethe

> Your talents are like the architectural foundations of a beautiful building.

> Doing what you like is freedom… Liking what you do is happiness.
>
> ~ Frank Tyger

45

If you are a parent, teacher, or leader you may find that your children, students, or employees are either unfocused entirely, or they are focused on a goal that is disconnected from a bigger picture or based on something external. You can help guide them using this concept of the building blocks of momentum—through individual elements and patterns—to view the larger perspective and create more joy and success in their lives.

When you use your natural gifts and when your vision, commitment, and opportunities coincide, an incredible energy ignites your life and drives your efforts. If you don't take advantage of your imagination to see the larger perspective, you end up in situations that cause sadness or discontentment. You might have made choices by focusing on more simple factors such as glamor, prestige, a certain title, or financial achievement alone at the expense of the entirety of your life experience.

EFFECTS OF IGNORING STRENGTHS AND TALENTS

Very few people have a sense of their natural talents, much less the ability to create their lives around them. People are conditioned by bosses, teachers, parents, and others, and might either believe something that isn't true for them or try to fix something they perceive as wrong with them. As a result, many people get stuck in situations that suppress their knowledge of their unique talents. This limits their success and the full expression of their individuality as a human being.

When you fail to take advantage of the opportunity to fully express yourself using your natural gifts, it feels toxic. You may experience illness, dissatisfaction, anger, and other ailments and negative emotions. Your natural talents are such an integral part of who you are that without them, you lose meaning and purpose. Your strong natural talent is the base from which you can create your life, make meaning, and find the joy within yourself. The problem is not only in recognizing, believing, and accepting what that talent is, but in using it to invent yourself and to contribute to the world in a meaningful way.

Hide not your talents. They for use were made. What's a sundial in the shade?

~ Benjamin Franklin
Poor Richard's Almanack

CONCEPT PRACTICE

You can use resources from the basic building blocks of the artistic process, choosing to move forward through tension with the desired release and momentum to help your children, those you lead, or your students tap into their natural talents. This does not mean that every child, student, coworker, or employee will choose the arts as a profession, but it does mean that the principles of the artistic process can be understood in ways that can allow everyone to develop and demonstrate their knowledge in many different ways. Along the way, many people will receive a depth of understanding and appreciation for the arts and the artistic process that will last a lifetime, and some will even choose the arts as a career.

CONSCIOUSNESS QUERIES

- How can you create experiences that will guide you personally to a deeper understanding of the artistic process and who you are as a human being?
- How can you create experiences that will guide your children or your students to a deeper understanding of the artistic process and who they are as human beings?
- How can you use these concepts to make leadership decisions that will positively influence your community, work, or business?
- How can you use these concepts to create experiences that will guide those you lead in the community, work, or business to a deeper understanding of the artistic process and who they are as human beings?

Frank learned this well. He was an accomplished artist, but had always been interested and skilled in designing toys and games for children, even as an adult. He built a small successful local toy business that fulfilled this lifelong interest. He had a big picture viewpoint so necessary for entrepreneurs who build small, profitable businesses like this and he knew his talents, passions, and natural gifts as well as his weaknesses. Frank's big picture viewpoint helped him assess the end goal, develop clarity, and create momentum toward his vision. He also understood the tension points in getting from point A to point B along the way. Finally, he knew from practice of his art how to take action, always looking forward and willing to learn along the way. He used his unique talents, and that continues to give him and countless children great joy every day. While he never gave up

We are most alive when our hearts are conscious of our treasures.

~ Thornton Wilder
The Woman of Andros

his participation in performing music, his success came from his local toy business—using his natural talents and loving his work.

The beauty of great art is in understanding the creativity, the artistic principles. When you gain depth of understanding, not only about *what* it says to you, but about *how* it moved you in the way it did, you experience the impact of the learning on your everyday life and work. You can use the arts not only to gain a deeper understanding of the beauty in the art form, but to widen the application of those natural principles that created that beauty.

The principle of creative tension in works of art ultimately has to do with the way you imagine the possibilities and create and manage tensions associated with those possibilities. The result is a certain kind of momentum that leads you forward—and in light of the whole—to the next series or the next work. One aspect that is often ignored in the creative process is the release. There are many ways to release or relieve a tension, and that combination of tension and release is what ultimately creates the motion. The release gives you the nature of the momentum you experience. There are three phases in this tension-release concept, all leading to the nature of the motion achieved: intensification, highest tension, and release.

CONSCIOUSNESS QUERIES

Think of a personal challenge that built over time—a situation at home, personal relationship, or circumstance at work. Perhaps you're even involved in a trying ordeal at this moment. Reflect on the following stages and how they relate to your experience:

Intensification
How long did it build before it was resolved? How much space did it take in your life? What elements created the tension? If it is a current challenge, how intense do you intend to let it develop to before you consider the way forward?

Highest tension

What was the point of highest tension? How long did you hold that high level of tension? Was it a single point or moment? Was it sustained? Was it stretched out over time? If a current challenge, how long will you hold the tension? What are its qualities in relation to time or space in your life?

Release

How quickly did you respond to the highest tension? What was the nature of the release? Was it natural? Did you resist letting it go? Did you let it go suddenly? Was it spread out over time? Did it diminish gradually? If a current situation, what factors will you consider in response to the tension? What are the qualities of the release you will choose?

- What kind of momentum did this combination of intensification, highest tension point, and release create?
- Where will that momentum lead you next?

The following chart outlines all of the principles discussed throughout this chapter—the concept of expanded building blocks. Imagine possibilities using the appropriate **elements** related to the activity or situation; find the **tension** and its characteristics; and choose the **release** that creates the **momentum** you desire. With the support of the information in this chapter, use this image as a guide in designing life experiences, business or organizational actions, educational activities, or creating art. The nature of the experiences can shift depending on the level of the individual or group involved, facilitating a lifetime of learning.

Imagine the Possibilities

Tension and Release

Momentum

INTENSIFICATION

How long will it build?
What elements are being used?

Elements you might consider in creating art
- Aural and tonal factors
- Physical aspects
- Visual qualities
- Descriptive features

Elements you might consider in guiding or teaching others
- Rapport
- Learning you plan
- Change the ideas to promote
- Knowledge to develop
- Physical arrangement of space

Elements you might consider in lending or managing others
- Collaborative effort
- Meaning and context
- Environmental and relationship

Elements you might consider in creating life
- Gifts
- Opinions
- Perceptions
- Natural talents
- Strengths
- Beliefs
- Character traits you value

TENSION

Visual, aural, or spatial moment?

A point or sustained or stretched out?

How long will you hold the highest point of tension?

How much space will you allow it to take?

What is the intensity?

RELEASE

What was the speed of your response to the tension you created?
Immediate?
Did it release naturally?
Was it sustained or spread out?

Did you experience resistance?

Did you experience ease?

END RESULT

What kind of momentum did you create?

How does it feel?

What are its qualities?

Did you move forward?
Quickly?
Slowly
Suddenly?

Where will it lead you next?

How does it inform your next beginning?

There is a gap between the possibilities and the end result or forward movement.

The way you move forward is a combination of intensification and the mixture of elements used, the nature of the tension point, and the qualities of the release.

An important part of the artistic process is how these individual decision moments are used to create motion. This chart represents the process for a single situation, experience, or challenge. Each single experience, however, can also be linked to another to form a series of experiences. When you look at your life, your work, or your art over time, you may see a superimposed intensification, point of highest tension, release, and momentum for an overall series of events or experiences. For example:

An example of a relationship—work, personal, romantic, family, committee, or relationship with yourself—over a period of time

I = Intensification
HT = Highest tensions
R/M = Kind of release and resulting momentum created

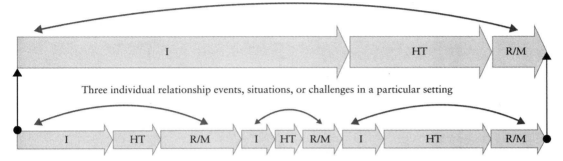

Overall superimposed intensification/tension/release/momentum over a period of time

I

HT

R/M

Three individual relationship events, situations, or challenges in a particular setting

I   HT   R/M   I   HT   R/M   I   HT   R/M

Refer to the details of the intensification, tension, release, and momentum phases in the previous chart.

A family relationship dynamic that intensifies and causes tension might be:

- The actions or behaviors of a teenager, grandparent, or family friend who causes disagreement between parents or among siblings.
- The disagreements between parents and the pressure of that conflict on the children and members of the extended family.
- The decisions that need to be made regarding the failing health of a child, parent, or grandparent.

There are limitless relationship possibilities in all areas of your life. The intensification and tension may even be within yourself—feelings of unimportance, not being valued, or looking unattractive to others. Experiment beginning with a situation in your life—a circumstance you are facing, an event at work, a personal relationship, or family dynamic—and list the factors in the intensification phase, the tensions, and the nature of the release you desire to move forward. Determine how this situation and the resolution fit in the overall bigger picture of your life. Make a note of your observations. Is it a momentary decision point or a major point of release that can carry you forward with new understanding?

An example of several areas of your life and how they are all connected to create your life experience over a period of time

I = Intensification
HT = Highest tensions
R/M = Kind of release and resulting momentum created

Overall superimposed intensification/tension/release/momentum over a period of time

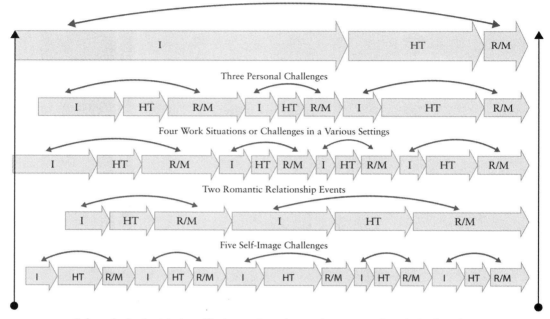

Refer to the details of the intensification, tension, release, and momentum phases in the chart above.

Experiment with how various decisions or possibilities have an impact on the momentum you achieve. Start anywhere. It depends on where you are at the moment—maybe it's the tension, the quality of the release, or possibly you're at the point of imagining possibilities.

Chance favors those in motion.

~ James H. Austin
Chase, Chance, and Creativity: The Lucky Art of Novelty

Summary

The main ideas and lessons of this chapter—the elements of your art, the patterns formed using those elements, and the quality of the tension-release-momentum created as a result—have an important connection to the other concepts presented in this book. Experimenting with the material of this chapter will help you take full advantage of the opportunity to create the highest level of artistic experience in all you do.

- Tension is normal and seeks release or resolution—it's natural. Use your full imagination, and remember that you have choices in creating the tension and resolving it.
- The basic concepts of each method of expression are essentially the same; only the materials differ from one artistic endeavor to another.
- The smallest elements, using the materials of the art form, create the patterns of these tension-release moments.
- We can learn to create meaningful momentum in our lives by deeply understanding the elements involved, the patterns, and the tension/resolutions, whether it is a single event, a project, or a series of experiences throughout a lifetime.
- The basic concept of creative tension in each of the moments is critical to the bigger picture; in order to create true art, you must have the sense of the bigger picture. The real meaning comes from seeing these moments in relation to the whole.

REVIEW QUESTIONS

- How you have moved through experiences in your past? Apply the concept of intensification, tension, release, and momentum to a work or family situation or personal relationship from your past and examine the various stages. Note what you discover.
- When reviewing your current or past experiences through this lens, do you find yourself seeing how you could achieve a different result? Did you get stuck in the moment or experience resistance? Did you remember to consider the moment in relation to the bigger picture?
- Identify all the areas in your life and superimpose an overarching flow to see where you are at this moment. Are you now at an overall tension point, a release, moving forward, or imagining possibilities? What steps do you need to take now to create beauty and flow,

moving forward in the way you desire? Is there any area that might take precedence over and impact the other areas in your life?

These questions are similar to what artists do in creating art, not only in the artwork or performance itself, but growing and expanding within themselves as human beings.

CONTINUE THE QUEST

Further explore the concept of tension-release-momentum in the arts. Use each of the four examples below to think about your home or work environment and how similar techniques might play out in your day-to-day life. Consider how you might be able to change the tension points and create a different kind of momentum.

- Listen to the *Amen* section at the end of the Chanticleer recording of *Ave Maria* by Franz Biebl. While there are several instances that demonstrate the tension-release-momentum concept throughout the six- or seven-minute performance, the last minute or so is an excellent example of building tension through unfolding points of tension and the final release at the end. It also shows us the moments of tension-release-momentum and how they move forward setting up the momentum and in this case, the end of the piece. This recording is available on YouTube at https://www.youtube.com/watch?v=XVyCJlPiHFg and on the CD—*A Chanticleer Christmas*, © 2010 by Mesa Blue Moon. B003XNKFPG, or individual mp3.

- Study designs used in advertising. Look at a design thoughtfully with the intent of finding the visual tension that is used to create a dominant element or design area that contains the most important message. Find the tension and sense how it evokes the feeling of energy and movement, directing your eye to the focus of the ad. Nearly every effective design includes some aspect of tension through the use of color, image, position, size, font, or shape. For example:

Explore the internet for the "Nostalgic Coca-Cola Polar Bear and Santa Art Cel Lithograph"—http://ecx.images-amazon.com/images/I/61vk218NBBL._SL1000_.jpg. The tension is created not only by the fact that there is a polar bear facing a Santa Claus, but the size of the bear related to the size of the Coca Cola. The two figures seem to compress the Coca Cola between them, creating tension and focus.

- Designers use the concept of tension and movement on book covers. For example:

  Examine book covers on the internet such as the cover of the first edition of *Leading Change* by John Kotter. Tension is created through the interlocking bold, shaded letters in the title as well as the penguins jumping across a crevice.

- Go to an art museum and study paintings that use a combination of contrasting elements or asymmetrical patterns. As your eyes follow the juxtaposition of opposing forces or the asymmetry of the design, find the tension and sense how it evokes the feeling of energy and movement. For example:

  Paul Cézanne is known as painter who expertly used tension in his work. Look at the images of his complete works—http://www.paul-cezanne.org/ —where you will see how he often painted a still life with things like books, cups, skulls, and bowls with items tilted or so close to the edge of the table that it felt as if they might fall over or off the table entirely. As you study his works, find examples of tension.

Some Abstract Expressionist paintings create tension by overlapping and interacting areas of flat color. These areas of color can be formless or clearly geometric. Look for the tension in the painting by Hans Hofmann displayed on the home page of his website: http://www.hanshofmann. org/. You can also explore other paintings in the image gallery section of the website.

- Look on the internet or in contemporary furniture or home decor stores for designers who create tension in their pieces by challenging preconceptions about balance, laws of gravity, or color contrast.

Study the lines of a bentwood chair, exploring the various ways the curved wood creates tension and a sense of movement as the curves twist slightly in order to connect to each other, to the back, the seat, and the floor.

The same sense of tension and movement can be seen in architecture like the Walt Disney Concert Hall in Los Angeles. Images and a virtual tour can be found on the internet at http://www.laphil.com/philpedia/about-walt-disney-concert-hall. Large photos of the building from multiple angles can be viewed at http://interactive.wttw. com/tenbuildings/walt-disney-concert-hall.

CHAPTER 3

ARTISTIC EXPRESSION: EXPLORING THE WHOLE AND PARTS

OVERVIEW

WHOLES AND PARTS

We sat in the audience enjoying an outstanding performance of the musical *Thoroughly Modern Millie* when one of the dancers suddenly lost her skirt. It fell off completely! The audience laughed at first, but as they observed what happened next, their amusement changed to admiration. The woman with the missing skirt kept singing and dancing as the others moved over and circled around her, still performing the song. They improvised their moves—still in character—as they gathered around while the actress replaced the skirt. Everyone moved back out to their positions and the performance continued as if choreographed. The performance as a whole was exciting, imaginative, and compelling. The audience offered tremendous applause throughout the performance, and especially during the curtain calls.

There are hundreds of such stories in the arts—artists moving forward through performance challenges. Piano and violin strings break during a concert performance, costumes malfunction, and numerous lighting and stage mishaps can occur. Artists learn how to manage the individual quality of each moment in relationship to the overall structure of the work as a whole. That missing skirt moment was not the artistic highpoint of the musical. To place too much emphasis where it's not structurally relevant can detract from the overall concept of the whole. The ability to hold back—

and not overdo—a certain phrase, section, movement, or visual aspect in a work of art is critical to a meaningful expression.

While many lessons can be learned from the missing skirt incident, the relevant point here is being aware so as to not indulge in the challenge or expressivity of one moment. If you indulge this way, you sacrifice the flow to and from the overarching structural highpoint of the work. Upon reflection, it became clear to me that this awareness was similar to what can be learned from a wide variety of arts experiences. Further thought revealed that the same awareness could also be used to understand context in relation to everyday life experiences.

For instance, one artistic challenge of conducting is to be sure all of the inner points of emphasis are felt, but kept in perspective in relationship to the whole. You can personally apply this concept when you feel you have made a mistake or when things don't work out the way you expected. This approach can help you practice placing your focus on solutions rather than regrets. A further benefit comes about as you learn to stand back and see the evolving bigger picture that comes in moving from one experience to the next. Each day, experience, success, and failure allow you to make new connections between events and to discover what kind of emphasis to place in relation to the bigger picture, over time.

You can experiment with emphasis and your own perspective in conversations, beginning in relationship with a single person and then later in small and larger group situations. After some practice you will find that to be understood, you need to consider what was most important and what played a more supportive role to the main point in a single conversation or series of conversations throughout a day or over a longer period of time.

Composers and performing musicians make something more important by using techniques such as a sudden silence, a change in the flow of the music, a longer duration, a repeated note or figure or phrase, an extreme volume change, or a change in the number of performers from many to only a few or vice versa. Similar techniques are used visually in art, dance, and theater.

Not everything is of equal importance. Being alert to how emphases are created and what they signify can help you recognize the most important moments, as well as the role of those that are more supportive, and how they all fit together to reach a goal or make a point most effectively.

For instance, a series of events led a former student, John, to experience the joy of teaching although he never considered the field of education during his college years. He had tremendous opportunity and support right out of college for a significant performing career, but he instead decided to place his focus on education. John chose to forgo the fulltime opportunities that awaited him in Los Angeles to serve the needs of students searching for meaning and purpose in their lives. Music performance supported his efforts and gave him remarkable opportunities to serve something larger than himself.

ARTISTIC INSIGHTS

Artists take the smallest elements, form patterns, create momentum, and consider what more those aspects can become. Exploring the smallest parts can be transformative; even greater beauty comes when putting the parts together to make a unified whole. Artists consider:

- The smallest parts—whether in space or time—in relationship to their function within the overall structure of the entire work or series of works
- The beauty of each part—or moment—regardless of its individual inherent nature, whether harmonious and tranquil or discordant and restless
- The potential of each part—and the unlimited opportunities for imagination and momentum—in relation to the whole

Pointillism offers an example of an artistic technique that allows the viewer to step back and see how individual points can come together to create a whole. The term is most closely associated with Georges Seurat and particularly his most famous work, *A Sunday Afternoon on the Island of La Grande Jatte*. The ten-foot-wide painting, which was the inspiration for Stephen Sondheim's *Sunday in the Park with George*, took two years to complete. In this technique, the artist expresses himself using small distinct dots of color applied in patterns to form an image. The technique allows the viewer not only to use the eye and mind to blend dots of color together into one image of the work as a whole, but to actually blend two or more different colors next to each other into a new solid color. When you step back and view the finished painting as a whole, the clarity of the image is remarkable. All of the individual dots, dabs, or strokes come together as a single meaningful and powerful expression.

QUICK TIPS

In many ways, we're all pointillists of one sort or another.
- Every day we view pixels as the smallest elements used to create images that are displayed on computer monitors, televisions, printers, and digital cameras.
- With our busy lives, each day is filled with individual moments that make up a larger picture. The complexity of these individual points in our lives is often enormous.
- As we move through each day, the days, months, and years become points themselves, continually creating a bigger image of points in time.

Stepping back to look at the points of time in your life can help you see the whole picture more clearly. Every day, month, and year, you create the moments that come together to shape and define the whole of your life through relationships, family, work, and private activities and thoughts.

The beauty of a work of art often includes the ugly and frightening as well as the attractive and soothing, decent and evil; moments of magnificent splendor along with those of doom; or the tensions of struggle and strength as well as quiet and chaos. Each part holds a story—or a memory—of its own. The importance of working with these individual building blocks cannot be underestimated. These moments deepen your knowledge and understanding and help you gain greater insight into the wholeness of your expression as an artist and as a human being.

The tension of these contrasting parts makes art meaningful. Art without any contrast is not necessarily appealing or pleasing. The tension of opposites fills our lives with the striving to move from one point to another. When we describe our emotional lives, we use words such as "happy," "sad," "angry," "calm," "quiet," or "chaotic." The contrast in good art often reaffirms opposites such as these; it can help us recognize and feel them as real and honest. Ultimately, a deeper understanding of how these bits of experience can fit together to create something new can provide you with ideas about how to resolve conflicts in your own life knowing that resolution is natural and achievable.

BRINGING IT OUT

In order to look more deeply into artistic expression, consider the meanings of the words—"artistic" and "expression"—separately. If you study all the usual definitions of the word "expression" they come down to one thing—the idea of something being brought out. In order to be brought out and made known, there must be a means of doing so—an action or symbol or series of events. In this case, we're talking about human beings creating art, so whatever is inside is expressed outwardly. The question then becomes one of how a person brings forth this outward manifestation. This is where the word "artistic" comes into play as the defining adjective to the expression. The word "artistic" possesses a variety of meanings, all of them tied to showing imaginative skill or excellence in the arrangement or execution of something. As artists, we use the word "artistic" to describe something that conforms to the standards of our art form. "Artistic" can also relate to sensitivity to the work of art or an appreciation of it. In this line of reasoning, "artistic expression"

> Music and silence combine strongly because music is done with silence, and silence is full of music.
>
> ~ Marcel Marceau

> Have a dialogue between the two opposing parts and you will find that they always start out fighting each other until we come to an appreciation of difference... a oneness and integration of the two opposing forces.
>
> ~ Frederick Salomon Perls

means that something is expressed or pushed outward in an imaginative and skillful way.

ARTISTIC INSIGHTS

The aesthetic of something being pleasing to our senses can be wide-ranging:

- Something truly beautiful, such as what might be found in a brilliant display of color on a canvas
- The coordinated dancing of a ballet troupe moving on stage in absolute harmony
- The sound of a single voice melody performed with haunting perfection
- Art filled with great contrast and expertly displayed within the beauty of the art form itself

Artistic expression can include ugliness, hate, and depictions of sin, brutality, and other things we hope never to see in real life. Excellent art often shows us great contradictions and crises, and we can learn a great deal from the resolution of those crises. Through our understanding of art we can gain a deeper understanding of how we might surmount challenges such as our own experience of ugliness or hatred, whether that comes from within us or from those around us. In understanding extremes of contrast, we can see the beauty in art with themes that are not simply pleasing for their magnificent features or qualities.

Benjamin Britten's *War Requiem* offers an excellent example of a work of art that brings great contrast within the structure of an eighty-five minute piece of music. When concertgoers heard it performed live by the Boston Symphony Orchestra, soloists, and choirs they were fascinated and deeply drawn to the qualities inherent within the composition itself that make it such a stunning tour de force. I realized—listening and later reflecting on the performance—that its power comes from the way Britten worked through and used the compositional elements in imaginative ways to express the tensions and contrasts of suffering and hope. In the end, the shock, pain, and revulsion of war brilliantly mix with the peace, comfort, and stillness of everlasting rest. The experience of opposite extremes of human emotion creates a special kind of lasting beauty, the mixture of elements creating a new wholeness of understanding. Even in our everyday lives, we don't truly ever forget the hopelessness of anguish. Instead, we're constantly renewed by its contrast with love and unity. When we step back and see things in context over a period of time we have greater awareness and understanding.

THE ELEMENTS

Nothing in the definitions of the words "artistic" and "expression" says that the expression must be done with any particular set of elements. It speaks only to how those elements are configured and pushed out into the world in a way that is imaginative and skillful using the standards of the specific medium to do so. When you understand artistic expression in this broader sense, it can help you understand your own life, guiding you to ways of dealing with the natural conflicts, pressures, and anxieties that occur in individual moments, in sequence, and in the span of a career or lifetime. This understanding allows for forms of artistic expression that include teaching, leading, and living your life in a creative and imaginative way, in addition to the artistic expression of traditional art forms. Since active participation in the arts can allow you to see, feel, hear, and truly know these things in great depth often without actually having the life experience, you gain considerable lessons from learning through various art forms. The more you take part in the experience of these concepts with the depth, breadth, and interrelated aspects of the various art forms, the deeper your level of understanding.

Artists plan their work by controlling and ordering the elements of their art in some way. When they try to combine these different elements into an organized whole, they use certain principles or guidelines. A unified work of art is a skillful blend of elements and principles to produce the best possible effect. It may seem like a cliché to say that the whole is made up of its parts, but all the same it is easy to lose sight of this in your life.

If the whole is greater than the sum of the parts, how does the whole come to be more? A former student told me a story about his young family. They experienced a series of losses and huge disappointments, and Jim struggled to find his way. One day, as he reflected on his difficult situation, the interactive environment of his college chamber music experience came to mind. It prompted him to consider the individual strengths of each family member and their contribution to the family as a whole. He immediately realized, no matter what each of them experienced, the powerful strength of the family together was magical. An awareness of the bigger picture transformed his view and his experience of the entire situation.

CONSCIOUSNESS QUERIES

Consider why you might lose awareness of the whole and parts:
- Do you take too narrow a view of the whole?
- Do you think that the whole is simply the mathematical sum of the parts?

The whole is a simple, yet complex, harmonious agreement of each part with all the other parts. The extent of the whole and the harmony of the parts—the way they hold together and relate to one another—is the important aspect to consider. The wholeness of things, of course, includes their parts, but there is an astonishing level of consciousness and unique aliveness to be gained when considering the bigger picture of the whole. Wholeness includes long term perspectives and realities. Although immediate problems and outcomes may be important, they are not the whole story.

A common understanding of the whole is that it is something like a car, a lawnmower, a human body, a building, or a bicycle. You obviously can't drive somewhere with just a few parts of a car, but you can go somewhere with the whole car. And the parts

So by craft or art
We can give the part
Wholeness in a sense.

~ Robert Frost
Kitty Hawk

can't go together in any random way. Each part has a function, and it's the unique combination of those roles which, in turn, creates an altogether new function that didn't exist before the parts were put together. Organized systems like this are the basis of everything we know, inasmuch as everything in the universe is, at one level, nothing but a part of a whole.

One of my former students discovered this concept as part of a performance experience. Deeply moved, faculty members and fellow student musicians quickly walked backstage to congratulate him on his powerful performance of one of the most difficult works in the classical saxophone repertoire. Everyone in the audience who had been on the edge of their seats during the performance now stood on their feet in appreciation of what they had just experienced. His confident stage presence along with the masterful rendering of wide ranging interval leaps, arpeggios, grace notes, dynamic contrasts, tempo changes, and articulations along with technically demanding thirty-second note runs was extraordinary. He performed the work as if it were part of him, but as we came around the back curtain to the stage entrance we saw that he was in tears and bent forward, leaning on the back of a chair for support. We were stunned.

Later, when he was able to talk, we found that he was disheartened over a note that didn't speak on the instrument as it should—as if that was all he remembered. After several weeks of reflection, weekly lessons, and rave reviews by fellow musicians from the audience, his awareness grew. He finally saw the performance in its entirety and accepted the praise he so well deserved. He discovered how that one moment, which most people never even noticed, was only a small part of what he expressed through the whole of the performance. This understanding became something he continued to investigate and his curiosity led him to confirm it in all his experiences: things exist in relation to each other. In his performance, the flow of the entire work was powerful.

His awareness grew to consider that moment in the performance at another level. He continued to develop what he considered to be the mishandled section as a whole, in and of itself, but now he had a new idea of how it would fit with the work in its entirety. High level artistic expression occurs when you can take these parts and develop them, work with them, utilize them, and maneuver them, focusing on how each particular part relates with the entirety of the work of art in a way that creates something truly new and meaningful, more than simply the sum of its parts.

This can be extended beyond the work at that moment to include the entirety of your creative work in a month, in a year, in several years, or in a lifetime. While it may seem a simple truth to say that artistic expression is putting all the parts together, the process is much more complex than that. For example, you can look at all the parts of a relationship experience and also examine the relationship as a whole. At the same time, the relationship can also be considered relative to other relationship experiences. The knowledge you gain can inform the future and allow you to create new, more meaningful, outcomes.

GENERATING WHOLENESS

Certain basic artistic principles generate wholeness in a work of art. To name a few: unity, variety, proportion, balance, movement, pattern, rhythm, harmony, and emphasis. You can think of unity as the wholeness achieved through the effective use of the elements and principles of the art form. Unity is like an invisible glue that joins all the separate parts together so they look, feel, or sound like they belong together—a sense of oneness, of things belonging together to make up a comprehensible whole. Generally, a work of art is strengthened by a sense of unity in form and composition. Works where all of the elements seem to fit together visually or aurally or in action or words allow the whole to become greater than the sum of its parts.

Variety and contrast, on the other hand, speak to the diversity of the elements in the work that are used together. Elements that conflict with one another create interest and are dynamic. There is unity in diversity—a balance between harmony and dissonance,

Individuality is only possible if it unfolds from wholeness.

~ David Bohm
in dialogue with
Renée Weber, *Re-vision*

between integrity and fragility. Not all differences can be held together. Some differences can create chaos in a work. Yet, not all contrast creates confusion. The contrasts and diversity often make the combination of elements more interesting. This joining creates momentum. In high level artistic expression, you consider what unites the work and what allows the contrasts to act together in innovative and unique ways.

RELATIONSHIP AND CONTEXT

Balance expresses the relative weight between harmonious and conflicting elements. Some contrast makes for an even deeper unity. Balance speaks to the way the elements and materials of the art form are distributed, the weight of one aspect or moment in relation to the others. In other words, the relationship between the elements links them or weaves them together. The relationship generates energy. Some relationships are naturally meaningful, deep, rich, resonant, or collaborative while some require more thought and attention. This uniqueness of the parts offers a vast pool of resources, limited only by your imagination. Since each part is unique and whole, you can tap into the potential of that individual part and utilize it beyond what may be its usual or expected role. Artists learn to balance the qualities of each part and arrange them so they complement each other. The unique combination creates the powerful effect of synergy—the whole and the parts in relationship become something new.

Context and perspective are important to the artistic process. Context—form and proportion, the use of space and time, and pattern and rhythm—consists of everything that is a part of the bigger picture. Expansion of your own personal sense of context will allow you to achieve much greater breadth of knowledge and understanding in your work.

Although artistic outcomes are shaped by context and perspective, it's also important to consider the inner quality, or character, of things. In other words, the awareness of what you're trying to create comes from within. The resourcefulness

I don't think of form as a kind of architecture. The architecture is the result of the forming. It is the kinesthetic and visual sense of position and wholeness that puts the thing into the realm of art.

~ Roy Lichtenstein

To be great, be whole: don't exaggerate. Or leave out any part of you. Be complete in each thing. Put all you are into the least of your acts. So too in each lake, with its lofty life, the whole moon shines.

~ Fernando Pessoa
Ode of Ricardo Reis

and motivation comes from within, as well. When you open to the artistic process, you find your way by delving into your own inner qualities, and when you can align this inner knowing with context, you have the potential to be truly innovative.

The artistic process calls for imaginative skill in arranging or interpreting elements in ways that move you to a deeper level of understanding. The process requires an understanding of synergy and momentum and their function in realizing the work as a whole. You consider what to leave out, as well as whether all of the parts that are needed are present.

ARTISTIC INSIGHTS

- Each part has a unique relationship to the work of art as a whole.
- There is also a unique relationship between the elements of that moment or part of the work as an entity itself.
- In other words, each part or moment of the work contributes in relationship to the whole and expresses its individual essence just as it also creates synergy with the other parts.

Filmmaking is not about the tiny details. It's about the big picture.

~ Ed Wood
Ed Wood

MOTIVATIONAL STORY—WILLINGNESS TO RISK

One afternoon, a longtime colleague shared her earliest memories about how she engaged with the artistic process. Jody explained she loved to explore things in great depth, truly getting inside them with playfulness and genuine interest. Looking back now, she realized that this natural inclination of delving deeply into things allowed her to expand her understanding. While the sense of knowing and discovery was exciting, she often felt frustrated when she didn't have the vocabulary to express the significant meanings of what she felt and saw. The arts gave her that opening for expression—a way of bringing what she discovered out into the world.

Jody learned from her experiences that not everything knowable can be expressed in words. This realization motivated her to begin a lifelong journey through the arts. She knew her life's work would involve the arts and she was convinced that it had to be in the performance of music. That is where she felt she could make the biggest contribution and realize who she was as a human being. It is where she felt she could take all of the parts of her life and put them together to feel most whole.

Jody mentioned that she felt fortunate to have excellent educational experiences in the arts. She naturally extended her interest in exploring the inner aspects of things to music. She constantly took risks, and while not all experiences were equally rewarding, all of them were crucial to the full acceptance and appreciation for the various twists and turns her life has taken since those days.

Although she studied flute privately, performed in several prestigious organizations outside of her public school experience, and received quite a few honors on that instrument, she seemed to have a natural talent to pick up any woodwind instrument and play it at a high level with ease. While in high school she played the instrument needed most, depending on the situation—flute in solo and ensemble festivals, oboe in concert ensembles, saxophone in jazz ensembles, and later bassoon in wind quintets. This breadth did not concern her—Jody enjoyed the variety of those experiences and the differences in the way the music felt from within the ensemble as a result of performing through those various voices. It seemed logical, though, that she audition and enter college as a flute major because she had studied it so intensely.

One day, early in Jody's freshman year, one of her professors said he had heard her every day in the practice rooms playing flute, as well as other instruments. He suggested she become a woodwind major and not limit herself to flute alone. At first she felt devastated because she thought that meant she could not perform at a high enough level on flute. When Jody told him a woodwind major option did not exist and that she didn't know what to do, he told her to simply go to the director of the school and tell him what she wanted. The director asked what she thought she should do to get a degree like that. Since Jody didn't know any better, she described the program of study and recital schedule for all five instruments. As a result she ended up

Unless you enter the tiger's den you cannot take the cubs.

~ Chinese Proverb

performing junior, senior, and master's level recitals on all of the five woodwind instruments. This experience became a powerful force in shaping her experiences from that time forward.

The willingness to take this risk led to a new degree and countless opportunities she would never have experienced otherwise. Jody took advantage of her natural desire to seek depth in her experiences and to do it through the wide-ranging voices of these various instruments. She gained a much greater breadth of knowledge, broader scope of repertoire, and more open-minded appreciation of styles than she could ever have experienced as a traditional flute major. She took parts of all of her experience to that point and created something completely new by being open, receiving an idea, and making things happen in a new way. It turned into something practical that dramatically changed the course of her career. Three years later, without realizing it at the time, the same kind of creative tension gave her the opportunity to create something new yet again.

When she was well on her way to a successful career as a performer in the Los Angeles area, a friend asked her to assist as a woodwind consultant with his large high school band program. Those who knew Jody well wondered what had happened to her. She fell in love with those kids learning to love music and she—a person who never considered teaching an option because she thought through observation in her public school years that her music teachers went through such incredible torture—taught high school band. Although she still actively performed at the time, she delved deeply into the work of an educator. She took the dynamic energy of expression she used in music performance and maintained it in the ideas she explored with students. It opened up doors to her future that could not have opened without taking this chance. After several years, all her previous experiences motivated her to move her woodwind performance, conducting, and teaching experiences to higher education. The move evolved naturally and she willingly took the risk to further develop her career.

As Jody entered the world of higher education, her evolving interests led her to complete a doctor of musical arts degree in orchestral conducting. At the same time, she continued to explore the elements of effective teaching as well as active solo and ensemble performance, and took a new interest in leadership as an extension of artistic goals and experiences. This interest gave her tremendous opportunities—life altering in discovering new ways of expressing herself. One of the opportunities that transformed her career—an experience in administration—allowed her to have an even bigger perspective.

While all of her experiences to that point grew increasingly to larger viewpoints—from flute to woodwinds, from performing to blending in teaching as a performing art, to conducting—administration in higher education helped her to learn about focus. Jody felt it gave her the opportunity to take the depth of her exploration of the insides of things to an entirely different level and to expand her awareness of the whole. Her experiences in educational leadership that have now extended over many years allowed her to take the flow of her artistic experiences and teaching into the challenges of academic administration. She learned to blend the power of creative momentum from the artistic process with the often analytical world of administration.

Near the end of our conversation, Jody shared that she viewed this sequence of events from an artistic point of view. She saw that in each of these experiences she created something entirely new. Each of them represented a building block, a moment or series of moments and experiences, which related to one another in ways that created the whole of her life path and career. The arts gave her a special experience, a way of exploring deeply, of risk taking without full exposure in every moment. Her experiences offered the opportunity to explore and balance the patterns and contrasts of transformational and transactional leadership. She came to deeply value the synergy of both styles in an integrated whole.

LESSONS LEARNED

EXPLORING THE INSIDES

Three lessons stand out as relevant to the concept of artistic expression explored in this chapter. First is the value of deep exploration inside things to see the relative weight of every detail. This led Jody to an understanding of the function of various elements and their tendencies, whether in music and performance, life, teaching, or leading. The dictionary definition of "details" explains them as particulars considered individually and in relation to the whole. In other words, without the details, it is difficult to understand and see the big picture. Jody came to understand that these small individual details can be skillfully used to make a work of art unique. At the same time, the good that comes from looking inside and scrutinizing the details is lost if you get stuck there because it is only a small part of something bigger. Although complex by itself, there is so much more than that one moment, that one work, or that one concert in artistic performance. This is true in all art whether it takes place in time, like music; in space; in words; or kinetically. Jody's experiences taught her how to focus and how to attain the big things by working on the little things.

MINIATURE WHOLE OF THE BIGGER PICTURE

It was clear from our conversation that Jody enjoyed an extraordinary feeling of freedom when she stood back and looked at the completion of each of these life segments as they occurred. She now realizes each was a miniature whole of a much bigger picture. When she reviews the combination of sequenced events, she finds it truly inspiring and encouraging. She came to appreciate balance from the perspective of the part and the whole while at the same time considering the importance and skillful use of movement in creating great art. As we talked, Jody reflected on the awareness and skill of being able to get inside things to explore, but also exit at will in order to gain a broader perspective.

…you take your day and artistically create it, so every moment has an artistic flavor.

~ William Shatner

POWER AND RESPONSIBILITY

Finally, she gained powerful overarching lessons from these experiences. She discovered the importance of the artistic process—of making something new out of things. She also came to value the willingness to experience what might sometimes be considered extremes in contrasts in order to facilitate the transformational process of her art and life.

The significance of using your passion and always making use of your natural gifts and abilities is critical to the artistic process. The skillful expression of your true essence as an individual is essential in the artistic process, no matter the medium. This skill also implies a willingness to immerse yourself in what you do in order to fully awaken your creative power. Lastly, when you truly understand that the breadth and depth of your expression as a human being is powerful and you accept this responsibility, you can become an innovative force in the world.

DEEPENING PERSPECTIVES OF WHOLES AND PARTS

THE ROLE OF EFFORT

The artistic process requires effort. Lengthy periods of reflection and observation are required in order to express something in a skillful and meaningful manner. An artist's work requires observation and sifting through things—getting inside them in order to extract emotion and meaning. For something to be considered a true artistic expression there must be imagination, an urge from within, and the use of all the senses—seeing and feeling things from more than one viewpoint. An artist achieves depth of understanding by using this imaginative skill along with what is known intellectually to create something new. Artistic expression involves peeling away the layers of something to get down to its core essence.

You, too, can compare the relationship between similar but seemingly different things and try to see them for what they might be rather than for what they appear to be at that moment. You can work to recognize patterns, form connections, and solve

My whole artistic life has always been about change, change, change, move on, move on. It's the only thing I find interesting.

~ Paul Simon

Creativity and artistic endeavors have a mission that goes far beyond just making music for the sake of music.

~ Herbie Hancock
  MusicWorld

problems, and almost become the thing you are trying to create. Most artists experience long periods of working and reworking their materials, often struggling; although they might succeed in some ways, they may not always know whether their work will be successful and endure.

Very few works of art endure without this undercurrent of effort. Once this effort is completed and the work shared with the world, it opens a conversation about its interpretation. Its greatness may appeal to others profoundly but in many different ways. You may ask why an artist would make such an effort. Artists must initially convince themselves that a new insight, a deeper understanding, or a new level of awareness will ultimately yield a reward worthy of their time and effort. The reward is often an incredible sense of freedom and new understanding that comes through the expression of the artist who creates the work. At the same time, the individual who experiences the work of art as an observer can gain a tremendous amount in his own way, expanding his knowledge and understanding, although it might ultimately be different from what the artist thought she expressed.

This artistic process resembles the energy you use every day to create your own life experiences. You have the tools to skillfully act as a guide, a solver of problems, and a decision-maker to bring life to your dreams. You have all the tools of imagination and reflection that an artist uses. An incredible sense of satisfaction comes from creating new ways of being and from the understanding and connections to the things in your life. Sharing the beauty of your essence as a human offers an incredible gift to the world, just as great art. Other people who observe your experiences, or share in some way what you have experienced, can benefit greatly from your growth. Think about how you feel when you see a friend recover from a difficult situation. Over a three-year period I witnessed a group of students grow dramatically as they watched one of their friends recover from an addiction. They grew well beyond what they ever previously

Vision is the art of seeing things invisible.

~ Jonathan Swift
The Works of Jonathan Swift: Miscellanies, by Mr. Pope, Dr. Arbuthnot, Mr. Gay, & C. Prose Miscellanies by Swift and Sheridan

imagined and became each other's support system. Their lives changed considerably. When you engage in an artistic process to live your life, you constantly work to make sense of yourself and your surroundings. Going within to find the essence, and using imaginative skill and effort to bring forth something new, gives you energy to continue to use your creative power.

RANGE OF POSSIBILITIES

With the power of the imagination you can see varied possibilities—both what can be expressed and how it can be communicated. Your imagination serves as your own personal studio of possibility. Here, you can rehearse the possibilities, map out plans, and visualize the momentum to move through obstacles. Imagination is the beginning of the creative process, the observation of what lies within. The inner vision of imagination is the ability to use all your senses to express something. You do this automatically when you worry or fear something yet to come. It takes work to develop your imagination in a useful way, to learn how to pay attention to it, and to bring it out into the world.

Once you are able to imagine something, you can work at creating the momentum to express it clearly. There is no limit to what you can imagine, but it does take effort to bring it to life, and many people stop before taking action. You can use your imagination to improve a relationship, engage employees, resolve a conflict, plan a party, calm an anxious child, and accomplish an infinite number of everyday, useful tasks. Artists often spend hours imagining something, inventing or experimenting with it before they even start to create it. You do the same thing when trying to solve a problem or find a solution to a challenging situation. You can improve your ability to imagine the possibilities and create momentum, whether in art work, teaching, training others, or leading.

Routine is the arch-enemy of musical expression. It is the interpreter's duty to find not only new ideas, but also a new vocabulary for old ideas. And it is important to remember that a musical masterpiece is not a communication to the world—it is the result of the composer's communication with himself. An objective reproduction of this communication is impossible because the very writing down of the composer's thoughts is in itself a transcription, a compromise between his independent thoughts and the limitation represented by the transmission of musical notation to paper.

~ Daniel Barenboim
  A Life in Music

The creative process is a process of surrender, not control.

~ Julia Cameron
  The Artist's Way

CONSCIOUSNESS QUERIES

Choose a current conflict or problem:
- Do you see any patterns associated with this situation?
- How can you use your imagination to create momentum and move forward in a new way?

At its core, the artistic process blends emotion with the disciplined pursuit of quality. Although you can seek the assistance of others, quality will ultimately come down to how you develop refined skills within yourself. This is why it is critical for students to have opportunities to explore arts processes, understand the patterns, and find what resonates most closely with who they are—their essence. Experiencing just one class now and then in the arts does not provide the deep and meaningful experiences necessary to stimulate the insight that comes with deeper exploration.

In order to open yourself to the stream of insights that arise from the artistic medium that most closely resonates with you as an individual, you must have the chance to explore it. When you engage in the process, you open to the flow of understandings that arise naturally as you work with the medium. A special relationship with the unconscious aspects of who you are—and the discipline to observe them in an objective way—brings useful information into your conscious awareness.

ROLE OF INTENTION

Artists see, hear, and feel patterns and even recognize patterns within patterns. They take the patterns apart and use the smallest elements in new ways that often lead to stunning and more complex final products. These discoveries open up whole new worlds of knowledge about an art form. In fact, over time, artists developed new techniques by transforming the use of pattern in their works.

For example, impressionist painters used freely brushed strokes that took precedence over previous strict lines and contours. Impressionist composers like Debussy violated traditional rules and patterns of harmony in an effort to express something new. Van Gogh quickly adapted impressionist painting techniques but changed the patterned short brush strokes into curving, vibrant lines. Expressionists transformed the concept further, manipulating patterns and line to convey their emotional states.

Patterns can be created out of almost anything—a certain behavior, a specific way of speaking, the way you interact with others, or your daily schedule. The ability to generate completely new ways of doing things is an important part of the artistic process. It's not about complexity but rather the discovery of a new way of doing things that transforms your previous understanding.

CONSCIOUSNESS QUERIES

Consider a certain time in your life, such as your college years or your first job experience, or a series of relationships.

- What patterns do you discover as you step back with a playful mindset and see the bigger picture of your experiences over time?
- Did you discover previously unrecognized subtle connections between events during these times or the series of relationships you explored?
- What meaning can you find in each time period or relationship situation? How do they fit together as a whole over time?

Your observations taken together over the years can reveal significant patterns and form a sort of guide as you move forward. In this way, you can use the artistic process in a way that leads to greater self-understanding.

The purpose behind the motivation to play and explore, to create, and to seek new ways of expressing ourselves is a subject of discussion throughout history. The more you see, the more you feel, and the more you explore. The process teaches you about yourself but also motivates you to truly know more about others and the world at large.

All around us are facts that are related to one another. Of course, they can be regarded as separate entities and learned that way. But, what a difference it makes when we see them as a pattern!...They begin to make sense. The world becomes a more comprehensible place.

~ Murray Gell-Mann
The Quark and The Jaguar: Adventures in the Simple and the Complex

Intention is important to the result of your creative process. Are you motivated to express yourself in order to engage and appeal to others solely for the benefit of a beautiful experience? You might be trying to draw others towards consideration of a higher level of thinking or deeper knowledge you discovered in the creative process. Perhaps you are driven to communicate a powerful raging about society, life experiences, or opinions on sensitive topics. You may be trying to generate strong emotions. You may be inspired to create purely for your own expression and deeper understating. Perhaps you are moved to explore the very nature of perception.

If you are open to the transformative nature of the artistic process and how to apply it to what you contribute to the world, you also know the feeling of creating something with intention. A difference between this artistic process and other forms of patterned, principle-based, process thinking is the involvement of all your senses in a deeply genuine personal goal. The outcome can take many different forms and serve many different purposes, from simple communication to the expression of profound insights or ideas to the world at large. Continuous reflection, observation, and organization of these outcomes can help you uncover ever more subtle relationships between both the external aspects of your experience and your inner world. You gradually gain greater awareness and can use your new understandings to form a new goal.

IMPORTANCE OF MATERIALS

The conventions and traditions of a particular art form enable artists to give shape to their materials: to shape sound into music, clay into a ceramic object, paint into a painting, marble into a sculpture, physical movement into a dance, and so on. Artists gain valuable information from the interaction of the materials with the principles and practices of the art form itself. This fluid interaction serves as a medium between their ideas and inner knowing to the outward expression of the work of art. The materials allow you to convey an artistic expression, to send it

So in many ways, art has as much to do with the artist's intentions as with the art itself.

~ Julie Dawson
How Art Works

out into the world. When you create art, you engage in a dynamic interaction with the artistic medium, bending and shaping the materials to express meanings. You engage with the materials, often changing direction as you respond to the resistance or yielding that are inherent in their qualities. Your decision to use certain materials, the way you relate to them, and the way you use or arrange them inevitably affects the outward impact and nuanced meanings. In the end, the materials almost disappear within the outward expression. The work of art becomes much more than the sum of the material by itself.

A few years ago I visited a new outdoor sculpture gallery on the Christian Science Plaza in Boston's Back Bay. The walk served as a retreat from the busy traffic patterns of the city, and those who took the opportunity found themselves in the midst of larger-than-life sculptures that appeared to invite you in to take part in the experience. If you looked closely enough you could see the transformations in the wide array of materials used and how they had been shaped and reshaped into something new. In some of the pieces, it seemed possible to see and know the past life of the materials—where they had been and perhaps even what they had experienced prior to their new life on the plaza. In others, the past hid deeply beneath a shiny mirror-like finish that reflected the passing clouds. The artists had chipped away at the stone and twisted and hammered the metal, teaching the material to yield and surrender to a new way of being. If you took the timer to linger, you sensed the natural movement inherent in each piece and how they connected as a whole, moving you along piece by piece as if encouraged by a gentle breeze.

The transformations experienced by the materials at the hands of the sculptors seemed much like our own personal experiences as we move through our lives. Just as the sculptor's tools transformed the materials they used, experiences in our lives mold and shape us, teaching us to surrender, to move beyond, and pushing us forward, in this way changing our understanding of who we are and how we fit in the world. The sculptors create their art by connecting things together in new ways and pushing their materials to the limits. Each of us evolve similarly through our individual and collective experiences, positive or negative, influencing the way we take on our work and everyday life.

At the conclusion of the walk, I felt inspired by the power of the art—how the sculptures worked together as a whole while taking advantage of their individual and unique beginnings, situations, and surroundings. Each piece came from the use of distinct artistic technologies and skill, yet they worked together naturally to create a unified whole.

As with the individual decisions in artistic creations, each situation in your experiences occurs as an organized arrangement of interrelated elements, and each element functions structurally within the whole. Collectively the functions determine the overall situation. To change something, you need to change the relationships that brought it about, and you must first discover how its elements work together. You can gain constant feedback when you work with these elements of your life, just as you do when you work with the materials of an art form. This feedback can help you change direction, molding and yielding the elements of situations and experiences to express new meanings and change the direction of your efforts. As with an artistic medium, to observe something externally is to simultaneously observe something within. Your perceptions include reflections of the innermost parts of yourself—symbolic elements relevant to you. As you come to recognize this, the disciplines and principles of the artistic process contribute to your relationships, your emotional well-being, and your productive contribution to the world.

RELATIONSHIPS AS ART FORMS

The dynamic synergy you experience through the artistic process applies to relationships as well. Whether you speak of relationships between two or more people in your life in general or in teaching or leading, the connections and interactions between the parts and the whole generate the power to create or enable something. Using the earlier car example, the pieces of a car spread out all over the ground are not a car. It only becomes a car when you assemble the pieces, arranging and connecting them into proper relationships. In works of art, the materials in effective relationship with the medium create an integrated whole. Diversity creates dynamic synergy in relationships. Even in the car example, you can see the importance of diversity, just as you can see its value in works of art. If every part of the car happened to be a steering wheel, there would be no car at all.

With groups of people, the relationship of each individual to the group—whether two or two hundred—also demonstrates an important aspect of dynamic synergy. The synergy between the individuals, as well as the synergy between the individuals and the grouping in its entirety, creates the whole expression. The richness of the whole depends on the uniqueness of the parts. We live our lives as individuals, but we also become a part of many dynamic systems throughout our lifetime.

The diversity of values and viewpoints in institutional or organizational management and leadership are similar to the way materials interact in the artistic process. Momentum comes from the creative tension of materials interacting in a certain way. The momentum in resolution of a conflict can lead to greater awareness for everyone involved. If you truly study the most profound pressing personal and economic issues the world is experiencing today, you certainly can see the value of greater awareness—outside in and inside out.

MAXIMIZE YOUR POTENTIAL

Real value comes from the genuineness of your everyday actions and the innermost quality of your mind and heart. Intellect is not enough. In order to create your life as art, you need a special relationship with intuition, feeling, and your senses. More information is not enough. You need the deeper understanding of seeing beyond appearances. You need to learn how to learn and how to actually use all of the information coming at you. Even though we live in a more global environment than ever before, we are at the same time responsible for individually managing our own circumstances. The contrast of those extremes requires emotional and mental flexibility.

It is an age animated by a different form of thinking and a new approach to life – one that prizes aptitudes that I call "high concept" and "high touch." High concept involves the capacity to detect patterns and opportunities, to create artistic and emotional beauty, to craft a satisfying narrative and to combine seemingly unrelated ideas into something new. High touch involves the ability to empathize with others, to understand the subtleties of human interaction, to find joy in one's self and to elicit it in others, and to stretch beyond the quotidian in pursuit of purpose and meaning.

~ Daniel Pink
A Whole New Mind

Any effort to maximize your potential and ability is a good thing.

~ Daniel Goleman
Share Guide

Engaging with works of art and expressing yourself creatively through the artistic process can be important to your overall well-being as an individual and to society as a whole. Artistic expression becomes more than physical objects, performances, or something mental. Engaging with specific materials, not just ideas, helps you create momentum and express yourself more effectively. As a parent, educator, manager, or community leader you must inspire and engage others and show them how you learn rather than just tell them what you know. Through the artistic process you can advance the value of a broader view of relationships and contribute to experiences that give others depth of understanding. When you become truly successful, the people under your influence will be eager to learn and will likely continue to grow.

The artistic process can help you identify your emotions and use them to help you think. You can explore the conflicts, tensions, and resolutions that create momentum and truly feel the movement as you observe. You can explore your experiences and the things you may be feeling in your everyday life. The artistic process gives you a way of playing with an expression of who you are and can influence your perceptions of everyday life. It offers a healthy means of expression and helps you shift to a place where you can more accurately identify what moves you and why.

QUICK TIPS

- Expression through the arts helps you discover your inner self and understand how you relate to the world.
- Expression through the artistic process is highly personal. It's instinctive and gives you new ways of moving through the world.
- Expression through the artistic process can help you understand and adjust the underlying patterns in your everyday experience.
- Expression through the artistic process can help move you beyond previously fixed views about the way things are done, about other people, or about ideas.

CONCEPT PRACTICE

Understanding the wholeness of a work of art and its relation to the parts—as well as the relation of the parts to each other—can be experienced in other disciplines, but the various combinations of elements in artistic expression work together to create something with greater depth. Becoming more than the sum of parts in artistic expression involves something meaningful, rich with emotional content and value. The artistic process can help you learn to see and experience both the whole and the parts at the same time. Engaging in the artistic process offers an experience of both discovering yourself and expressing yourself.

In his first year working full time in public school education, a former conducting student prepared a high school wind ensemble to perform one of the most difficult works in the wind repertoire for a festival performance. Todd studied the piece in great detail and prepared plans to help the students in the group overcome the challenges and learn the style and flow of each section.

He worked tirelessly day after day on these individual sections of the piece. He became excited when the group accomplished all of the sections and he began putting them together in larger groupings, connecting the smaller pieces into larger parts of the work as they rehearsed over time. He finally felt they could read through the entire work from beginning to end. To his dismay, when they reached the last section, which he hadn't touched with them because it just repeated the opening portion of the piece, the music fell apart completely. The students didn't recognize it even though it was a repeat of the beginning!

Once he explained that this ending simply repeated the opening section and they practiced it a few times, they put it all together in an excellent performance. Todd realized that although the students completely understood the smaller sections and how they worked together, they never understood the whole piece. Since he hadn't seen any purpose in rehearsing the last section because it repeated the opening, they did not understand the concept or flow of the overall work. The restatement of the opening surprised them, appearing utterly new. Although he personally understood the piece as an entire work, this lesson helped him learn how to guide others to that understanding as well. He learned he could work on individual parts, but needed to help everyone see the overall larger structure all along.

While Todd used this concept regularly in his own music performance, this experience proved invaluable to deeper understandings that guided him in other situations, from personal relationships to community gatherings to meetings at work. He understood that in the complexity of relationship experiences of any kind, everyone involved must be connected to the bigger picture all along so they do not get bogged down in details that could slow their momentum or stop their progress altogether. You, too, can use the concept of parts and wholes to expand your own understanding and guide your children or those you teach, lead, or manage to see and feel the bigger picture as well.

CONSCIOUSNESS QUERIES

- In what ways can you use the concept of parts and wholes as an artist in creating meaningful relationships in your life?
- How can you create experiences to guide your children, students, or others in your community to a deeper understanding and value of the bigger picture?
- How can you use this concept of parts and wholes to make decisions to positively influence your community, work, or business?

In music practice and performance, an artist pays attention to, and monitors, the parts while simultaneously having an awareness of how they fit into the whole. The performer considers everything from the smallest details to patterns formed using principles of the art form. Performers consider the relationship of those patterns to the overall context of where musical ideas fall within the structure. They accomplish all of this at the same time in order to express the fullest sense of the work as a whole. A sense of all of these things is experienced in every moment.

The same simultaneous sense of the whole and parts can be experienced in group settings—chamber music, dance, theater, collaborative art projects, and choirs, bands, or orchestras. In practice, you take things apart and work on them, often gradually building larger and larger parts of the work until the entire work flows in a meaningful way. This kind of practice becomes critical because just being able to play all the notes, perform each movement, or manage each dramatic section does not necessarily predict a cohesive expressive result. Artists must be aware of every part or moment and match that awareness to how it fits with the mental image of the work as a whole.

The same technique can help you recreate sequences of past events in your personal experiences to gain understanding and add meaning that can give you good information to use right now in current situations. For example, isolate a time period in your life or work, such as your college years, when you worked in a specific job, the time you lived in New York City, or your twenties.

- Examine the various aspects of your experience during that time. Is there a unifying theme? How did events in that period fit together, one leading to another in a meaningful way? Think about how the highpoint of that time period took place and how each part shaped the whole experience.
- Try the same thing with another period of time and consider how both series fit together as one larger whole. Think about what might be the broader meaning of both, now, as a bigger connected structure.
- Continue the process, gradually building a larger understanding of the whole.

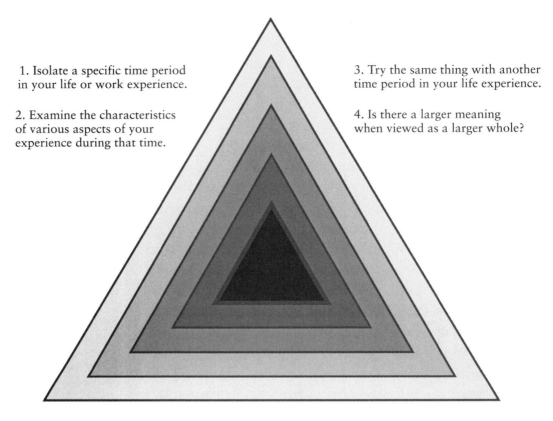

1. Isolate a specific time period in your life or work experience.

2. Examine the characteristics of various aspects of your experience during that time.

3. Try the same thing with another time period in your life experience.

4. Is there a larger meaning when viewed as a larger whole?

Continue the process, creating a larger and larger whole.

Experiment with these approaches to add meaning and depth of understanding to events in your work or personal life and to inform decisions as you move forward. Once you understand the concept, create ways of guiding your children, your students, your employees, or others in your community.

SUMMARY

With our cognitive ability, we can understand a concept in its wholeness and also break it down into its basic parts. When you think about it, you likely analyze or take apart almost every aspect of your life, including your emotions, your relationships, and your career. Breaking apart a concept and piecing it together again is important, but you must also use a process that helps you understand the balance between the parts and wholes. In using the artistic process, you need to understand how each part functions by itself, how each functioning part relates to the other parts, and how all the parts work together to create the whole. The ability to examine things in such depth allows you to think in innovative ways and develop the more entrepreneurial attitude necessary for success in the world we face today. Experimenting with the material in this chapter will help you express yourself as an artist, taking advantage of the beauty found in wholes and parts. Consider the beauty and elegance of three universal truths of the wholes and parts:

- Pattern becomes fundamental to artistic expression and experience—one part, or moment, allows you to express beautifully and simply the phenomenon of relationship and wholeness from within itself. A pattern can also be seen in an experience or situation in your personal or work life.

- Proportion occurs in the relationship of connected patterns to one another. While sensing the wholeness of the part, a clearer, broader structure reveals itself as the parts are placed in relationship. The links between patterns in life occur in the same way.

- Perfection reveals the full realization, the completeness and fulfillment of the work as a whole. Personally, this relates to success, joy, self-realization, completion, or accomplishment—seeing *beyond the trees* to a full view of the forest.

When you primarily focus on the parts, you miss translucency in understanding the whole. With a primary focus on the whole, you miss the collaboration and complexity of the parts. The effort then becomes one of seeing both the parts and the whole at the same time as well as learning how to imagine creating something new out of old parts.

REVIEW QUESTIONS

- Select a relationship, work situation, or family dynamic. How do you view the various parts of this experience from the past or in current time? Apply the concept of looking at pattern, proportion, and perfection in your work or personal life. Make notes of what you discover.
- When reviewing your experiences in this way, whether current or from the past, were you able to see the wholeness of an individual event? Of how a series of events or situations over time relate to one another?
- Can you see the individual parts, their relationship with one another, and broader structure at the same time?

The thinking processes in the arts can help you find more meaning in your personal experiences. They can help you develop relationships of consequence, design learning experiences fitting for the skills needed in the twenty-first century, and create institutions, organizations, and companies that move forward out of seemingly narrow viewpoints and limited resources.

CONTINUE THE QUEST

Reflect on how the concept of wholes and parts can work in your life, career, and community as you explore various art forms, nature, and other things in your environment.

1. Study images of a famous painting like Leonardo da Vinci's *Mona Lisa* or his drawing *Vitruvian Man.* Read about the golden ratio and da Vinci's deep understanding of proportion. An image of da Vinci's *Mona Lisa* is available at *http:// uploads6.wikiart.org/images/leonardo-da-vinci/mona-lisa.jpg*
An image of da Vinci's drawing *Vitruvian Man is available at:* https://upload.wikimedia.org/wikipedia/commons/2/22/Da_ Vinci_Vitruve_Luc_Viatour.jpg
In the *Mona Lisa*, the most prominent elements of the painting are her head, the neckline of her clothing, and her arm. How does da Vinci achieve the sense of completeness in the painting?

Read about the golden mean from different viewpoints at http://www.geom.uiuc.edu/~demo5337/s97b/art.htm and http://www.livescience.com/37704-phi-golden-ratio.html.

2. Nature offers a wonderful way to explore the concept of wholes and part. Examine the parts and the whole in a sunflower. Inspect the plant life in your area.

3. Listen to the first movement of *Symphony No. 5 in C minor* by Ludwig van Beethoven.
    A recording of the entire symphony with Leonard Bernstein conducting the Vienna Philharmonic Orchestra can be heard at https://www.youtube.com/watch?v=1lHOYvIhLxo
    In this video—http://www.wimp.com/appreciatesymphony/—Ludwig van Beethoven's *Symphony No. 5*, the first movement is performed and animated with a bar-graph score that helps you see the patterns as the music is performed.
    The symphony opens with four notes that have become quite famous. This rhythm becomes central to the entire movement and it also ties all the movements of the work together. Find the patterns and consider how they relate to other parts of the movement.

4. The first theme of Mozart's *Symphony No. 40 in g minor,* KV550 includes another well-known theme. How does it fit together as a thought in and of itself? How does it relate to the other parts of the movement?
    You can listen to a recording of the symphony with Leonard Bernstein conducting the Boston Symphony Orchestra at https://www.youtube.com/watch?v=qzBwa2jI1Oc.

5. Look at everything in your experience with the same awareness—architecture, furniture, book covers, interior design, television advertisements, or a series of conversations. They all incorporate small elements that create patterns, they all generate a feeling of relationship between the patterns, and they all produce a wholeness that projects some sort of overarching meaning.

CHAPTER 4

PASSION: CRITICAL PARTNER TO MEANINGFUL ACTION

OVERVIEW

CURIOSITY, OPENNESS, RESPECT

Painter, classical musician, and arts colleague, Paul clearly remembers being bashful as a child. He was not only afraid to speak, but one morning over coffee he shared a story about how the exact words couldn't come to mind for the powerful feelings that seemed to burn deep in his innermost thoughts. His shyness was a shield that protected him and helped him find his way through difficult circumstances. As a young musician, he found music and art to be a means of expression that might ultimately reveal the meaning of those deeply hidden thoughts. Although still not finding the voice to express them to the world unaccompanied, the arts offered him a way to channel his energy. As time went on, Paul recognized a growing awareness that led to greater understanding and confidence. He told of one particular experience that was transformative.

He was in a new performance environment, inexperienced in playing the trombone and unfamiliar with the musical style of jazz. Even though he practiced by himself and in rehearsals many times, he was terrified of standing up and playing an improvised solo in public. When the director pointed at him in a performance as an indication to stand and play an improvised solo, his natural shyness and fear of personal expression rose to the surface. At first, he felt immobilized by the feeling of tensed-up muscles and shallow, constricted breaths. Although he felt frightened, he had no choice but to stand. He pulled himself together with a big deep breath and played.

He recalled that he sat down after the solo not remembering a thing about what had happened. He received an immediate and enthusiastic response from the audience. Later, when he had the courage to listen to a recording of the performance, he realized he followed the chord changes in an imaginative way. The solo was rhythmically interesting and there was a structure to it that felt like a complete thought. Paul revealed that the experience in its entirety helped him form a deeper relationship with himself, his fellow musicians in the ensemble, the composer, the people in the audience, and with elements of the music itself.

He said the expression came from deep within his innermost being. This new awareness of relationship transformed his fears and the shield of his shyness. The genuineness of his expression, his curiosity to find what was trying to speak from within, and his respect for the music and the other people formed a motivating bond that gave him the confidence to speak. The energy of everyone working together toward a shared expression of the music helped him to rise and face his fears. It literally moved him to achieve something that wouldn't have been possible otherwise. Over time he understood that, even without the words, his curiosity and longing for expression led to a new way of being in the world.

Not only was his performance ability changed dramatically, but as he moved forward in his life as an artist and educator, he found that the combined voices of everyone working together to achieve a goal led to imaginative results that went well beyond what any one person could achieve on his or her own. It was the same creative passion of the jazz performance experience: a relationship environment that generates energy and brings people together in a dynamic way. He also learned that the same understanding could enhance his experiences with other people, both in his community and personal relationships. Paul feels this awareness continues to grow today.

There is great opportunity to experience a feeling of passion through the processes involved with creating art. When you learn to fully engage in artistic processes, it stimulates a meaningful connection of your heart and mind, and it generates the qualities of curiosity, openness, and respect. It is what ignites desire and drives effort. When you access passion, you will find the greatest probability for change, forward momentum, and reaching goals. Creative passion adds richness and meaning to your experiences. The artistic experience leads you to make empowered choices over limiting beliefs or behaviors. Motivated by passion, the artistic process gives you the opportunity to use your imagination in order to see, hear, and feel things you could not otherwise understand in such great depth.

You may have experienced something similar in your own expression or in those around you. Words just flowed seemingly out of nowhere. You had no idea where they came from. I am not speaking here of the kind of unconscious expression that might come from rage, anger, or a strong opinion. It is a sincere awareness you feel that rises powerfully and undeniably, and it flows forth from within. The depth and integrity of the feeling may have even shocked you. If you observe it in someone else, you may be completely taken in by that insight.

ARTISTIC INSIGHTS

Creative passion helps artists move beyond their comfort zones to find and develop stronger relationships with their inner and outer worlds. Creative passion can help you:

- Take risks and face your fears.
- Move past self-criticism to a new level of openness that motivates you to interact with the world around you.
- Move past simple enthusiasm to full expression of what you discover within yourself.
- Navigate through changes with confidence.

Creative passion as used in this *Fieldbook* refers to the ability to enjoy the artistic process for its own sake. When fully engaged, you gain a profound sense of being part of something greater than yourself.

There is a boundary to men's passions when they act from feelings; but none when they are under the influence of imagination.

~ Edmund Burke
  The Writings and Speeches of Edmund Burke

PERSONAL ENGAGEMENT

When you become personally engaged and motivated by your own imagination, the enjoyment is felt by others in your environment. Whether in a family setting, the community, a teaching environment, or in the role of a manager in a work situation, your creative passion can pave the way for significant learning experiences and growth for everyone involved. The genuineness of your effort is critical. If your passion is authentic and comes from an honest place within, your creativity and motivation will unconsciously and instinctively expand. When you have genuine desire for something, you are more able to generate the emotional or expressive energy to uncover it and communicate it creatively. The artistic process can help create the curiosity and openness needed, but it requires the choice to give it your focused attention. When you truly want to create something, you need to put forth a strong, purposeful, concentrated, and balanced effort, which in turn generates momentum and gives life to imaginative outcomes.

John was a college student with many challenges in his personal life. He attended all of his music classes, but he wasn't making any progress toward his degree because of his absences in other subjects. He never missed a trombone lesson or ensemble rehearsal, but continuing in school required attending the other classes on his schedule. As it turned out, he was the first person in his family to go to college, and his parents had mandated that he work rather than attend his classes. A trombone scholarship paved the way for him to begin. All along he had been carefully balancing his schedule so he could work to meet the demands of his parents and at the same time continue to express himself through music performance.

In a formal hearing, the music faculty told John that he could not continue in the program without making a full commitment to all of the courses required for the degree. His scholarship depended on steady progress and a certain grade point average. He left horribly disappointed and near tears, but then something remarkable happened.

Experience shows that success is due less to ability than to zeal.

~ Sydney Charles Buxton
The New Dictionary of Thoughts

He found the internal strength to speak openly and honestly with his parents. He told them of his desires and dreams. His voice came forth as it never had before. His parents were so deeply moved by his confidence and what they heard in his words, they abandoned their previous restrictions. They allowed him to live at home while he completed the degree.

Perhaps the most rewarding turn of events was that once he became more self-assured he didn't have to hide his desires from his parents any longer. They became fully committed to his activities and attended nearly every recital and performance. Furthermore, under the supervision of members of the music faculty, he started making more money than he had ever previously earned by teaching private lessons to young children through the Community Music School.

The possibility of losing his scholarship, his connection to the faculty and students, and the voice he found through performance was more than he could bear. It meant so much that he became willing to face the fear of speaking honestly with his extremely demanding parents in order to continue. The opportunity to learn through the artistic process and engage with the elements of an art form can be life altering and open doors you may have never before imagined no matter what you ultimately choose as a career.

CONSCIOUSNESS QUERIES

- What can you do now to develop a deeper relationship with your innermost being?
- How can you connect more closely with others?
- In what ways can you use creative passion in your life to generate energy and bring people together in a dynamic way?

Creative passion exists in the spaces between thoughts and actions. When you focus your attention in that space, you can become so involved that times passes without your awareness. This timelessness is often the part of the artistic process that makes the difference between imaginative and productive outcomes and

> Without the passion, we soon lose interest in a difficult task. Yet without being objective about it, our work is not very good and lacks credibility. So the creative process tends to be what some respondents called a yin-yang alternation between these two extremes.
>
> ~ Mihály Csikszentmiháli
> *The Creative Personality*

> Making the simple complicated is commonplace. Making the complicated simple, *awesomely simple,* that's creativity.
>
> ~ Charles Mingus
> *Mainliner Magazine*

My interest lies in my self-expression—what's inside of me—not what I'm in.

~ John Turturro

those that are uninspired and ineffective. We all have a need to express ourselves. It is a deep passion hidden inside all of us. We often spend a lifetime trying to find the way to express it, many times without ever having conscious awareness that we were looking for it.

An extraordinary experience comes to mind. The faculty in our instrumental department sat together listening to an entire day of scholarship auditions. The day was fully scheduled at thirty-minute intervals. Near the end of the day, a young clarinetist entered the room. She barely spoke. In fact, we not only had to strain to hear her small quiet voice, but she used very few words to respond to our opening questions. Everyone appeared to dread what might come from the instrument. One colleague stared at the floor and another turned his head away in discomfort awaiting the upcoming audition

Meanwhile the student settled into her chair. She stared at the music in silence. She raised the clarinet to her mouth, took a deep breath, and played. We were stunned. She performed with extraordinary confidence and grace, using her clarinet in a way she had not been able to use her voice. An expression full of meaning emerged from deep within her soul. Her creative passion for expression came forth from absolute silence.

With the challenges in contemporary society, creative passion is essential in order to effectively navigate the sudden changes we face nearly every day. The curiosity, openness, and respect that come from creative passion, along with its unique relationship-building potential, are greatly needed not only in relation to others in our environments, but also within ourselves. We can thrive in the swiftly changing local, regional, and worldwide challenges if we are willing to consider less competition and a more wisdom-building, synergistic approach to solving problems. Now is the time to step up and find your true inner voice.

Artists, arts educators and administrators, and arts leaders in our communities can assume a unique and critical role as long as they reach deeply to find the creative passion of the artistic process and then strive to share that wisdom with those around them. All of us can acknowledge the need to look more deeply within and strive in this way to express ourselves. Whether you are an artist or not, the situation we're facing does require that you step out of what may be your comfort zone, explore your choices more deeply, and engage in conscious, well-thought-out, and passionate risk taking.

GENUINE DESIRE

You may wonder what risk there is in passion. The difficulty for many people is likely the fear of what will be found deep within. Passion demands a strong desire to know and grow; at the same time, the learning process often includes isolation, pain, and anguish. This tension between the powerful desire to learn and the real fear of truly knowing is exactly what ignites the creative fire. Even within the genuine desire to know lurks a craving that builds creative tension.

Choosing passion means that you also choose to make great demands of yourself. When passion is sincere, you choose to focus with a balanced and concentrated effort; you learn that you have the strength to struggle to the brink in order to expand your knowledge. Once you experience this process of passion to its fullest expression, you can never go back to indifference. You learn that, when you gain the ability to carry it through, you thrive on the power to guide your energy time after time into actions that further strengthen your growth and understanding. Through the challenge of passion in artistic expression and the pioneering nature required to navigate the ever-changing brink—the highest point of tension—of the creative process, you can constantly expand to successfully achieve your potential. Passion gives you the energy and enthusiasm to persist and persevere.

Brad never lost the openness of creative passion he learned during his years of music instruction through public school and college classes. When the company he worked for entered an extremely difficult financial situation, in the middle of chaos and fear, he chose to make a difference. Everyone felt that the owners were making random decisions that threatened everyone's livelihoods. In this stress-packed, challenging environment Brad

Of this I am certain, nothing great in this world was ever accomplished without passion.

~ Georg Wilhelm Friedrich Hegel
Lectures on the Philosophy of History

Origin of "passion"

Middle English, from Anglo-French, from Late Latin *passion-*, *passio* suffering, being acted upon, from Latin *pati* to suffer. First known use: 13th century.

~ *Merriam-Webster.com*

opened to the imaginative space of creative passion that he learned to practice in music. Risking the wrath of his panicked bosses, he confronted them with what he saw. He reached deep within the core of his being to suggest a different way forward. As he entered this passionate creative space, he noticed emerging patterns; he saw relationships between aspects of the company and their clients that no one had previously detected. Through the tension of the situation, he remained focused and found the strength to face the owners and share what he saw.

Although trying times continued as they worked through the difficulties, Brad's calmness, and the genuine enthusiasm that came from the desire to help the company and his coworkers, changed everyone's energy. The company established new policies and together the team all contributed to a new way of doing things. The company is now growing and on its way to a new era of success.

Creative passion makes it possible for artists to learn to remain simultaneously focused on both the quality of each moment and its integration into the artistic whole. They can be aware of everything going on around them without becoming distracted. This is precisely what happened to the woodwind section when I was playing in an orchestra while we were in the middle of performing an important soli passage. We sat on risers a couple of feet off the main floor of the stage, and noticed movement and whispers coming from behind and below. The orchestra members, assembled on the jam-packed stage, were performing beautifully to a full house. But this peripheral activity was quite unusual.

As we finished the soli and unobtrusively looked for the source of the strange sounds and movement, we heard the principal trumpet player whisper in an alarmed and urgent tone that his third valve slide had flown off. He had to find it before his next entrance, coming up momentarily. If you're not familiar with the ins and outs of the trumpet, the third valve slide moves for tuning purposes. It is important to keep it oiled so it moves easily. We weren't certain what he did that caused it to fly off the instrument, but he seemed terrified.

He quietly leaned forward, got on his hands and knees, and crawled around on the floor near where we were seated frantically searching for his third valve slide. While he crawled around, the flow of the music continued. In fact, many of the other musicians were completely unaware of his emergency.

Remarkably, he found it with seconds to spare, and crawled back up on the trumpet riser level, carefully slipped onto his chair while placing the slide back on the instrument, and led the entire brass section entrance with great skill. We later laughed at the scene within the orchestra that went unnoticed by the audience. The trumpet player remained fully engaged with the flow of the music the entire time, even throughout the tension of his predicament. Although his attention focused primarily on locating the missing piece from his instrument, he simultaneously kept track of the overall flow of the music, the approaching trumpet entrance, and his role in leading the entire section. The other musicians aware of the predicament remained attentive to the demands of the music, continuously pulled forward by its momentum.

QUICK TIPS

Use creative passion in your own life to transform everyday experiences. In the midst of the confusion of a group situation—a family gathering, a meeting at work or a community gathering—consider the following:

- Take part with genuine awareness of everything going on around you.
- Contribute with a full understanding of your role in relation to the overall picture.
- Pay attention. Balance your effort with others.

Presence is more than just being there.

~ Malcolm Forbes

Work is love made visible. And if you cannot work with love but only with distaste, it is better that you should leave your work and sit at the gate of the temple and take alms of those who do work with joy. For if you take bread with indifference, you bake a bitter bread that feeds but half of man's hunger. And if you grudge the crushing of the grapes, your grudge distils a poison in the wine. And if you sing though as angels, and love not the singing, you muffle man's ear to the voices of the day and the voices of the night.

~ Kahlil Gibran
The Prophet

MOTIVATIONAL STORY—FREEDOM

DEEP LONGING

From her earliest memories the freedom Cathy found in artistic expression completely absorbed her. She openly explains how every level of her musical life became a learning experience that set up a series of events for which she is incredibly grateful. It wasn't just an escape; she found the arts to be an expression of emotions, and also an expression of her innermost being. It helped her see her relationship to the world and the universe. Cathy found herself enjoying the freedom of music performance—the right to speak, to think, to discover, and to act within the music itself. She willingly explored this delightful inner experience and stepped into it as a child at play. She practiced a lot, fully immersing herself into the sessions while freely enjoying what she discovered. Cathy speaks of finding joy in seeing and feeling what she was learning. She eventually noticed this strong desire enter into everything she did. Her childlike, pure and somewhat naïve desire to know and learn about how things worked and to truly understand overrode everything else, even if it meant uncomfortable moments or the threat of being judged by others. She was so eager in seeking awareness and understanding that this possible consequence didn't even occur to her.

For example, an experience in her sixth grade music class affirmed her joy of discovery. The teacher had spent a large part of class time trying to fix a classmate's clarinet; she finally gave up, not only because the rest of the class sat waiting, but because she could not see the problem. As the class went back into the group activity, Cathy quietly asked the fellow student to let her see the broken instrument. She studied her classmate's clarinet intensely and then looked at her own instrument. It was suddenly clear. The problem had a simple solution. A spring on the broken clarinet had slipped off its support. She gently pushed it back in place and the clarinet worked beautifully. While the teacher expressed anger at Cathy for her lack of attention to the work of the class, the internal joy of discovery and opportunity to help her classmate overrode the fury of the teacher.

As a child, Cathy privately wrote pages and pages that she never shared with anyone. She didn't often express her thoughts publicly because she was afraid of the bullying and mistreatment she saw aimed at others who did express themselves freely. Even though she occasionally took part in family singing at home, she preferred to play instruments and write rather than use her voice. Music became an incredible gift for her because it allowed her to see, know, and—most importantly—express many thoughts and feelings that came from the depth of her soul—things she had no idea about how to express out loud in words.

When she entered high school, besides participating in instrumental music, her friends encouraged her to join the choir so they could all be together. In preparation for the holiday season, the director assigned Cathy a solo speaking part. The music stopped at various places and individual members of the choir were selected to speak certain lines; Cathy was thrilled to have this opportunity and practiced until it flowed naturally. At the dress rehearsal, she carefully listened and blended with all of the voices, watching the conductor and paying close attention. The music rose, fell, and moved forward perfectly. Then came the time for the first person to speak; the conductor pointed in her direction and she said her line—"On, Comet! On, Cupid!" The music moved again. Cathy's turn—the conductor pointed at her and she said her words just as they had rehearsed—"On, Donner and Blitzen."

But something was wrong because, even though it was a dress rehearsal, the conductor stopped immediately after her lines. Cathy remembers feeling the sensation of air leaving the room and the deafening sound of the wall clock. The instructor paused, turned away from Cathy, and said in a disgusted voice, "You do it" as he pointed at another person. He started the music and went on with the rehearsal. Cathy remembers feeling a strange combination of embarrassment, dignity, and pride. At the end of the dress rehearsal they all left the room quietly and Cathy never went back to choir. She could not do it even with the assurance of her friends. With the energy of freedom and an unconditional devotion to inner joy, she had a strong stirring

The word freedom comes from German (literal, modern-day translation, "Freiheit"), but is actually closer in derivation to the German word "Friede," which means "peace" and is a word of pre-Christian, Germanic origin (originally "Frith"). The archaic term was used to signify the period following the termination of a bloodfeud between two Germanic clans when the softer, feminine qualities of the god "Freda" or "Frita" held sway. To achieve such a peace, some consideration had to be given up on the part of the clan whose member had committed the most recent wrong against another clan…

~ *Etymologically Speaking*

inside to express herself fully and she intuitively knew this class would not let her flourish in this way.

PLANTING A GARDEN

Although Cathy originally never intended to teach, once she experienced it she felt a strong desire to learn everything she could about teaching. She made every effort to understand the impact of her instruction for the benefit of her students. At the same time, as she sought to provide her students with rich and meaningful learning experiences, she discovered the gratifying benefit of gaining ever increasing knowledge and wisdom herself. The energy she put into her work as an educator led to an ongoing unconditional devotion to learning, for her students and for her own personal growth. She soon found the same vitality in assuming leadership roles and working with groups of faculty in her schools. She truly loved the work of imagining the possibilities and creating the momentum to help move institutions forward in their organizational lives—the whole being much more than the sum of its parts. Cathy found great joy in witnessing everyone experiencing things at a much higher level than they might ever realize separately.

At each juncture, whenever she chose to move on, she said it felt similar to the choir experience in that she found the strong desire to express her inner creative voice, and that may mean the need to move to a new environment to have the freedom to do so. Cathy believes it has been difficult at times for others to understand that she is "in love" with what she does, whether at work or in daily activity in her private life. She describes it as an interesting mix of excitement, enthusiasm, delight, longing, and desire all put together into one package. She further explains that her experiences in music helped her learn how to use this energy.

This feeling might be compared to that of planting a garden and wisely caring for it while waiting for it to grow, all along the way yearning to see the results. Or imagine pulling the weeds, trying your best to get all of the roots, raking out the remaining clumps of dirt, and then—when it's all over—standing back to

If you can give your child only one gift, let it be enthusiasm.

~ Bruce Barton

enjoy the beauty of the fresh earth and simpler, cleaner, more beautiful part of the garden where you were working. When you become captivated in this way, the world is a great place and you enjoy your life and work. You can become fully engaged in the innermost aspects of any activity.

This is where real artistic expression comes from. But it doesn't mean you become lost in disconnection; you find balance and learning, too. For Cathy, the balance comes from seeing and feeling what is happening in the world around her. Learning comes from fitting together what that means in every moment. It is not false, overly cheery optimism or the blind foolishness of "Pollyanna-ism"; it is real and genuine. Cathy feels she discovered a radiance and resonance that comes from knowing and learning about herself, the people around her, and how it all fits together to make a whole. You too can create this sort of environment for yourself. When you do, you will find you want to dream bigger. You become more engaged and create things you previously considered impossible. You become a motivating force of enthusiasm and inspiration for those around you.

> Gardening is learning, learning, learning. That's the fun of [it]. You're always learning.
>
> ~ Helen Mirren

LESSONS LEARNED

LIMITLESS POSSIBILITIES

Cathy learned to go beyond the usual experiences of daily life and become more deeply engaged in a way that ignited her imagination. Music helped her discover how the future moves forward from what happened in the past. Music moves along in time with various kinds of momentum between tension points and an overall climax for the work as a whole. Everything that occurs arises out of what happened leading to that point. It is never possible to hear an entire musical composition at once as you might view a painting, seeing its entirety sitting before you. The individual points move the music forward, but the result of the series of points combined create the quality of the more global end result. The choices available to conductor or performer, in the quality of each moment in relation to the overall outcome, offer limitless possibilities. Similarly, a series of moments in life can help you understand a single event, a series of events that lead to a resolution, or the entirety of points throughout a lifetime. This experience might be compared to a segment of a composition, then the series of segments of a composition, next the composition as whole, and, ultimately, the entirety of an artist's work over a lifetime.

Through the inner work of creating passionately, Cathy learned who she is, and in truth who we all are. She learned:

- The value of each moment and how it shapes the music—and life.
- The value of putting everything you have into the things that you do, ultimately reaping benefits beyond what you could ever imagine without this inner effort.
- The value of expression and the balance of inner work, gently and sensibly balanced with external pressures.
- About points in time and the variety of decisions that can be made to create different end results.

Every time she hit a turning point, Cathy discovered a satisfying sense of the whole—how the pieces fit together in a new way. Time and again, she saw an ever-expanding picture that increased her awareness.

Not only did she find the power of passion for herself in the creative process of life, but she realized its influence regarding everything and everyone. The discoveries led even further to awareness that the sustaining of sound in music is comparable to the endurance and staying power of life. In music, it takes a certain amount of energy to begin a sound from silence; the energy to sustain it is supported by choosing from a wide range of intensities; and, finally, varied qualities of energy are involved in ending the sound to take it back to silence.

In more recent years, the opportunity to engage with the processes of other art forms allowed Cathy to search inside the structure and language of each and make expressive connections related to her experiences in music. These latest discoveries—

the movement of the human body in dance, the complexity of dramatic interactions, and the widely varied materials, methods, components, and structures of visual art—gave rise to a deeper understanding of the manifestation of creative passion and its role in seeking and speaking. The imaginative energy of all the art forms continues to add even greater depth to Cathy's awareness. She loves the discovery of finding the relationships between them and exploring the ways they communicate. She feels it is such fun and it never ends; there is an endless reserve of knowledge.

CHILDHOOD INNOCENCE

The willingness to have fun and enter the unknown is critical to artistic expression—to truly be out of mind, that is, outside of how and what you think and believe. Otherwise, you only recreate the past, time after time. An honest openness allows you to enter the creative chaos of the world with an imaginative spirit; it calms the anxiety of not knowing how your creation will unfold or how long it will take. The qualities of creative passion help you face obstacles as they arise. You become more able to take action with the spirit of genuine openness.

For instance, a colleague who enjoys technology invented a new app that used his experience as a dancer to help people reduce tensions that build up in the midst of stressful days. This innovative solution to a problem came from the creative passion that grew out of his performance knowledge, his general love of technology, and the desire to make difference in the lives of others. He worked in a job that required him to sit at a desk most of the day, and in his willingness to use a playful frame of mind, he saw an opportunity to create something truly valuable for people.

With the imaginative spirit of an adult at play, you can hold your focus and move through the creative process without being hijacked by the past or distracted by other things in your life. Curiosity and openness can give you the willpower to create with unwavering faith and trust. It may not always be easy because everyone experiences occasional interference—deceptions or

I wish to sing of my interior visions with the naïve candor of a child.

~ Claude Debussy
Claude Debussy: His Life and Works

A problem is a chance for you to do your best.

~ Duke Ellington

If it's not fun, you're not doing it right.

~ Bob Basso

Never, ever underestimate the importance of having fun.

~ Randy Pausch
The Last Lecture

I keep turning over new leaves, and spoiling them, as I used to spoil my copybooks; and I make so many beginnings there never will be an end.

~ Louisa May Alcott
Little Women

disappointments. When trust wavers, you can learn to use the artistic process to consciously practice holding focus and working with a playful mindset. Conscious practice rekindles your confidence. It strengthens the relationship between yourself and the external world. Sometimes subconscious response patterns stimulate you to take creative action and, other times, another person may inspire you.

At a difficult decision point in her life, Kate—a gifted artist—drove to the beach every afternoon after the work day. It was only about ten minutes away, and she found the rhythm of the waves, the occasional ruckus of the birds as they searched for food, and the movement of the breeze a welcome synthesis of sound and sensation. One day, along the way, she was lost in thought when a huge billboard caught her attention. It said in big bold letters, "If it's not fun, you're not doing it right." It immediately jolted her from her serious thoughts and she laughed. Of course. That was the answer. The sign reminded her to take the next steps in her career using the creative passion she learned so well in her arts experiences. She had for a time forgotten her playful imaginative spirit. That reminder not only transformed her beach experience that day, but it influenced everything she did from that time forward. She promised herself she would always remember this important aspect of her expression, creating her life as art.

As Kate continued to learn through the artistic process, she discovered more about the depth and breadth of her creative ability. With each discovery, she had a better understanding of how to take control of her own creative efforts in the way that best served her in everything she did. Passion gave her the energy to do what needed to be done. This is passion that went well beyond the concept of what is often referred to as "finding your passion." Kate's experience in the arts gave her the desire to care and the power to try, time after time.

Kate feels she was fortunate to experience the arts from an early age. Music particularly appealed to her because it literally "moved" her. She remembers she actually felt the vibrations and the rise and fall of creative tension within her body. Rather than just an escape, Kate found that her understanding and awareness expanded with each new experience, not only in her various work-related roles, but in finding wisdom and meaning in life in general. Because the time element of music means that it needs time to unfold, there are no shortcuts. There is a beginning and an end, but in between Kate recognized a feeling of freedom. The sense of a certain amount of autonomy in creating the flow from beginning to end inspired her.

> ...It is when we act freely, for the sake of the action itself rather than for ulterior motives, that we learn to become more than what we were.
>
> ~ Mihály Csikszentmihályi
> *Flow: The Psychology of Optimal Experience*

DEEPENING PERSPECTIVES OF PASSION

WHAT IS PASSION?

Passion is an incredible gift central to the artistic process. Passion gives you the power to live, create, and communicate with natural, unrestrained joy. Passionate energy arises from within the depths of your innermost being. When you approach your life and work with the openness and curiosity of passion, the results of your effort go well beyond anything you could have previously imagined. You build a new relationship with yourself and everything in the world around you. Passion gives you the power to work hard at something and keep going even when the going gets tough. It pulls you along to grow and learn through moments of creative tension. You participate in things with a playful mindset.

QUICK TIPS

- Passion helps you reach outward and create a wide array of options and opportunities.
- Passion gives you the ability to see the world as a place of infinite potential.
- Passion liberates you.
- Passion gives you self-confidence and the energy to follow through.
- Passion helps you reclaim curiosity and a childlike openness.
- Passion helps you find the balance needed to sustain creativity and be able to stand on the highest tension points of the artistic process, time after time.

Things are only impossible until they're not.

~ *Gene Roddenberry STAR TREK: The Next Generation*, by character Jean-Luc Picard

Real passion allows you to experience genuine self-expression. It calls for continual personal, professional, and imaginative growth. It gives you the energy to move forward through what might appear to be overwhelming barriers to full expression. Passion is expansive; it gives you a way to grow and achieve your potential.

Unaware observers might view genuine passion as driven or obsessive behavior. This is a considerable misinterpretation by the observer. What makes the difference between the creative passion necessary for artistic expression and driven, obsessive behavior is twofold—one is motivation and the other is the experience at the highest point of creative tension. Even though they may look like the same thing to some, the truly passionate creative individual willingly struggles to find his or her way to growth and expansion and maintains objectivity through reflection on motives and reasons. The shadow of passion is far from this expansive and deeply meaningful inner effort of discovery. It is rather more focused on escape or attachment to something; it might indifferently happen to find its way to the highest tension point only to be unable to muster the strength or desire to sustain it; it is devoid of inner self and motivated by an external objective rather than growth.

If the passionate creative process is ultimately so joyful, it is curious to consider why many don't strive in every moment for this growth. The reasons vary. For instance:

- You may, consciously or unconsciously, choose not to go there for fear of what you will find.
- There may be a conflict between a strong desire and the difficulty of learning something that contradicts a previous understanding.
- It may be that without ever knowing it, you have become so anxious through life's experiences that the demanding, but often exhilarating, combination of love and pain leaves you unwilling to take the risk.

It is, however, exactly this synthesis of love and pain that is needed to develop this process of passionate creative expression.

Passion is fundamental to the process of artistic expression. This is true whether you are creating or performing works of art or living a more passionate existence that enhances your own life and the lives of those around you. It motivates you to take your inner life seriously. To be passionate and creative is at the heart of what it means to be human.

THE IMPACT OF PASSION

The path of passion is an important choice for all of us if we are to be effective participants in the dramatically changing environment of this day and age. The willingness to grow and search inside the process of artistic expression will ultimately transform your relationships with yourself and others. Whether you are currently an artist or not, the commitment to experience what creative passion can do for you will change your vision of arts in education. It will also change your view of effective organizational, institutional, and educational infrastructures as well as your expressions as an innovative human being.

The relationship-building aspect of passion—as learned through the artistic process—might cause you to pause and examine your connection to some of the institutions and organizations you are affiliated with; you may begin to question things from a more critical standpoint. While the new knowledge you gain may cause discomfort, your own creative capacity can make a positive impact. At the same time, if you find yourself in a situation that appears to be inflexible, and in an environment unable to move beyond old paradigms, it could be time to move on to other opportunities. With the right motivation and environment, you can make a difference.

Few things are more critical to the future than this concept of passion, which can shape your existence. Passion allows the creative process to be self-integrating; it makes us whole. It helps us develop a creative relationship with the past, the present, and what we anticipate for the future. Creative passion inspires meaningful action and opens our hearts and minds to change—a key quality, given how quickly things move nowadays.

Self-expression must pass into communication for its fulfillment."

~ Pearl S. Buck

Children need this knowledge. Everything is changing so rapidly that very few people are in a position to identify the careers and life's work they will create for themselves, even in the arts. Passion will help children use the skills and knowledge they gain throughout their lives to take risks and to see things through to the end. Ultimately, passion will give them the motivation to do things because of an intrinsic reward rather than the external incentive of simply pleasing someone else or winning a competition of some kind. They will collaborate and build meaningful relationships with everything in their environment, transforming organizations and institutions.

How Passion Manifests

Passion manifests in what you do through the individuality and genuineness of who you are as a human being. Your personal expression comes about through the interesting mix of internal knowing and external experiences specific to your life. You constantly shape and reshape things as this motivating mixture develops throughout your lifetime. Passion has a lot to do with how you choose to work with the tensions that arise in personal and work environments, both one by one and collectively. It has to do with how you engage with the bigger picture of who you are and what you have to offer the world regardless of your role.

Artists become artists because they engage in a productive way with the materials and elements of their art forms. Educators, managers, parents, and leaders who engage productively with the materials and elements of their life experiences become artists of a sort in the same way. Their passion leads to ongoing personal growth as they share their knowledge with others. Not only do they love helping others, but they love what they do. They feel complete in the sharing. Others respond with fully engaged hearts and minds. Creative passion sets the foundation for high levels of performance.

Things won are done, joy's soul lies in the doing.

~ William Shakespeare
Troilus and Cressida

Love is the spiritual essence of what we do. Technique is the manifestation of the preparation and investment as a result of the love.

~ Wynton Marsalis
*To a Young
Jazz Musician: Letter
from the Road*

ARTISTIC INSIGHT

- Artists reveal their passion through expressing within their art forms.
- The depth of expression in a work of art extends well beyond the mere technical use of the materials and elements.
- The uniquely individual mixture of internal and external aspects of the artist speaks through the technical manipulation of the artistic components.
- When you go beyond mere technique and express yourself from a position of passionate inner awareness, the world around you is dynamic.

PASSION IS CRITICAL

The changing nature of the twenty-first century requires the skill of adapting to—and growing into—increasingly complex roles and environments. The capacity for flexibility, openness, and the willingness to learn is essential. Increasing in importance is the ability to draw information together from disparate sources and the insight to fit it together in new ways. Real passion does not come and go. It endures and matures. Passion is critical to success in your work and to happiness as a human being.

When others sense your passion and sincere conviction, they feel the truth of your commitment and will respond enthusiastically. A wholehearted commitment is contagious. This is not shallow enthusiastic behavior, but the sort of enthusism that sparks curiosity and creates confidence. Perhaps you have a difficult time tapping into true inner passion, confusing it with hype. You are not alone. Many people spend a large portion of their lives searching for something more, often confusing caffeine-induced excitement for passion. They may search for it with little sleep, shallow breathing, or a fast paced enthusiastic voice. When you feel it deeply, and can sustain it, everyone around you can sense it. Passion that is critical to creating your way in the world is authentic.

Passionate people continually tap into their innermost sense of things; they pay attention and see the bigger picture. They serve more than just themselves. They are inspirational and move others. Just as in the work of an artist, the expression of a passionate person is enlivening. Passion is critical to meaningful learning and creative consciousness.

FINDING PASSION AND HELPING OTHERS

Motivation is the essential element in developing passion. The energy that comes from motivation drives everything else. Emotions are fundamental to motivation; in fact, the two words come from the same Latin root, "to move." When you are motivated, you are inspired to take action of some sort; you are literally moved. Passion requires an intrinsic motivation that embraces personal growth and understanding. While no one can make a person have a state of mind that enables them to explore the inner requirements of passion, you can communicate directly or indirectly in ways that encourage them to take action. Artists inspire others through the messages they promote in their works of art. You can do the same by the way you express yourself in everyday life.

You may experience a lessening of motivation or the ability to find and maintain passion as you grow older. Throughout your daily experiences you are often encouraged to become motived and act from purely extrinsic rewards, such as grades, pleasing someone else, money, or other material rewards. This sort of incentive is not sustainable. If you think about these experiences in your own life, you may notice the feeling of bouncing around and leaping from one external reward to another. True motivation is a personal decision to activate certain behaviors from within, it persists with continued effort even through adversarial issues, and it carries with it an intensity that gives you the ability to concentrate deeply and maintain your energy.

Ted found himself in a debilitating state of depression. He was extremely busy and never took time for himself. He went on like this for years, but illness finally dictated that he stop

Art is not a thing; it is a way.

~ Elbert Hubbard
In the Spotlight: Personal Experiences of Elbert Hubbard on the American Stage

everything. While at first he had a difficult time slowing down, the free time allowed him to reconnect with the theater and music experiences he had enjoyed throughout his years in school. The opportunity for artistic expression reminded him that he had been on a rollercoaster, financing the desires of everyone else in his life at his own expense. He went back to his work and achieved greater success than he could ever have imagined prior to this experience. While he became busy again, this time he was motivated to approach things from within his own internal guidance system rather than the pressure and judgment coming from others. It changed everything.

You can certainly stimulate the interests of others in ways that influence their desire to seek growth and ultimately creative passion, but it requires that you do it with more than just sharing information. It involves creating a vision of the future and a movement toward results in a way that leads to internal seeking. In finding passion, you learn to enjoy the process, even through experiences that may look like failures. The joy in these instances comes from the ever-expanding wisdom you discover as you move forward.

CONCEPT PRACTICE

Passion learned through the creative process comes from the depths of your being, not from a job or in what you do. It is possible to find it even if you never remember having experienced it. While you cannot do it for others, you can help build that capacity in your children, students, or those you lead; it takes practice. Everyone is "trained" in some way by the conditions and experiences in life; the only way to overcome those habits is to practice, just as artists consciously practice their art. To effectively teach or lead others, you must be able to show the way. You can inspire others by allowing them to watch you grow. There is nothing more disingenuous than fake passion created purely from external motives. Learning passion is like learning a language—you can learn it and use it. It comes from being involved as a creator rather than as a spectator. It is remarkable

I can't imagine a person becoming a success who doesn't give this game of life everything he's got.

~ Walter Cronkite

what you can learn when you let go of conditioned beliefs and fears about yourself that may have limited your creative power. As a parent, educator, or leader in your community, it is your obligation to learn to create from a passionate perspective.

Some people experience resistance when learning the concept of practicing passion. If you recognize it as a true treasure, you learn to appreciate its value and can more easily move past self-doubt and fears. Until you know genuine passion well, you may be misled by the false enthusiasm of those who are more externally motivated without the depth of the inner experience. You can create experiences tied to your daily activities that help you grow as an imaginative and resourceful creator just as an artist creates a masterpiece. The time it takes to connect to this concept of practicing passion is unique to each person, but it is well worth the effort. Spend more time in your creative domain and have fun.

If you apply this concept of passion to the concepts of building blocks of momentum and artistic expression, there are four basic steps you may use creatively to develop various levels of awareness and depth of knowledge:

1. Realize that resistance is similar to creative tension in creating art. It has similar power to transform your awareness and ability to create momentum.

Practice getting inside the resistance; get inside the tension with focused attention. The more you get inside the challenge and put your full attention on it, the easier it is to resolve it and move on with deeper understanding.

One of my college friends recounts a story about her cello instructor who wandered around the room when she played. It was a large room and Annie never knew exactly where he stood. He fiddled around with various things as he wandered. In one lesson, she was performing as if in a recital, expected to focus her attention internally and solely on the music. Although she didn't know his motive at the time, he deliberately did things to cause distraction. Sometimes he might come up behind her and place his hand on a shoulder or turn her music, or make noise. He expected her to go on as if nothing had occurred. This was a great lesson in focused attention. Now, every time Annie meets a distraction, challenge, or confusion she uses the distraction to focus herself. If you want others to be truly inspired by your example, show them how to use the tension of resistance and distractions to focus even more, not less. The more attention you give to your focus, the deeper your interest and passion.

2. Choose to take on the tension and generate momentum that moves you beyond it. Or sit in the tension and experience the emotion of being in resistance. If you choose to sit in the resistance you may experience anger, fear, stubborn denial, depression, or apathy. Once you decide to move forward, you have a choice of the quality or characteristics of that movement. You soon discover a world rich with possibility. The motivation can move you from desire to courage, willingness, acceptance, and enjoyment.

As Annie's cello instructor wandered around the room, the first time he placed his hand on her shoulder while she internally focused on the music, he startled and terrified her. She jumped and cried out, completely disrupting the flow of the music and losing her focus. She was lost in the experience and somewhat taken aback that he did that. Over time, she understood the experience as an important part of her education and she loved to experiment with ever increasing focus through these distractions.

3. Explore the ways the tension can be resolved, the possible results of each method and then choose how to move into the resolution. It's like a game. As in any game, you may fall and scrape your knee, but you go on because you have come to trust and believe in the resolution.

The cello professor never discussed what was happening in Annie's lessons, but once she realized his intent, she began to experiment with various ways to overcome these distractions. She learned to use her internal focus in practice and in performance. She loved the opportunity to experiment with using this new knowledge in everything she did.

4. Recognize the value of creative passion and move forward. The more you practice passion, the more you love it. You feel energized. Once you experience the motivation—and the relationship of your inner life with your outer experiences—you begin to truly enjoy what you discover. Ultimately, you can never go back to old ways.

Annie's desire came from the collection of experiences, not only in this series of cello lesson episodes, but over time throughout her life. She noticed she could simultaneously create new and meaningful relationships with the music and the composer, with the instrument, with her teacher, and—most importantly—with her own sense of power as a creative human being. She became curious and, even though there was a sense of vulnerability, she is always willing to learn more. Creative passion is a contagious creative experience.

External Experience
Judgement—Distress—Pressure

Internal Guidance System
Heart—Honesty—Sincerity

Creative Passion
Unique individual synthesis of external and internal experience

Your journey is yours to create. Even if it is hidden, everyone has an inner spark of passion that can be roused and set free. Passion is your choice. You can connect with your internal guidance system and express it out into the world. Finding and respecting the genuine core of who you are takes you well beyond self-criticism and judgment. You are the only one who can create your experiences—regardless of what others do or how they behave.

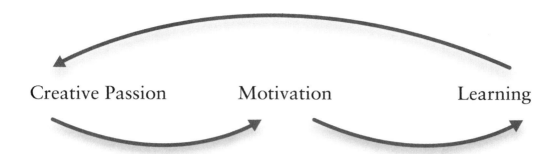

Creative Passion   Motivation   Learning

It's not necessary to scare others with such lessons as described in Annie's experience. You can learn to use a more playful mindset to create activities in your life and work that will allow you and those around you to learn this concept.

Understand that this requires much more than just making a big effort. It is not simply working harder. With passion, if you make a big effort to reach a goal it must also involve your heart, the core of your being. With the inspired synthesis of your effort, heart, and mind you can achieve more than you ever thought possible. Although a playful mindset is essential, this does not mean you are play-acting. Instead, you employ a genuine involvement with the enjoyment of what you are achieving. Passion is an expression that goes beyond a particular talent.

It will certainly take more than one lesson to understand passion and use it effectively; in fact, the steps in the model above may need to be repeated time after time before you achieve a sense of step four. Once you experience passion, you can practice it time and again over a lifetime, evolving to increasingly higher levels of understanding. Whether passion comes easily or is more difficult, you can learn it. You can design ways that incorporate your own personality and style into passion. There is no magic prescription—just desire and commitment.

SUMMARY

Passion is essential to everything you do. It can give you the energy and power to move forward as a creative human being living in a rapidly changing world. Passion requires that you

> This is the real secret of life—to be completely engaged with what you are doing in the here and now. And instead of calling it work, realize it is play.
>
> ~ Alan W. Watts
> *The Essence of Alan Watts*

Nothing is more reveal-
ing than movement.

~ Martha Graham

seek depth of understanding and learning from your innermost self. It is an instinctive natural power that can be explored to create opportunity out of dissolution, synthesis out of seemingly disparate or fragmented elements or situations, and focus out of conflicting understandings. The concept of passion explored in this chapter is expansive, moving well beyond the usual definition of having a "passion" for a certain thing. It is balanced with external influences. Passion in the sense explored here leads to a more far-reaching level of enjoyment and achievement:

- In most aspects of life, an endeavor will have much more success when passion is put into it. Passion has energy and power. Everyone is capable of having the passion to creatively express.

- When you don't feel passion, the result of your efforts may come with an experience of dissatisfaction. Everyone has the ability to choose to move beyond these feelings with a willingness to risk and explore. You can become motivated to do this by focusing your attention, and seeking motivating situations or assistance from inspiring mentors.

- When you are passionate you are expressive, you want to learn, you persevere, you take responsible risks. You truly enjoy what you are doing, you think independently, and you are productive.

- Passion can create excellence.

- Observing passionate people is uplifting and exciting. False passion is draining and deceptive.

Passion generates the qualities of curiosity, openness, and respect. It can help you move forward in the most imaginative way out of what has happened in the past. It is critical to artistic expression and in living life more fully. Quality learning experiences in the arts can provide a complete and balanced means of exploring creative passion.

REVIEW QUESTIONS

- How high is your motivation to learn and achieve your goals?

Examine the reasons for your efforts. Search your motives deeply. Did they come from a pure connection to your innermost self? The effort may have come from an external requirement, an effort to please another person, or a reward of some sort. Note what you discover.

- How high is your energy level and joy in terms of following through with things?

Consider whether your approach came from fear or anxiety, in some cases, and a sense of curiosity and openness in others.

- How do you model this expansive concept of creative passion for others?

Examine your relationship with others—children, students, employees, community—and think about how you interact, encourage, and allow them to seek their internal voice.

CONTINUE THE QUEST

Further explore the concept of passion. Use the suggestions below to think about interaction with the roles in your personal and work life. Consider how you can begin to make changes— even small ones—to live with passion and inspire those around you to do the same. Accept responsibility and put passion into everything you do. You can bring true passion into any area of your life.

- Observe people who exhibit the qualities discussed in this chapter. Take one thing that you observe and try it out in your life. Don't give up when a challenge arises. Focus and stretch yourself.

Around here we don't look backwards for very long. We keep moving forward, opening up new doors and doing new things.

~ Walt Disney

- Read about artists such as Ludwig van Beethoven, The Beatles, Stephen Sondheim, Paul Gauguin, Steven Spielberg, Fred Astaire, Anna Marie Robertson Moses, Jackson Pollock, and others. Think about how they used passion to express themselves even through challenges.
- Examine your motives. Listen—really listen at the core of your being. Spend time in silence.
- Take care of yourself. This might sound simple, but taking care of yourself means getting enough rest, eating well, getting enough exercise, and dressing in a way that makes you feel good about yourself.
- Trust yourself, avoiding the inclination to work or live for the approval of other people.
- Be understanding toward yourself when you make a mistake.
- If you are an educator, manager, or leader dedicated to helping others become self-responsible, self-integrated, and creative, you will get exactly that. If you don't have that genuine desire, you won't get that result. Be a learner yourself and take full responsibility for your effort and performance.

Practice this concept with focus on a certain element or idea; explore it deeply and ask questions. Inner knowing and passion will be the reward.

CHAPTER 5

POTENTIAL:
THE POWER OF POSSIBILITY

OVERVIEW

Your unique blend of experiences allows you to make a special contribution to the world. If you are willing to step out of your comfort zone and face the unknown, you open yourself to the true power of possibility. As an artist, you learn that the times of greatest discomfort can also be the most creative. Artists learn to face fear and disappointment with confidence. Their experiences teach them that they are always on the verge of something greater, regardless of whether that point is initially one of success or failure. They learn that the special blend of all of their experiences brought them to that point and will continue to shape their future. Through expression as an artist you understand that this mix of experiences helps you realize your potential.

Karen was in her freshman year performing in a wind quintet and strapped into the bassoon with both a neck strap and a seat strap. If you are unfamiliar with the bassoon, a seat strap is usually used while seated to hold the weight of the instrument, freeing your hands to play. When the bassoonist is standing to perform, a neck strap is typically used instead. The weight and feel of the instrument is slightly different in each case. You may wonder then why Karen used both while seated. The only analogy that comes to mind is the comfort of using training wheels on a bicycle. Since Karen was inexperienced as a bassoonist, she was insecure with the instrument. Her classmates in the quintet had played their instruments from a young age.

If you learned to ride a bike with training wheels, when it came time to take them off, you may have felt a little scared, not because pedaling was difficult, but because it was tricky to learn to balance. The bassoon is a large instrument—four feet five inches tall with a total of eight feet four inches of tubing folded back on itself. At first, Karen felt more comfortable to use both the seat and neck straps.

She found herself in this position when selected to perform with the honors wind quintet—flute, oboe, clarinet, horn, and bassoon. Although she had more experience on the clarinet, the dearth of bassoonists put her on the bassoon, strapped in and ready. They were in the midst of performing the last work on a recital program before they left campus for a featured performance at a major conference. The repertoire was difficult, but they were well prepared.

The enjoyment of the quintet members was obvious: they communicated expertly with a nod here and there, a movement of the body to reach the next emphasis in unison, connecting to the audience as if they were one instrument.

They were performing the final movement of Anton Reicha's *Wind Quintet in E-flat,* skillfully building momentum to bring the piece to a close. With only about two minutes to go, it was clear the audience was excited, sitting with anticipation on the edge of their seats, when out of the blue came a loud squawk, sounding very much like the quack of a startled duck. They looked at each other startled and confused. The music had stopped. What happened? Although it seemed like hours, it took only seconds to assess the situation. They all realized the squawk had come from Karen! Her reed was in her mouth but not connected to the bassoon! The reed had slipped off of the instrument as she played the solo E-flat arpeggios that led to the clarinet entrance and the finale of the entire piece. A bassoon reed is a double reed, so when it is not connected to the instrument it still produces a sound—a duck-like quack as the two pieces of the reed cane vibrate against each other.

No one could continue without the bassoon arpeggios setting up the ending. There are no apps for a situation like this. There are no touchscreens or interactive elements, just the deafening sound of blood rushing to Karen's face in embarrassment. The quick and joyful *Allegro molto* of the movement had been stopped in its tracks. Within seconds—and without any conscious thought that Karen remembers—she placed the reed back on the instrument and performed the arpeggios in a quick and joyful style. The clarinetist entered at exactly the right time, and everyone joined in to end the piece with great enthusiasm.

As they stood to acknowledge the applause, they all smiled with a strange mix of amusement and joy. Karen later realized from her musings after the performance, and through the years that followed, that she learned a lot from that performance experience—in fact they all did—and it has stuck with her all these years. The real opportunity of the experience came not only from the challenge of the situation, but from the joy of discovery when perched on the precipice. Even though the music stopped, it started again and reached an even higher level.

OPPORTUNITY IN EVERY MOMENT

At many points throughout her life, Karen is transported back to the memory of that concert hall. She gained an understanding of the opportunity in every moment. In performance, you are physically involved and all parts of your heart and mind are fully engaged. You are carried forward with the emotive aspects of the music, the technical characteristics of playing the instrument, the mechanics of your thinking, and your relationships with the other performers, the composer, and the audience. This creates an environment rich with possibility. With this knowledge, Karen is now able to move more easily beyond difficult circumstances and fully enjoy the easier moments, all the while knowing that the potential for what lies ahead is in her hands alone. The skill and capacity for expressive communication that came from experiences such as this heightened her awareness and aligned her innermost being with behavior that helps her maneuver in the world.

For example, she encountered a difficult work relationship that caused her a tremendous amount of anxiety. She worked for two years to resolve the situation, and ultimately recognized that the solution was to move on. As it turned out, her choice led to extraordinary opportunities that went well beyond what she could have found if she had stayed. Sometimes the greatest success comes from the most difficult circumstances. Karen reached deep down into the core of her being, all the while not knowing for sure where her choice and effort would lead.

Charles had a similar experience. He was pressured for time to complete a project for his company. Besides the tight deadline, a lot of money was riding on the outcome of his work. He tells a story of feeling overwhelmed when he suddenly remembered a lesson of potential and possibility from years of playing the oboe. The solution came to him clearly. Although this current work experience did not involve an audience, it was transformative nonetheless. Despite Charles having completed different versions over a two-day period, the project remained in a format not ready to present to the boss in the morning. None of the versions held together as a viable plan, and he knew it. He finally went to dinner on the last day thinking the whole thing a failure, and that his boss would see the plan as not practical or sustainable. After eating, he returned to his office for one more look before wrapping it up for the night. As he read his various versions, he realized the solution as more or less a combination of all of them. He spent several hours combining the major elements into a single proposal before he went home to prepare for the morning meeting.

The next morning, he felt exhausted as he walked to the scheduled meeting to present the plan. He knew the material well, but without the opportunity to test it properly, he wondered if his plan held together. After several tense minutes of review and questioning, his boss looked at him with a curious expression and told him he was shocked that no one had thought of this before. Huge success came from taking a chance. Charles used the knowledge he had gained from years of practice in the arts and found the strength to keep searching for a solution, and did not try to take the easiest route just to complete the proposal. He never gave up. His motivation came from the possibility thinking of his earlier experiences in the arts rather than from the fear of failure and rejection. While not all of the results he achieved throughout his career were as productive as this one, he found that each time he practiced this kind of effort it got easier.

In essence, the potential in these examples is in the openness to all the possibilities. While the concept of passion discussed in the previous chapter provides the position from which to fully use your creative power, potential gives you the power to make use of all the techniques possible to realize outcomes and create forward momentum. The same force that generates creative tension in works of art becomes the starting point for possibility and the opportunity to move forward to develop full potential. This is true in the exploration of daily individual and organizational life as well. Potential is energy ready to go—to move. It might look and feel like a decision point and an opportunity.

In a visual sense, potential can be compared to a ball precariously balancing at the top of a slope.

Aurally, it might be the consonant harmony leading to a sustained dissonance that seems to beg for resolution.

Physically, potential might be a group of dancers who move into a position on one foot while reaching out in front of the body with their arms. The gravitational force is a signal that tells the body how to act.

Potential energy might be waiting for a bus to go to a meeting or, in the Newtonian sense, the water stored behind a dam.

These are simple examples, but when they release, the potential becomes kinetic—energy that moves. When an artist begins a painting, a sculpture, a musical composition, or performance, there is potential for that artistic expression to develop into something. There is a constant and recurring transfer from potential to kinetic energy throughout the creation of the work both within the artist and within the work of art itself. Potential energy is motion waiting to happen, and through the artistic process you discover that even the smallest moves, elegantly made, can set in motion magnificent artistic moments, resolution of significant personal stress, or major transformational evolution in organizations and institutions.

When you sense the momentum that can come from these kinds of experiences, you find the increasing ability to uncover even more possibilities. When you learn the essential aspects of an art form and participate fully in the artistic process, you discover that your potential is far greater than you previously believed. The rewards for artists increase as they gain deeper understanding of artistic principles and master the techniques of their art forms. The power of potential is one of enormous rewards.

ARTISTIC INSIGHTS

Potential driven by passion requires much more of the artist. It compels an artist to:

- Get in touch with the innermost aspect of his being.
- Relearn how to be in order to more effectively become.
- Engage in her world with genuineness.
- Use his constantly growing inner knowledge to connect more broadly with the world around him.

DEEP LISTENING

In your personal and work life, increasing motivations and potential come from a deep understanding of your beliefs and values. First you must identify whether specific beliefs and values are genuine or externally focused. The sincerity of your efforts will create a wealth of possibilities. If you are an educator, manager, or leader, potential requires a considerable understanding of the methods and systems of your institution, organization, and community. When you gain this knowledge and master the broader aspects of living and working together with others in your environment, you begin to see things differently. Your imaginative capacity soars and you are able to explore possibilities and potential, not just for yourself, but for your family, students, employees, or members of your community. You begin to realize what the potential could be and that you

Things do not happen. Things are made to happen.

~ John F. Kennedy
University of North Dakota Address by President John F. Kennedy

can play an expanded role in bringing it to fruition. You will also notice that you are more open, and you learn to take part with an attitude that is very different from what might have been a tightly structured mindset.

The power of possibility allows you to adopt a more organic perspective, perhaps more like that of a gardener who seeds, feeds, and weeds his flower garden. All along he carefully shapes the vegetation in ways that will not only create beautiful individual plants, but in a way that is full of potential for all the plants together. You can do the same and create a more fulfilling experience for everyone. This is the power of understanding potential. You have the real opportunity to become who you are, and more importantly, who you are meant to be.

Beth fully realized the power of possibility near the end of her first year of teaching public school music. She went to work every day with the knowledge that she was well prepared as a musician and teacher. Even though it was her first year and the students exhibited a wide variety of levels of experience, she felt comfortable with the progression of steps she needed to take to prepare each of them for a festival performance. The artistic process was an important part of her life and she understood the power of potential. She was able to translate her depth of understanding to help students realize their potential.

Even more significant, however, was Beth's growing sense of how their personal musical growth could contribute to the collective result by productively working together. She helped her students understand the impact of their personal growth, not just for its value to their individual development, but for what it can do as a contribution to the whole group. As the students gained a tremendous amount of knowledge about the potential of the music—how it moved forward and evolved in time just as their experiences in life—their awareness of the power of collaborative experience deepened significantly. Their performance level rose to a level much higher than any one of them could ever achieve on her or his own. The heightened possibilities of relationship with the composer, the elements of the music, the conductor, audience, and other members of the ensemble expanded their understanding

It is the province of knowledge to speak and it is the privilege of wisdom to listen.

~ Oliver Wendell Holmes, Sr.
The Poet at the Breakfast Table

of potential. The festival performance was exceptional, and it set in place a beginning for all of them that went well beyond the evolving momentum they found in the music alone.

THE ROAD TO DISCOVERY

The arts and the principles of artistic expression can play an increasingly important role in the evolving situations and events of everyday life. You can achieve your own potential while at the same time pursuing the enormous potential in your families, classrooms, communities, and the organizations and institutions you serve. The artistic process is a powerful tool if you are willing to immerse yourself in the truths embedded within the various art forms and the real beauty of what can be found there. It means working your way through resistance and stress to create momentum and find the way forward. On the road of this discovery you will learn the empowering potential of moving beyond what at first glance appears to be a hindrance to what is in reality the tension needed to create momentum. You become ever more capable of expanding your capacity for risk and failure and for beginning another time; and you discover the potential of each moment to create the momentum your desire. With the potential of moving through the challenge of creative tension and seeking various forms of release, you become more skilled, gaining multiple layers of new knowledge. Once you understand the positive incentives shaped by this constant rediscovery and passionate pursuit of potential, you and all those close to you will be attracted to the possibilities and drawn into the journey.

Life as an artist or as an arts-related creative professional offers a constantly winding path of many twists and turns. Through the process of discovery along these zigzagging pathways, you are increasingly aware of what is truly aligned with your essence as a human being. You even find yourself learning to welcome those twisting and turning paths. They are essential in discovering the potential of what is possible—of what you want to do and where you want to go. Yes, the creative tension can at times appear

You see things, and you say, "Why?" But I dream things that never were; and I say, "Why not?"

~ George Bernard Shaw
Back to Methuselah

It isn't where you came from; it's where you're going that counts.

~ Ella Fitzgerald
ellafitzgerald.com, official site of the first lady of song

overwhelming, but sitting in that uncertain and uncomfortable place is where you find the potential, and it is what helps create the energy to move forward. There is a tremendous opportunity now to make a huge impact on the world, one that is greatly needed; you can use your wisdom and your understanding of the artistic process to "pay it forward" in a way that can powerfully and positively have an impact on the lives of others.

The artistic process guides you to an understanding of what you can and cannot control. You learn to be fully present with what is happening in the moment without trying to control it or judge it. The potential gives you the strength to move forward, creating opportunities you might have never before considered. There is no longer an attachment to a fixed perspective. The power of this concept comes from knowing yourself deeply and considering the potential of all the possibilities to create momentum and accomplish your vision. Through the trials and tribulations of daily events, you learn the value of the reflective process and the deep listening critical to the development, growth, and understanding of your own creativity.

MOTIVATIONAL STORY— IT DID THE BEST IT COULD

Several years ago Bridget lived next door to a retired couple in their late eighties who truly enjoyed every aspect of the natural environment of the area where they lived. Jack and Sarah created a beautiful garden of vegetables and a yard full of stunning plants. Every day they worked outside, carefully trimming, weeding, raking, and protecting the garden and landscape plants from disease and the frequent visits of the varied wildlife in the area. The javelina, rabbits, deer, spiders, and birds were particularly fond of the garden and were frequent and persistent visitors. The couple loved the wildlife—Jack was a retired veterinarian—and they strived to provide for the wildlife while also providing for their own table.

Free the child's potential, and you will transform him into the world.

~ Maria Montessori

I love those who can smile in trouble, who can gather strength from distress, and grow brave by reflection…

~ Leonardo da Vinci

Bridget delighted in watching their progress and the careful balance of maintaining the integrity of their garden and landscape with the closeness of the wildlife. They worked diligently to get the fruits of their labor to the dinner table. The javelina proved particularly courageous and challenging, as they eat almost anything edible they find in their environment. The javelina realized the potential of what the contents of the garden could provide for their family. The persistence of the javelina—often seen in herds of as many as twenty animals at a time—forced the couple to meet the situation with increasing ingenuity. Without running from the situation, the couple matched the javelina in their persistence, though always with care for both the javelina and the garden. Jack set up an alarm system that sounded in the middle of the night when the javelina got close to the garden. It created just enough of a racket to startle them without disturbing the neighbors. Some nights he got up several times to go outside and drive them away. He also planted javelina-resistant plants—chrysanthemum, eggplant, and low-growing juniper—around the garden. He finally planted some javelina favorites—cactus and succulents—at the edge of his property to encourage them to eat at a distance.

The rabbits were another story since they have an incredible ability to hide. Their determination to enjoy the various treats in the garden amazed Bridget. They dug under, hopped over, and went through nearly all the fencing Jack devised. The couple learned to be particularly resourceful in rabbit garden-defense techniques. They constantly changed their strategy, careful not to foreshadow their moves or they would come out the next morning to discover that the rabbits had seen what they were up to all along. Then there were the deer that not only loved to nibble on the abundant foliage, but created wonderfully soft and comfortable beds in the nice loose garden soil. Many times, the morning reviews of the garden revealed the deer had visited, and not only were sections of the garden eaten but large sections were crushed. The deer were particularly skilled at finding alternative paths to their goal of gaining access to the garden. Night after night, they literally mowed down or crushed the fencing to gain

I have been impressed with the urgency of doing. Knowing is not enough; we must apply. Being willing is not enough; we must do.

~ Johann Wolfgang von Goethe
Wilhelm Meister's Apprenticeship: Johann Wolfgang von Goethe

access. When Jack put a bed of pine needles below a tree in the yard next to an old bucket filled with various selections of acorns, grass, an occasional bird seed block, and some of the fruit from their trees, the deer often stayed well into daylight feeling comfortable and safe in their surroundings without ever touching the garden. Another frequent visitor was the blue jay. These tenacious, loud, and beautifully colored birds used their natural abilities to their fullest potential. They are aggressive birds and have the reputation of being bullies in disguise. But Jack planted sunflowers in various locations around the property, and they loved to pull the fresh sunflower seeds right out of the sunflower heads. It appeared that these birds even tried to help the garden produce by "planting peanuts" in the garden that they gathered from various feeders in the area. They loved hiding them in the soft garden soil so they could return later to eat them. Perhaps the most alarming visitors were the tarantulas. The couple often worked in the garden alongside these hairy creatures. While these large spiders didn't do much to harm the garden's produce, they enjoyed all kinds of insects the garden environment provided. They moved slowly among the plants with somewhat unnerving strength and confidence, fully aware of the potential for a meal. With their yellowish markings, they were relatively easy to spot if you paid attention, and Jack and Sarah did their best to keep a watchful eye and either relocate them if possible or stay away until they moved on.

As you can see, Jack and Sarah achieved an admirable balance between care of the garden and landscape and care for the wildlife visitors. Bridget enjoyed seeing the couple carefully walking and bending down or moving to their knees to care for the garden. With the shade of protective hats to keep the sun from their faces, and with trowel and clippers in hand, they created a healthy harvest all season long. Beyond the delight of seeing the garden, Bridget enjoyed the fragrance each day—the aroma of the plants and the fresh earth turned and kept aerated and loose. The old couple regularly shared their bounty with Bridget. The vegetables were beautiful to look at from her yard as Bridget peered into theirs. And they were as beautiful to eat as they were to view from afar, particularly the fresh tomatoes that were such a beautiful shade of red with perfect texture and mouthwatering flavor when cut open to eat.

One late afternoon, Sarah walked through the foliage to visit Bridget on her back patio. As usual, she carried a variety of produce to share. She handed Bridget one item at a time, first a zucchini and then two cucumbers. Finally, she presented a tomato which she knew was Bridget's favorite. As she handed it to her, she said in a gentle and soft, caring voice, "Here is this tomato, and it may not look very good, but it did the best it could." After closely examining the tomato, it was easy to see what she meant. It was an odd shape with various bumps sticking out awkwardly all over it. Obviously a misfit in this garden of perfect plants, it looked like it worked very hard to become a tomato but didn't quite succeed. Later that evening, Bridget prepared a meal and sliced the tomato. At the first bite, it was clear that the way the tomato looked had nothing to do with the taste. It was absolutely delicious, so full of flavor and the perfect texture. Fulfilling its potential as a delicious tomato plainly did not come from its physical external adornment.

LESSONS LEARNED

Bridget tells of how enlightening it was to observe the resourcefulness and adaptability of her neighbors. She grew to admire the depth of their dedication, responsibility, and commitment in their daily garden rituals. They never gave up and followed through on everything they started, never leaving something partially completed. Clearly, Jack and Sarah derived great pleasure from their daily discoveries, as setbacks appeared to be viewed as opportunities to overcome challenge. Careful balance between the desire for perfect plants and produce and the natural wildlife and habitat of the area required an ever-increasing skill combination of gentleness and strength. They became capable of detecting subtle movements and appearances, always seeking new ways to honor the opportunity to express themselves through their deepening understanding and respect for the fact that everything had a purpose. None of the visitors were intrinsically bad. The couple realized that every plant, weed, insect, and animal had a role to play within the garden ecosystem. Sharing the produce with Bridget at the end of many days throughout the summer, even if it didn't look perfect, expanded her understanding of the freshness and beauty of potential inherent within her work as an artist and allowed her to further explore the concept in other aspects of her life. The artistic process can help you learn that every one of your creations—whether as artist, educator, parent, or entrepreneur—has value, even if it is only to learn how to move forward in a different way.

The old couple certainly had ample opportunity to develop and use their energies to honor the truth of possibility and potential. The experience strengthened Bridget's arts learning to constantly be on the lookout for yet another way to move forward, reaching full potential and at the same time keeping in mind the impact of decisions on everything and everyone. Watching them brought to mind further knowledge gained from the artistic process—to always be open to outcome, but not attached to it. They knew they couldn't control what was really uncontrollable or become attached to a certain fixed perspective. They remained open to new ideas, they were flexible, and they had the capacity to care deeply from an objective point of view.

Jack and Sarah held the creative tension in perfect balance, knowing their own power to create momentum and accomplish their vision. What an incredible lesson for an educator or leader. Handing Bridget a tomato that looked so ugly while saying "it did the best it could" might appear to come from a simple and naïve place, but the words held much greater knowledge than might be recognized at first. At the heart of what the couple achieved was the power of possibility and potential. They held incredible poise in the chaos of creative tension and had a childlike wisdom in response to the world. This sort of mindset is a true teacher to the reawakening of our intellect, our creativity, our artistic awareness, and our natural intuitive capabilities.

CONSCIOUSNESS QUERIES

No one is immune to setbacks and adversarial situations. Consider your response:

1. Are there situations in which constructive use of creative tension could help you move forward to something better?
2. Are you placing blame or using your energy instead to explore ways to achieve your goal?
3. Each time you move on, are you open to possibilities you never before considered?

The more you practice moving on from obstacles, the better you become at creating the kind of momentum you desire. Experiences in the arts teach you a deep understanding of the possibilities that can be found in creative tension.

DEEPENING PERSPECTIVES OF POTENTIAL

WHAT IS FULL POTENTIAL?

Full potential means that something is everything that it can be. It is the synthesis of all elements that creates something meaningful. Potential is ever evolving; it continues to change and grow as you gain experience and understanding in life. More importantly, potential is the synthesis of everything within you, just as potential is everything in a work of art. Developing something to full potential requires the deliberate and disciplined practice used in artistic expression—in the process of creating works of art. Reaching full potential requires the synchronization of your body, your mind, and your heart. Higher levels of awareness are achieved through a disciplined process of reflection and introspection. Reaching full potential as a human being has been a major objective promoted in various ways throughout history. The concept of reaching your highest potential is often expressed in the word "areté," a frequently declared value in ancient Greek culture. In its basic sense, it means excellence of any kind, but ultimately was used to mean something closer to the act of living up to one's full potential. In one word, "areté" wraps up the sense of virtue, bravery, strength, excellence, being the best you can be, highest effectiveness, and reaching your highest human potential.

QUICK TIPS

- Use the mindset of an artist to discover the principle of potential.
- Consciously practice every day.
- Open to moving beyond challenges with new knowledge gained in the process.
- Focus on creating momentum, whether in the moment or over a period of time.
- Understand that reaching potential is a never-ending process of continuous growth.

UNFOLDING TENSION—POSSIBILITY FOR POTENTIAL

One of the most beautiful aspects of artistic expression is when creative tension itself develops with unfolding layers of consciousness that are revealed in a continuous stream. These unfolding layers are developed throughout an entire work, a series of works or performances, or the work of an artist over a lifetime. The potential, as revealed through layer upon layer of creative tension in more complex visual images or ever-expanding levels extended in time or space, promises an incredible reward of understanding and depth of knowing. These moments might be spread out over an entire work or isolated and focused. When viewed from a more expansive viewpoint, the creative experience in the arts can open up a connection between your own consciousness and identity as individuals, and it can awaken the vital energy of your innermost being that leads to self-transformation. The often misunderstood value of the arts in education would be resolved if the process of artistic expression were truly understood as a way of living life in today's expanding consciousness environment. Through the process of performing or creating art, you have the opportunity to achieve a potential that brings real meaning and depth of understanding to your life.

I am not a has-been. I am a will be.

~ Lauren Bacall

IS POTENTIAL THE SAME FOR EVERYONE?

Abraham Maslow created a theory predicated on the idea of reaching one's potential as the highest expression of a human's life. This concept goes well beyond having or being a certain something—an artist, a teacher, or in another role. It has to do with recognizing and using your talents, interests, and gifts. Full potential involves uncovering the true nature of who you are, along with a deep understanding of the creative nature of that expression. Self-fulfillment, the unfolding creative tension of becoming ever more what you are capable of becoming—in reality, "what you are"—is not something you can do through a rigid set of ordered events. It comes from everyday experiences and deep reflection, from observation and using your talents to express that essence. As a result, your individual needs are different. While everyone certainly has potential, you are at the same time unique in your expression of it. All of your inner and outer experiences—your own set of circumstances—helped guide your understandings to the point where they are today. You may have used these events and conditions to discover and learn or you may have instead put these things aside, fearful of what they represent, not fully understanding their value.

You might ask what full potential looks like or how you know when you are achieving it. Certain qualities help reveal your progress:

- You experience a tireless curiosity.
- Daily experiences are filled with a childlike focus and wonder.
- You are open-minded and willing to learn.
- You accept full responsibility for momentum in your life.
- The richness of what life has to offer is apparent every day.
- You fully commit to things you do.
- You enjoy others, even in disagreement.

Your potential is a personal journey filled with ever-expanding self-awareness. It involves the wisdom of the creative blend that

What a man can be, he must be. This need we may call self-actualization.

~ Abraham Maslow
Motivation and Personality

comes from bringing together your mind, heart, and body. The strength of that synthesis determines the speed, the smoothness, and the steadiness of how you move forward. Ultimately, just as in creating or performing art, the power of that inspired strength will determine your ability to achieve your potential.

THE ROLE OF PRACTICE

Artists become great by making the most of their potential. Several things need to come together for this to occur. Most people know that one of the most important elements in the artistic journey is practice. In order to succeed in creating or performing art, you must practice. There are no quick fix solutions to replace this focused and disciplined work. Practice is more than just working hard at something. While it might be challenging work, real practice refines your mind, your body, and your heart to perform a particular task beautifully and effortlessly. In practice, you learn to use your skills and build on them. Practice takes you beyond former limitations, pushing past what you were capable of doing previously. At the same time, it creates new challenges in an unfolding higher level of achievement.

ARTISTIC INSIGHTS

Artists use practice to make things possible. Practice has the power to stimulate non-linear expansion around any initiative:
- Artists concentrate deeply, fully engaged.
- They structure their practice with an objective in mind.
- They are flexible and make adjustments as new challenges arise.
- They make full use of the elements and materials of their art form.

The confidence and power you gain from consistent, unshakeable practice is remarkable; it is something you can count on. Practice is never rushed; it is conscious. It pulls you forward and increases your passion. When you develop the discipline to

Practicing is not forced labor; it is a refined art that partakes of intuition, of inspiration, patience, elegance, clarity, balance, and above all, the search for ever greater joy in movement and expression.

~ Yehudi Menuhin
   The Musician's Way:
   A Guide to Practice,
   Performance, and
   Wellness

do the slow and steady work of real practice, you continue to reap the rewards of newly found self-awareness and strength.

A colleague shared a story of how a commitment to practice truly changed his life. He was having a difficult time communicating and relating to his students. It seemed to him that no matter what he did, the result was one of frustration and mutual disrespect. The students wanted to connect with his teaching as much as he wanted to succeed, but nothing seemed to work. He was on the verge of quitting his job and moving into another field. When a friend suggested he try the same technique of practice that he used to achieve a high level of performance on the tuba, he felt he had to give it a try.

To his amazement, the immediate result showed incredible promise. He understood his goal, and he remained flexible as he made adjustments in his approach. He continued his practice day after day, gradually shifting the atmosphere in the classroom. He not only found new interest in his subject, but he understood in greater depth why he chose teaching as a career. His students became increasingly enthusiastic and they jointly sought the opportunities that came from this new relationship. They shared the understanding that the possibilities were limitless.

One of the most inspiring truths found in the artistic process is that through the discipline and discoveries of deep practice, it is possible to develop an overwhelmingly sincere commitment—a passion for what you are doing—regardless of the initial motive for serious practice in the first place. Learning to love the learning helps you take a different perspective and enjoy the process. This powerful commitment comes from letting go of the mind and surrendering the self in contemplation. With this deep attentiveness, time seems like it passes without your conscious awareness. Achievement won in this way can be felt in your innermost being. Dedicated teachers are highly skilled at helping others with this practice and "passion-building." They use a deliberate progression of experiences designed to build your knowledge. You learn how to:

- set clear goals and objectives.
- focus and break down skills into parts.

- work with intensity on the element that needs the most attention.
- gain an understanding of how that part will fit back into the whole.

Quality in artistic expression is more than a simple expression of feelings; it is an exploration of the language embodied in the material of the art form itself. Creating art requires an understanding of that language and the ability to speak the language of the art form as if it is your native tongue. The skill of deliberate practice takes time to develop; it is a lifelong process — with a sincere commitment, the process is well worth the effort.

ELEMENTS OF THE REFLECTIVE PROCESS

Potential is uncovered through a reflective process critical to the development and appreciation of your own creativity. This reflective process reexamines what you have done and captures the moment to assess what you are doing. Reflection influences the future. The practice of reflection can include a variety of elements.

In artistic or performance work, reflection might be used to look at the way you use the elements or materials to create something meaningful. It may possibly involve the connection you make between various sections of a work of art or the way you use the elements to create momentum.

Educators might examine the way they design a particular instructional sequence or the way they interact with students to create a meaningful learning environment. They also review how they managed the class.

Your reflection as a business or community leader might include the techniques you used to generate momentum or change. Your reflection could be based on the way you lay the groundwork to shape the foundation for your work.

Parents might use the reflective process to review the methods they used to empower their children.

Journalist and author Daniel Coyle, whose work draws on neurology and personal research, identifies deep practice as one of the three key elements that allows you to maximize your potential.

~ *Talent Code*

The same concept can be carried into personal relationships or the direction of your personal life. The reflective process can be applied to any number of things you do. It requires you to become an external observer of sorts with the ability to consider the decisions and assumptions you make as you move forward toward your potential. It is essential in the process that you learn from the reflection, and that you remain open to new or different perspectives. Real reflective practice takes you beyond learning to that of learning how to learn. At the same time, you must also take whatever action is necessary to align yourself with the new understanding that arises and to move on at a higher level of awareness than before.

Justin shared a story of how the students in his middle school classes used the reflective process without at first knowing that that was what they were doing. He leveraged his rehearsals to the fullest, using the techniques he knew from his own work as a performer. He accomplished outstanding performance results and, at the same time, encouraged students in rehearsal each day to reshape and reflect on the insights they gained about the music. He found that they were so engaged with the process that it didn't end when they left class. They frequently came back to class the next day excited about the new ideas that emerged after leaving the previous day. They were inspired to have the opportunity to consider the multiple possibilities in the music, and the potential for their own growth as well. He said that students often returned years later to thank him for allowing them to learn in a way that helped them, well beyond that class experience, to discover relevance and meaning in their lives. They shared stories of how the reflective process he encouraged them to use in middle school band helped them continue to learn and make choices in their lives.

Another student shared a similar experience with the reflective process. She found that the wisdom she gained as a "triple threat" artist who excelled in acting, singing, and dancing was instrumental to her success in the investment banking business. She became an expert at experimenting with various combinations of elements to make decisions that produced the best possible results for her clients. She could rethink her choices and continually discover the most effective investment formula tailored for the specific needs of the person she was advising. She knew from her education and success as an artist how to embrace the process of constantly assessing her methods and their connection to portfolio success over time. Her approach gave her a competitive edge and she quickly rose to the highest levels in the business.

Through curiosity and the emerging ability to explore your own experiences and actions using the reflective process, you open up possibilities of purposeful learning that comes from your own life and work rather than through external means. It allows your unique expression to grow and change over time. In reflective practice, you gain the ability to deal with greater and greater complexity, ultimately leading you beyond knowledge to vision and wisdom. Reflective practice gives you a new relationship with momentum and emotion. Knowledge is embedded in the work of artists, and reflection allows for ever-deepening awareness.

> Without reflection, we go blindly on our way, creating more unintended consequences, and failing to achieve anything useful.
>
> ~ Margaret J. Wheatley
> *Finding Our Way: Leadership for an Uncertain Time*

QUICK TIPS

The reflective process in your own experiences is transformative.
- It gives you mental, emotional, and physical flexibility.
- It leads you on the journey through change and a continuous path of lifelong learning.
- You gain an increasing capacity to make innovative and informed creative choices.

BEYOND COGNITIVE INTELLIGENCE

The reflective process requires listening from a deep, receptive, and caring place within your self. Often referred to as "deep listening," this ability is an important part of your creative intelligence. Deep listening opens your awareness to the unknown and unexpected. It allows you to produce something meaningful to your own sensibilities, while at the same time communicating more effectively and developing a genuine feel for the expression of others. This kind of listening requires that you suspend your

Pauline Oliveros is an important composer and performer in contemporary American music. She has dedicated her life's work to a unique meditative and improvisatory approach to music called Deep Listening. Her Deep Listening concept is about opening to the universe and facets of sounds. She describes Deep Listening as "listening in every possible way to everything possible to hear no matter what you are doing. Such intense listening includes the sounds of daily life, of nature, of one's own thoughts as well as musical sounds." She explains, "Deep Listening is my life practice."

self-oriented, reactive thinking to the expressions of others and to quiet your own persistent inner thoughts. You become more able to see and hear without being hijacked by your own emotions. The ability to listen deeply goes beyond cognitive intelligence. Listening is a competency critical to artistic expression, but it is also a vital skill for everyone to achieve in order to effectively express themselves; and it has the potential to extend its powerful influence to group settings. For this sort of listening to be effective, it requires that you actively participate with an open mind. The nature and qualities of artistic expression provide the means to develop this expansive aptitude and integrate it into your everyday experience, influencing those around you with the promise and potential of continued growth throughout your lifetime.

ROLES OF GIFTS, OPINIONS, PERCEPTIONS

Your potential is often shaped or even distorted by your sense of what you hear, see, or feel. This is true for everyone. Your gifts, talents, opinions, and perceptions significantly impact your experience of the world. While deeply understanding these personal elements can lead you to a high level of creative expression as an individual, they can also work in a way that limits your vision and imaginative power. The limiting aspect often comes from personal characteristics that you learned through your life experiences—patterns of thinking, expectations, self-concept, attitudes, moods, motives, and interests. The reflective process, practice, and deep listening mentioned in the preceding paragraphs are critical to expressing yourself honestly and can assist you in seeing yourself and others more accurately. These practices support your creativity by expanding your capacity for openness and sincerity.

Not only do the creative elements of who you are influence the way you move forward toward creating great art, they have a considerable impact on achieving your personal potential and goals. At the same time, the creative elements—your opinions, perspectives, beliefs, and values—are also sometimes the very things you are afraid to consider. They may seem private or personal and you may fear uncovering something you don't want to find or something that surprises you. Yet, practice, the reflective process, and deep listening can transform experiences for everyone and inspire you to grow and evolve with the eyes and ears and heart of an artist. From this more vulnerable position you can better consider the significance and scope of what you're trying to achieve. You can imagine the possibilities and create just the right balance of episodes of creative tension and forward momentum to determine how you reach your goals. Artists have a great deal of choice in the artistic process, and while there is not only one way, it is critical that everyone learn to make the choices that create meaningful momentum in everything they do. The result will be the enjoyment of lifelong learning and creativity.

CONCEPT PRACTICE

You can use the power of possibility in everything you do. Through learning in the arts you can develop the cognitive skill of imagining possibilities that create real momentum toward your goals. Once understood, you can experience the benefits of this way of thinking repeatedly as you move from one experience to the next. The competence to fully use your imaginative power and create momentum while considering all possibilities is becoming ever more vital in today's global society. You must take charge of your own momentum. If you simply allow the chaos around you to shape your goals and hijack your imagination, you limit the possibilities you see for yourself. If you open to the power of possibilities, the only limits are those you place on yourself. Openness means being vulnerable and flexible, willing to experience incredible opportunities you might never have known existed.

CONSCIOUSNESS QUERIES

These are some questions to ask yourself to consider your openness and the ultimate benefits you might gain from this concept of potential:

And I believe the distance between **good** and great that the Itzhak Perlmans of this world have travel**ed** is a distance we can all travel because it's the **distance** between being us and being ever more **fully** ourselves. It is what's inside you—whether you're in music **or the** fire service, busin**ess or** education—that **makes** you unique, special, **or** even great.

~ Barry Green
  *The Mastery of Music:
  Ten Pathways to
  True Artistry*

- Do you feel you know or need to know exactly how things are going to turn out?
- Are you flexible and receptive to new possibilities?
- Do you see each moment as a potentially significant occasion for new possibilities rather than a predetermined course?

Potential in the arts requires you to go beyond technique—to "get inside" what you are doing with a genuine openness, one that allows you to freely explore the opportunities of every moment. As Philip moved from one position to the next in his career, he found the increasing ability to use the power of possibility in all his work. It was so much a part of his effort as an artist that he was naturally drawn to the potential, even as the supervisor of his department at work. He found that the same intentional effort toward potential he used as a performer could pull people together and allow them to take part in a process. It helped everyone connect with each other in a meaningful way and make connections between things they may have never before considered.

While artists focus on creating their art, an effective leader focuses on creating an environment that allows people to move through challenge and change with the grace and motivation to consider all the possibilities before them. With the power of possibility, you can establish an environment where everyone simultaneously grows and learns more about themselves and the organization. The capacity to experience the emergence of new hopes and dreams, along with the potential of new possibilities, creates a rich and fulfilling experience for everyone involved.

Deep listening is a way of exploring the opportunities of every moment. You can practice deep listening by observing your thoughts and feelings even while maintaining focused attention on a conversation. If you find yourself planning your next statement or interrupting another person when they are speaking, explore a more attentive form of listening:

Unless you try something beyond what you've already mastered, you will never grow.

~ Ronald E. Osborn

1. Practice living in the moment and let go of any idea of a certain result.
2. In your practice, make an effort to respond authentically and allow all possibilities to unfold.
3. Examine the relationship between what you hear and what you think, and discover any connections that can guide you to consider possibilities you never imagined.

Artists learn to explore every moment as a creative experience. They learn to practice, listening in every possible way to everything in their environment. With experience, they discover their own inner voice amidst the din of the world. Over time, newfound self-awareness gives them the confidence to risk and communicate with others in creative ways.

Roger, a professional actor, learned to take risks and step into the unknown many times throughout his career. He practiced and developed a personal sense of expression that came from looking deeply into the character's subtext when he performed. The thoughts and motives of a character, although only implied by the writer, are brought to life by an experienced actor. In order to achieve the implied meaning of the character's motives, it required Roger to look deeply at himself as well. His self-awareness grew over time, and he learned to trust his innate sense of things freely without conscious thought. He tells of how his growing level of awareness helps him make good creative choices and alerts him when it appeared the choice might be a poor one.

In essence, Roger not only learned to tell a story as a character from the inside out, but he learned to express himself from the inside out as well. Each of us has the responsibility to find that kind of truth within ourselves, especially in today's digitized media environment. The artistic process can teach you to bring out your true inner voice and help you make informed choices.

During a break from his acting work, Roger had an opportunity to visit some longtime college friends at their home on the beach along the Southern California coast. As it turned out, he found

Acting is not about being someone different. It's finding the similarity in what is apparently different, then finding myself in there.

~ Meryl Streep

himself in the middle of a challenging family situation. He told a story of how he used his acting training that summer to help his friends, their son, and four other teens completely transform their experience, preventing the troubles that seemed imminent.

The world of teens is often extremely difficult with pressure coming from many sides. All five teens in this particular group felt ostracized from the world around them, and each of them was also completely disconnected from his own inner world. They were on the verge of making decisions that would have a negative impact the rest of their lives.

Roger became interested in their situation and spent time with them, asking genuine questions and listening with curiosity and the skill of an experienced artist. He pulled them out of their constant refuge in digital immersion. As it turned out, the teens were craving that sort of connection. They looked forward to the time together.

Finally, Roger took their stories and convinced them to share them as a drama. He taught them to act out the stories skillfully and to find the subtext meaning that brought the stories to life. In searching for the character subtexts in the stories, they looked deep within themselves. The results were fascinating. Without even knowing it, each of the teens found healing through the nuanced honest expression. It became obvious they had been searching for the truth of their inner worlds all along. Now, they not only had a way to find it, they had a way to express it.

Take the time to reflect on your decisions and the momentum you create toward your goals. The reflective process is sometimes challenging and you may experience some fear of what you might discover. Let go of fear and worry. Some decisions work and some do not. It really does not matter. What matters is the willingness to continue to seek the potential of every experience with the creativity of an artist, making an ongoing effort that moves you forward toward your goals. Uncover what it is about this moment that makes it important for you to consider the potential of the decisions you make. Determine whether your priorities are restricting the potential for all possibilities. Ascertain whether you are willing to learn and try out a way you never considered before.

I believe the most important single thing, beyond discipline and creativity, is daring to dare.

~ Maya Angelou

You can explore a continuous cycle of discovery by testing your decisions over time. Give yourself permission to explore options, make an informed decision, and consider the results.

POTENTIAL

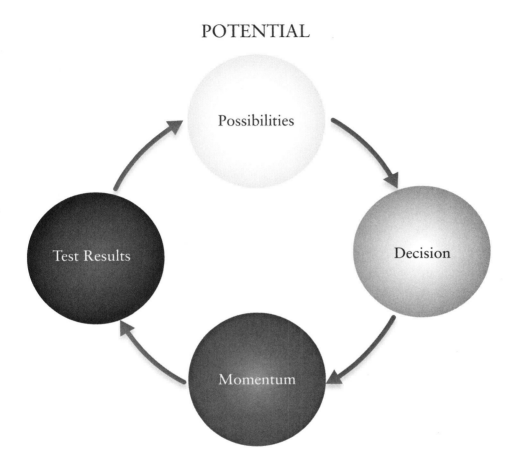

Does the momentum you generated make sense in and of itself? And if so, does it make sense when considered as a part of the bigger picture? Is there anything you want to try the next time to create a different kind of momentum? There is no judgment here. Simply learn from the experience and try out what you learned in your next opportunity. You can learn to use your imagination and your unique blend of inner and outer experiences to influence the world in an important way. Open to all the choices before you and discover the power of possibility.

Vulnerability is the birthplace of innovation, creativity and change.

~ Brené Brown
Listening to Shame

SUMMARY

The concept of potential helps you realize the outcomes you desire. When you experience the momentum that can come from the choices you make, you discover an increasing ability to uncover even more possibilities. The potential is far greater than you ever thought. Your imagination alone doesn't necessarily mean a productive outcome. When an artist begins a work of art, there's potential for that expression to develop into something, but it takes practice and a playful, contemplative mind—one open to all possibilities—to actually achieve a meaningful result.

Openness to all the options before you gives you an advantage and helps you take actions that move you forward. Everyone experiences times of difficulty, boredom, or frustration, but you can choose to move on, not getting stuck there. Every day offers the potential for new possibilities. The teens in the previous story transformed their experience by taking a risk and opening to a new adventure. They learned, changing their daily immersion in digital technologies; even the smallest shifts in what you do or think can create the biggest opportunities.

The desert garden successes of Jack and Sarah came from openness to possibility. They did not let the constant challenge of the daily garden visitors change their goal of bountiful produce. They were vulnerable as desert gardeners, but they were willing to repeatedly change direction to achieve their goals. They were fully present, interacting with the environment, open to the unfolding opportunity of each moment. You, too, can find yourself on a productive path in alignment with the boundless true power of possibility.

With practice, deep listening, and the reflective process, you can uncover the path that creates something truly meaningful to you. Artists consider the elements of their art form to find the potential in a work of art. Basic features like color, texture, rhythm, harmony, and intensity are used to create possibilities and momentum. You can consider your values and beliefs—their benefits and limitations—as the elements of potential in your personal and work life. The willingness to adjust and relearn or take another direction helps you reach your goals and express your potential. Your inner awareness grows as you experience the results of your choices over time.

Consider the power of possibility and experiment with the choices you make to create momentum in your experiences.

Every moment offers the opportunity to create momentum regardless of the nature of the experience at that point in time. In the earlier gardening story, even when the javelina ate his plants, Jack did not waste time complaining. Instead, he focused on what he wanted and took action to get it. He avoided a victim mentality and looked instead for opportunity in each situation.

Involve yourself in what you do with the full capacity of your innermost heart and mind. Learn to listen deeply and look within yourself. Allow your self-awareness to grow over time as Roger did as an actor in the earlier story. Use the power of your true inner voice to inform your choices and communicate with others.

Allow yourself to be flexible, creating momentum that carries you forward toward meaningful experiences in everything you do. Roger adjusted his summer plans in the earlier story. His flexibility gave him the opportunity to use his acting knowledge in a new way, to create more meaning in the lives of the five troubled teens.

Potential involves an active process. It requires vulnerability, openness and risking, and a dynamic approach that can be developed and refined through practice.

REVIEW QUESTIONS

1. Think about how you use the power of possibility in creating momentum. Are you curious and open or indifferent and closed in your approach to each moment? Are you afraid of being vulnerable and exposed to the judgment of others?

2. Consider how a series of events in your life evolved over time. For example, choose something like a search for a job that never materialized, or the evolution of a series of work experiences that were difficult and unfulfilling, or the evolution of a relationship. Did you try out what you learned

from each experience to influence the potential of the next? Were you able to try out what you learned and see evolving results of achieving your goals?

3. How have you developed the ability to listen deeply to the nuances of the words you choose in conversation? To see and feel the sensitivities of your heart, mind, and body when making a decision about a way to move forward? To discern the subtle details of the events happening around you?

CONTINUE THE QUEST

Further explore the concept of potential. Use the suggestions below to consider potential and the power of possibility in the artistic process and beyond. As you explore the examples, think about how you can use the concept to create more imaginative experiences out of every decision you make.

Explore the concept of unfolding potential in works of art.

- Listen to a cappella recordings by ensembles such as Chanticleer.
- Study the increasingly complex drama of *Downton Abbey*.
- Explore the works of Pablo Picasso, Martha Graham, Igor Stravinsky, and Frank Lloyd Wright.

The following techniques are often used by artists as deep listening and reflective practice.

Alexander Technique can cultivate your awareness and influence your ability to explore feelings and nurture your innermost self. This technique can guide you to live more fully in your body and anchor to the present moment in all your activities so you can open more easily to potential.

Read about Mindfulness (MBR), a program launched by the University of Massachusetts Medical School in 1979. It helps you maintain a moment-by-moment awareness of your thoughts and feelings without judging them, leaving you open to consider possibilities.

When artists consider movement in their art form, the technical aspects of expressing themselves in the medium almost naturally take care of themselves. The ideas explored here can help you take full advantage of the concept of potential and make decisions that lead you forward with a wider range of possibility. They help you develop the skills necessary to manage challenges and make choices that make use of everything imaginable to realize positive outcomes, create momentum beyond technique, and make the most of the seven concepts.

CHAPTER 6

PLANNING AND MOMENTUM:
AN UNFOLDING AND EVOLVING PATH

OVERVIEW

STRUCTURE AND FREEDOM

With her hands wrapped tightly on the steering wheel and her shoulders tensing up in apprehension, Abbie drove through the four lanes of traffic, making her way to the rehearsal of the *Trio Sonata* from Bach's *Musical Offering*. She focused on how to get through the experience. She felt certain all four members of the ensemble wondered what might take place once inside the small practice room. This rehearsal marked one of the final commitments of their chamber ensemble before final exams. The building tensions of previous weeks triggered bewildering conflicts, and all four of them were on the verge of walking away altogether. Challenging personal issues and the usual pressures at the end of the year had an impact on each of them in ways they never before experienced. In addition, the recent and dramatic changes in the university influenced decisions in the music school. The faculty members were anxious about looming budget cuts, and the financial burdens of college life were taking its toll. All of these issues seemed to multiply and weave together into a complex web of weight and worry. It impacted their relationships with one another, even though they all worked so closely together for the past four years.

Upon arrival, they gathered and prepared their instruments to begin the rehearsal. The room felt still and heavy, and the first notes of the music sounded with unusual reserve. They expertly worked their way through Bach's music, from the momentum created during various highpoints and releases in each section to the climactic highpoint of all four movements as a whole. They engaged fully with the journey of the music, and the flow of the musical elements pulled them forward through the overarching structure of the nearly eighteen minutes of music. At the end of the rehearsal Abbie thought with interest about what happened. Time passed—a two-hour rehearsal flew by seemingly without their awareness. The mood shifted dramatically. They laughed and enjoyed themselves, talking as if there were no problems anywhere in the world.

Bach's works are structural masterpieces. They can move you through the emotional highs and lows with a complex mix of formal architecture and technical compositional skill. The complexity of the music matched the complexity of the situation and the two blended together into a uniquely therapeutic prescription. All four members of the ensemble engaged so deeply with the movement of the music that its strength and sheer joy carried them forward toward a common goal of technical and interpretive excellence. The glorious blend of elements created a deep and lasting emotional impact. Insurmountable problems seemed to disappear within the intricacies of structural changes in the music as it unfolded over time.

In a rehearsal, if something limits or halts the flow of the music, you stop and communicate, practice the challenging pattern, then connect it to the surrounding parts and move on. You and the other players experience rising tension that not only comes from the structural aspects of the music itself, but also from the problems that might arise as you move through the music together. The beginning of the music sets the stage for what is to come. The tension rises to a climactic point and the flow moves away from that point to the conclusion. At the same time, many tension points in the underlying structure support the overarching climactic movement. Everything must balance to effectively portray the full depth of meaning that can come through the music. In this final rehearsal, the members of the group so engaged with the music that they moved easily and effortlessly through the musical architecture as a cohesive ensemble.

The structure of the music drew them forward and provided the context for a heightened experience that they could not have otherwise known, particularly at such a challenging time. It gave them a sense of the bigger picture. Over time, Abbie reflected on the meaning of what they experienced together and, as time passed, her learning expanded. It made such an impression on her that she considered how she might use this sort of structural support when creating momentum in other settings. The structural arrangement of Bach's music served as a planning springboard for many of her future efforts.

Abbie learned that with each new beginning there is a journey that can lead you on to new opportunities. The experience provided a dynamic framework from which she could initiate change and stimulate a driving effort, not only for her personal goals, but in the commitment from others. In a variety of organizational and group experiences, whether with four or four hundred people, Abbie found that the enthusiastic willingness to begin a journey together came with an understanding that there is a sense of both stability and flexibility within the beauty of a well-designed plan.

People learned in these situations that planning or structure is not limiting or restrictive. Rather, it provides freedom that cannot be known without it. This is a valuable lesson for anyone who manages or leads other people, whether in business, educational institutions, or organizations. In Bach's music the plan is clear, but there is still an opportunity for individual choice in collaboration with everyone involved. The concept of planning and momentum gives you the freedom to follow an ever-evolving path to completion of a single project, a series of decisions, or your work over a lifetime. Everyone wants freedom—freedom to create their lives, to do their work, and to build their relationships. Artists have an unusually keen sense of what it takes to express themselves without restrictions through their art form. They create their art within a context, and that context is structure. Artists have learned that, despite what seems counterintuitive, structure actually creates freedom.

The beautiful thing about learning is nobody can take it away from you.

~ B. B. King
The Charlotte Observer

While it is natural to think that you are more limited by structure, without it things can be in constant chaos. Structure—the knowledge and practices of the art form, business, organization, institution, or group—allows you the freedom to perform meaningfully as an artist, a leader, an employee, a friend, and as a human being. It does not mean you must follow an extreme hard and fast set of rules with no flexibility. Structure simply provides the discipline and order that gives you stability, direction, and power.

ARTISTIC INSIGHTS

Each day, artists practice, produce, and perform their art, freely expressing themselves within the context of their art form. They do this by expertly manipulating three basic dynamic forces within the parameters of their particular mediums:

- They know *what* they need to do to put their art into practice.
- They know *how* to take the steps to create meaningful art and achieve success.
- They are *consistent* in applying their knowledge.

Only by learning to use the elements and structures of the particular art form can artists communicate expressively. In fact, they know the formal structures so well they can use them without being stuck in a box of strict rules. The structural plan of a work of art does not dictate, but rather adds to its value.

In everyday life, you might be fearful of the extreme structures you see in work environments, family circumstances, or on the news broadcast from countries around the world. As a result of these experiences, you might try to abandon the very thing that can lead to your greatest success. For example, Martha was so fearful of the unclear and questionable directives she wasn't allowed to challenge in her work in a major medical industry that she was on the verge of burnout after only three years. Because information was closely held and career-ending decisions were made by upper level management without any understandable reason, she and

Some people regard discipline as a chore. For me, it is a kind of order that sets me free to fly.

~ Julie Andrews

her colleagues became paranoid. The demanding and inflexible work schedules along with questionable evaluations that left many in fear for their jobs made it nearly impossible for them to be anything but order-takers. The seemingly deceitful behaviors of the upper management started to strip her of the desire to continue. Martha—usually filled with creative passion—felt bored, unappreciated, and frustrated. There appeared to be no options for her to realize her creative potential or grow in that environment. Working on non-productive goals day after day consumed all her energy. She felt smothered by the daily stress at work that gradually crept into her personal life.

In the end, rather than leave a thriving field of medical research, she relied on her years of music and visual arts training to reflect on her goals. Martha searched within herself through reflective practice and found the underpinning truth of her desire to make a difference in the lives of others. She practiced the attitude of this truth every day, approaching the situation with a more playful mindset, facing her fears, and creating a sort of game each day that tested whether the behavior of others in reality had the power to hurt her in any way. With this new approach, she used her artistic process experience to break down the elements of the structure and find meaning. Ultimately, she reconstructed her relationship with the way things were and found openings where the management occasionally considered suggestions. She took advantage of opportunities to share her ideas. Martha learned how to move within the structure and maintain her personal creative power. She felt re-energized and more determined than ever to create momentum in her work. While not every situation would be as successful as this—and she eventually moved on to a more open and collaborative environment—the depth of understanding from Martha's arts experiences made a huge difference in her evolving medical career.

By contrast, some of the things you experience are actually a result of the other extreme: the absence of structure. Without structure in an organization or group of any kind, there are no decision-making boundaries, and as a result, decisions have to be made from the top. There is no freedom in this sort of situation.

Instead, individual and organizational growth is limited and creativity is stifled. People have no way to learn or contribute in a meaningful way. Artists know that creating or performing art with weak structure—poor composition—produces no meaningful result. Even though the design elements are often hidden, artists constantly consider the overall framework and things such as:

- The shape and flow of the work
- Selection and grouping of elements and materials
- Signs or symbols planned and used
- The values and beliefs they are representing
- Balance and emphasis

One of my students learned to use her musical knowledge of this concept in her summer job. She worked for a youth program in her town, saving money for the next school year. Her frustration with the behavior of the group grew day after day. It seemed that every time she told the teens to do something, they refused to do it. A constant power struggle developed over the first two weeks of the program, and she felt forced to confront the eleven- to fourteen-year-olds with punishing consequences several times a day. She went home day after day completely disheartened, unsure how she would survive the summer.

One evening, when her roommates were out of town, she took the opportunity to reflect on her experience in the quiet solitude of her apartment. She was jolted out of her misery by an image that came to mind from the previous semester. Although she worked hard on a complex piece of music, it felt like each day of practice drew her deeper into what seemed like a power struggle with the composer. The music was challenging and difficult to learn and play with good musical results. Finally, at one of her lessons, her private instructor told her she simply had to pay closer attention to the design of the piece and to use that in her practice to overcome the difficulties. She went home from her lesson that day and conscientiously studied the music. The close examination of the inner workings of the composition as a whole helped her see the work with new eyes—how the elements shaped the music and held it together—almost as if she saw it for the first time. She immediately practiced the music with this fresh view and achieved outstanding results.

The next day she went to work with a plan. The memory of the lesson experience transformed her attitude into determination to change the situation with the children. She set up a structure so they knew what was expected of them. She involved them in planning some of the rules and routines. They practiced the new structures each day and loved the experience. Over the next weeks, they enjoyed the prior knowledge of what to expect each day and looked forward to the special event days on the schedule, even monitoring some of their actions on their own. The power struggles ended completely.

Connecting Fiber

Planning is critical to artistic expression and full realization of creative endeavors. It serves as the connecting fiber that sets you in motion and helps you move from an idea toward the ultimate end result. Planning and momentum work together as a team. While planning provides the structure or the concept of an artistic project, and serves as the map that gives form to the ideas, momentum provides the energy to stay focused. Once you move forward with a plan, even if it shifts and changes as you go, it is much easier to stay engaged to the end because there is a basic framework from which to proceed. Planning involves experimenting, seeking out, and designing ways of presenting ideas through the material you use. There is no set way, and there are many planning models. In creating art, common elements in each art form are basic considerations in the planning process. One of the goals for pursuing and developing your ideas is to establish a sense of purpose in what you are creating. In the end, this "planning and momentum team" concept helps you apply your techniques and skills to bring your ideas to life.

REGENERATING POWER

You have an opportunity in the artistic process to move forward and discover what fascinates you the most, and what intrigues you to the point that you want to explore it more. The details of the artistic work you undertake begin to fill in with the power of newfound motivation. The closer you look, the more you see, and the more momentum takes over. When the momentum gets going, a regenerating power drives you forward. At that point, you do your creative work because it is out of the question to think of not doing it. You begin to pay attention to clues, connections, and opportunities as the work unfolds. Your future evolves in ways you might not have imagined when you started your planning process. The plan is a work in progress. While it is important to have a goal in mind, it is also important to remain flexible. No matter what your goals are, or how difficult to achieve, creating momentum to reach them starts with commitment—commitment to create an initial plan without doubt and procrastination.

One of the greatest sources of procrastination is deep-seated fear—fear of success, fear of change, fear of failure, fear of ridicule, fear of the unknown, and so on—in an endless cycle. It is essential to recognize these fears and use the concept of planning and momentum to help you take daily steps to continue to move forward. This process removes you from the chaos of flitting around from this to that, starting over each day to the satisfaction of steady progress and ultimate accomplishment. It is much easier to keep moving once you have momentum than it is to start from a complete stop. Planning gives you the power to keep moving, and it is much easier to stay focused and move obstacles or distractions that might come up.

IT IS WHAT WE MAKE IT

The artistic planning concept has a particularly important role to play in contributing to your ongoing growth as a human being. This tremendous gift in an increasingly complex environment gives you rich opportunities to take control of your own learning and behaviors. Not only do you learn to get started and work through obstacles by creating momentum, but you learn how to troubleshoot problems in the midst of the process. With thoughtful participation in the planning process, you also develop an ever-deepening self-awareness and self-motivation to carry out your goals. The abstract nature of learning in the arts allows you to acquire a great depth of knowledge, often without your conscious awareness of the full power of your learning. It can help you develop and build on valuable skills, such as:

- How to begin with an idea—either one that is original or inspired by someone or something in your environment
- How to develop a plan for the idea that forms the structure for your effort
- How to become engaged and moved, allowing momentum to take over
- How to check in to determine what is or is not working
- How to restructure if new things arise or obstacles block the path
- How to finish the project and carry forward all of the layers of knowledge you gained to influence an expanded new beginning

David used these skills to recover from a debilitating dance injury. He was in the middle of a rehearsal and in immediate pain upon landing after a jump; it drastically changed his life for more than a year. He had a history of knee pain and tried to follow the treatment and more limited schedule previously recommended by his doctor. But this time, the injury—a tendon rupture—required surgery. The removal of the damaged tissue from the tendon was needed to stimulate blood flow and promote healing.

David knew that some dancers never return to the level they had before this sort of operation, but surgery was the best option considering both his history and the level of the injury. He also knew that even after a successful surgery, he would not immediately feel better. His body had been through a major physical event, and recovery meant a commitment of time and diligence to the rehabilitation process. It took a year of strengthening exercises and massage. Although there were difficult moments, he followed the rehabilitation strategy and gained momentum as he ultimately reached his goal. With appreciation for the opportunity of a new beginning, he developed a strong commitment to injury prevention and dedicated himself to a routine that maximized the strength and flexibility of his quadriceps and hamstrings. He consistently followed a good warm-up regimen, stretching his quadriceps, hamstring, and calf muscles. He never gave up.

Your confidence and perceptions about your own strengths can influence your progress. Begin the creative process without judgment and doubt. Sure, you have to be somewhat realistic— to think that you are going to perform a Beethoven piano concerto when you have never touched the piano, or paint like Leonardo da Vinci when you have never picked up a paintbrush may not be practical. But, whether it is a project at work or a desire to dance, you can develop an increasing awareness and explore trust in yourself:

- You can learn to hear, see, feel, and appreciate multifaceted connections between that trust and awareness and what it is you do in your everyday life.
- You can learn how to respond instinctively to obstacles and twists and turns.
- You can develop the ability to deal more effectively with complex problems and difficult situations.

HOLDING ON AND LETTING GO

You might wonder how planning and momentum look and feel in each art form and, perhaps more importantly, how you can use the knowledge for your own growth and then positively influence those around you. This is an interesting and somewhat difficult question to answer because most people likely parent, teach, manage, or lead with the same perspective they were taught or that they learned by watching others. That may mean that the in-depth, more holistic investigation and understanding described here was not part of your experience. While a portion

Life is what we make it, always has been, always will be.

~ Grandma Moses
Grandma Moses: My Life's History

Just living is not enough... one must have sunshine, freedom, and a little flower.

~ Hans Christian Andersen
The Complete Hans Christian Andersen Fairy Tales, "The Butterfly"

of the wisdom might seem familiar, the realization that your experiences lacks a more comprehensive viewpoint can serve as the inspiration to craft a plan and create momentum.

ARTISTIC INSIGHT

Making art is a unique blend of planning and spontaneity. The particular mix of control and freedom in the process is unique to each artist. Creating a work of art might involve decisions that are:

- As simple as exploring the color red.
- As complex as writing a fugue or a composition in the sonata form.
- As challenging as performing a dance sequence that includes techniques the dancer never attempted before.

While an artistic structure might initially hold a typical organization of the elements and materials of the art from, they evolve as the work unfolds. The same is true for anything you do—you just work with a different set of elements and materials depending on the nature of the effort. No matter what you do or what endeavor you undertake, you can only use well what you truly know. It takes practice to create a direction, build momentum, and make adjustments as the plan unfolds.

MOTIVATIONAL STORY—WHERE'S THE MUSIC

Some of Joanna's earliest memories as a child are those about music and music-making. The individual and collective sounds that she heard come out of the television, radio, and record player (yes, the record player) attracted her full attention. The fascinating sounds seemed to float or march or sing in patterns that drew her into their vibrations and held her there, miles away from whatever else was going on. The sound and the feeling of music gave her an understanding and a sense of freedom she did not know otherwise. There was never a question about whether music would be in her life. It was there, and it was there to stay.

All the art of living lies in a fine mingling of letting go and holding on.

~ Henry Ellis
Affirmations

Her family owned an old upright piano as she was growing up and Joanna remembers having fun with her siblings, singing and making their own music. She recalls they more than likely got this from their mother, who played the steel guitar. All of her brothers and sisters loved to sit for long periods of time, spellbound by the sounds their mother could make picking and strumming with one hand and using the slide—the steel—in the other, often singing words that led them to new worlds they could only imagine. She remembers they treasured the times when their mother played. They all made requests, especially for "My Little Grass Shack in Kealakekua, Hawai'i."

Joanna believes it was because that song was light and fun and happy and they loved to see her that way. Their mother also liked to take the words and rhythms from songs she heard on the radio and act them out, singing and dancing as she performed this new version of her own.

Joanna finally had an opportunity to take music in fourth grade. The pull-out program allowed her to leave her regular classroom and go to music class. She learned to play the recorder and the accordion; yes, in fourth and fifth grade she played the accordion in her small town school. She also took private accordion lessons in the town music store and played in an accordion band! Reading music seemed to come naturally. She realizes now what an incredible experience this was, particularly the knowledge she gained from the accordion. The accordion is set up with a piano keyboard on the right side and the bass and preset chord buttons on the left. Joanna could change the combination or quality of sounds by using the "stops" located on either side.

Later, as her music study progressed, she realized that the accordion gave her an advantage in learning music theory and harmony without her full awareness of it at the time. The bass buttons of the accordion are set up in the circle of fifths—a major structural element in music theory. Besides that, the preset chord buttons with each bass button included all of the main chord structures—major, minor, seventh, augmented, and diminished, and so on. Joanna became quite accomplished and continued to play this instrument for many years, well beyond the time when she started with other instruments in sixth grade.

Joanna felt music gave her the ability to keep going amidst some rather challenging circumstances. For instance:

- Musical form gave her an understanding of structure that helped her continue to move forward even in difficult situations. It grounded her a little and made everything less confusing. It helped her think more clearly.
- It provided the framework for a driving effort, the enlivened willingness to keep looking ahead, and the readiness to keep starting anew even when she initially felt defeated or unsuccessful.
- Music practice prepared her to reach for an existence she did not yet know from actual experience.

As she now reflects on her childhood experiences, Joanna has a sense that practicing and reflection helped give her gain a deeper understanding of who she was and where she was going.

With a plan to major in music performance, she thought she knew where she wanted to go to college. As it turned out, when the time came, she felt unsure of whether the school she dreamed of for years was really the right one. Joanna never travelled very far outside of the small California community where she lived, and when she took the 3,000 mile journey to visit the school in New York, it did not match her expectations. Joanna adjusted her plan and looked beyond a childhood dream to find a location that resonated more deeply with her. As she reflects on that experience now, she realizes that the school she chose in her home state was without doubt the right choice for her. Her plan was still intact, but enriched through the willingness to change and make a choice.

Joanna's performance career started immediately out of college, as planned, but she discovered she also enjoyed teaching others about music. From there, her musical life evolved to a place she could never have imagined. The experiences were not even in the scope of possibility when she began her childhood music journey. Joanna speaks of how she found great joy, satisfaction, and a sense of accomplishment when she taught. Teaching brought her increasing insight about music as an art form. Working with other people resonated deeply within her, as profoundly as the music itself. While she still continued to perform, she studied human development psychology and other subjects relevant to her daily experiences and life in this new expression of herself as an artist.

When conducting became an interest of hers, it came to her as yet another expansion of her ongoing life in music. With this new discovery, Joanna found she could combine her love of music and performance with her love of people, and it led to an additional form of expression that gave her an increasingly broader point of view. In retrospect she feels that this new role revealed the lineage we all have as artists—our own experiences, the experiences of our teachers, those of our teacher's teachers. If you are honest with yourself and explore your work with integrity, the patterns you develop in your expression as an artist come from a rich and meaningful position that values everyone. To truly speak with the highest level of artistry means you are not exclusive, limiting, or self-serving in what you do.

This deepening awareness allowed Joanna's initial plan to evolve. Her move to organizational leadership grew out of everything she learned from previous experiences. You may not think of organizational leadership or management as a form of creativity and artistry, believing it is simply arranging pieces of things in the right place or completing forms. This is an extremely narrow and mistaken point of view. The new leadership role offered Joanna the possibility of using her imagination and further expanding her artistic abilities from a broader perspective. She found a treasure trove of expressive opportunity and rewards, not only for herself, but for the organizations she served.

Through her more wide-ranging organizational work, she learned to have even greater appreciation for other art forms and how they all connect to function together as a discipline, a concept that is important and critical to the education of young people. Joanna continued to develop her library and studied not only music, but also visual art, theater, dance, and creative and dramatic writing as well as the multifaceted aspects of organizational leadership. She still performed as a musician for many years, and still finds time to do some conducting now and then. Yet, the full efforts of her artistic expression shifted to the imaginative and creative possibilities of organizational development.

LESSONS LEARNED

FLEXIBILITY

As Joanna reflects on the knowledge she gained from this unfolding plan in her life, she still sees clearly the ongoing thread of music. What she started with is still in place as a framework and, although she is constantly gaining momentum, it just looks different from what she originally could conceive. She learned to extend the flexibility of performing music to other areas of her life. This flexibility allowed her to build constant momentum, enjoying ever-evolving and expansive growth all along the way.

QUICK TIPS

- Flexibility is essential to your full expression as a human being and the development of a successful career and productive life.
- Openness to consider options and opportunities while continually moving forward is critical to success.
- You can accomplish much more in this way than if you stick doggedly to whatever you are doing without consideration of all possibilities and where they might lead.

Flexibility does not mean that you flit around with everything that comes your way. In fact, a plan that is too loose, causing you to jump from one thing to the next without ever completing a thought or a task, can lead to an unproductive and diminished result. Joanna never planned to teach, become a conductor, or become an organizational leader, but her openness to exploring these things as they arose naturally out of her experiences paid incredible benefits. She never became so singularly focused on a goal that she became blind to other choices that arose. If artists get stuck on the exact way they think something should be—such as a certain design in visual art or music composition or a certain way to perform a particular passage—they never open themselves to possibility, momentum, and the innovative expressions that can come from openness and flexibility. In fact, real vision and insight seem to come out of that uncertainty of not knowing exactly—from that chaos.

ENERGY TO KEEP GOING

Planning is not limiting or restrictive; it gives you a sense of freedom you could never know without it. It provides the structure to build, not only a strong foundation, but also the possibility of what was not conceivable at the start. It moves you forward in a way that allows you to follow an ever unfolding and expanding path to completion of a single artistic project, a group of works, or your work over a lifetime. You become who you are as an artist from what you individually put into your work in combination with the unique collection of opportunities and experiences you enjoy along the way.

The momentum initiated by planning gives you the ongoing desire to learn and a deepening awareness of where you are going. Without momentum, even small problems become magnified. Momentum creates the sense that things are happening, that you are going places and getting results. Lack of momentum makes you feel as if everything is difficult and nothing seems to get done. It may sound obvious to say that the key to creating momentum is to keep going, but there are many people who give up and do not follow through with their goals. The more you experience momentum, the more unstoppable you become.

A predisposition for continuous growth is an important contributing factor to the successful development of your ongoing artistic and personal expression. Lifelong learning builds momentum—it keeps you moving. While Joanna's study of music started her on the path, her interest in other art forms, human development psychology, and leadership further expanded that knowledge in a way that contributed significantly to her expression in every way. Perhaps the most significant understanding that Joanna acquired came from the willingness to reach deeply within everything and look at it from both an internal and an external perspective, whether the art itself, education, leadership, or herself and her values.

QUICK TIPS

Exploring everything from both the inside out and outside in can help you express yourself with authenticity and integrity.

- It helps you adapt to change.
- It helps you find meaning in your life.
- It increases your wisdom and opens your mind.
- It helps to develop your natural abilities.

Gaining knowledge and skills as you move through your life makes you more interesting and better able to communicate effectively with people of all kinds. Continuous self-motivated pursuit of knowledge enables you to take a different perspective and make more informed decisions. The ability to expand your mind and strive for continuous education is critical to your success and the success of those you influence. The arts provide a rich and meaningful framework for learning of this sort.

DEEPENING PERSPECTIVES OF PLANNING AND MOMENTUM

ROLE OF SCOPE AND INTENTION

In order to accomplish the desired effect, artists narrow the creative possibilities when they begin a work of art or prepare for a performance. This process allows their work to be accomplished in a more meaningful and manageable way. In fact, the initial planning stage in any endeavor helps to establish the scope and focus of your work. The structure of your plan is a unique mix of order and adaptability that helps you most effectively work toward the goal you hope to achieve.

To survive, you've got to keep wheedling your way. You can't just sit there and fight against odds when it's not going to work. You have to turn a corner, dig a hole, go through a tunnel— and find a way to keep moving.

~ Twyla Tharp

Never look back unless you are planning to go that way.

~ Henry David Thoreau

It may seem obvious, but the first step in narrowing the creative possibilities is to choose the ideas that will help you accomplish your goals. You make the choices that appear to guide you to the greatest success. While taking risks is an important part of the creative process, the planning stage is where you consider which possibilities are most likely to succeed. It is important to take the time to consider all the factors involved.

- Determine which possibilities will bring about the most desired results.
- Decide which possibilities you are most passionate about.
- Consider whether you have time and resources to reach the goal you desire.

Once you achieve the focus of a well-thought-out plan within the scope of your time and resources, momentum begins to build and you become more excited about what lies ahead. More possibilities are likely to be uncovered as you move forward. You never know what might turn up that can lead to more choices in relation to the plan you have in place. It is amazing what can come to light when you are enthusiastic and moving forward.

You might experience the importance of narrowing your choices and focusing on your objectives by simply walking through the grocery store without a plan. Aisle after aisle you pick up whatever appeals to you, and when you get home you look at your receipt and realize you spent much more than intended, and can find nothing to make dinner. In contrast, when you plan ahead, you know what you are looking for and, although you may add and change some things as you shop, you arrive home with all the ingredients you need, and you stay within you budget.

Like an architectural drawing for a building, planning serves as the basis for creating momentum and accomplishing something. Too many choices can become numbing; a well-designed plan for your goals sets necessary limits. Once you narrow the path, the realization of what you imagined begins to take shape. The same is true for any artist. In carving a statue, a sculptor starts

Life is the sum of all your choices.

~ Albert Camus

with something such as a big slab of stone and chips away from the outside in to gradually turn the large lump of material into a work of art that resembles a person or an object. While they have an image of the inside all along, only near the very end do the intricate details take shape. The same is true in any artistic endeavor. Sculptors, architects, and other artists know in advance what they want to create. While things may change along the way, they start by narrowing the possibilities. The choices might begin as simple decisions. For instance:

- What material will I use?
- What shape?
- What character and style?
- Is there a time factor and, if so, can I accomplish what I plan to do in the time available?

Without narrowing the possibilities before beginning, the work may never take shape and the details that lead to completion will never be revealed.

While making choices is important to planning, you might realize from the examples above that it is also much more than that. Make your choices with intention. Aim with purpose to stimulate your thinking about how to realize the result you desire. Just as in the Bach rehearsal at the beginning of the chapter, not only was there a solid structure for the work itself, but consideration for the possibilities in performance meant that the ensemble members made meaningful choices to bring the music to life. The rehearsal plan involved decisions about how to use the time and what actions would help achieve the performance standard. Their plan took into account the need in advance to determine how to recognize problems along the way and anticipate the outcome of all the work.

There are many purposes for a plan and, as a result, the steps you take may vary with both the field and the goal. The artistic process provides a freedom in planning that is not necessarily experienced in many business, institutional, and organizational environments. Leonardo da Vinci carried notebooks to write

> The first step to getting the things you want out of life is this: Decide what you want.
>
> ~ Ben Stein
> *Out of the Blue: Delight Comes into Our Lives*

down his ideas immediately. Throughout his lifetime, he had accumulated more than 7,000 pages of notes that included observations, letters, reflections, drawings, and plans about a wide range of subjects. While the notebooks developed into an art in and of themselves, he likely started out using them as a way to plan and improve the quality of his paintings. Composers often carry a sketchbook of ideas for similar reasons. If you use this aspect of the artistic process in general planning, keeping an open mind will allow you to consider a wide range of creative possibilities, even if they do not initially relate to what you are doing at the moment. While you ultimately focus on the project you engage with at the time, the openness to such a wide range of thinking truly expands the creative possibilities and allows you to achieve an outcome that moves you well beyond your present reality. While you are pulled forward toward your new creation, the path yields new associations and connections that add richness and complexity to the outcome. Perhaps what you are planning is not as relevant as the true beauty of where you are, where you are going, and how you get there through the underlying structure you achieved from all the possibilities you considered.

STARK BEAUTY OF STRUCTURE

I remember an occasion, walking through the streets of Boston, when I felt drawn to the stark beauty of the bare shapes of leafless trees and shrubs that stood out clearly against the city landscape. The trees stood securely on the bare ground; except for a few broadleaf evergreens, the color had vanished completely. A wide array of browns and grays filled the street landscape. The unadorned shapes made a stunning contrast to the mixture of sunlight, clouds, and blue sky in the background. It occurred to me that, just as in a work of art, the structure was there all along, hidden beneath the leaves, to offer support and give them life.

The beautiful visible tree structures resemble "structural bones" that support any great work of art. Hidden structure gives life to a work of art and allows it to speak. The bare structure of

There are three classes of people: those who see, those who see when they are shown, those who do not see.

~ Leonardo da Vinci

the work of art is pure potential. Even with the same materials and intention, different artists can create completely distinctive works based on shifts and differences in the underlying structure. In previous weeks, I had been drawn to and fascinated by the shapes and colors of the leaves of similar trees. Now, in their plain bared state, no two branch structures looked the same. Their true essence was revealed when their colorful leaves no longer hid their character.

CONSCIOUSNESS QUERIES

- How can you use this knowledge in everyday life?
- How can you use structure to support what you do without it becoming the focus at the expense of everything else?
- Consider the qualities of communities, organizations, and institutions in your life and work. Explore beneath the surface, "stripping away the leaves." Can you see more clearly the fundamental nature of your personal and professional life experiences?

As you explore core structures, you can work with the foundations and resources of the various aspects of your life to build fresh, creative experiences at home and in your work environment. If you manage or lead others, you can use this knowledge to bring about clarity and a new sense of purpose for everyone involved. The beauty of structure is in the powerful promise of energy and enthusiasm that allows you to move forward in new ways.

THE WHOLENESS OF ALL THE PARTS

From the *Arts Awareness* perspective, two important considerations can guide a successful initiative in more complex organizational and institutional planning. First, it is vital that the goal not be focused purely around one element, such as monetary goals. While financial considerations are important, that is only one element of a successful planning process. Artists use a wide

My mother said to me, When one sees the tree in leaf one thinks the beauty is in its leaves, and then one sees the bare tree.

~ Samuel Menashe
Samuel Menashe: New and Selected Poems,
"The Bare Tree"

I prefer winter and fall, when you feel the bone structure of the landscape. Something waits beneath it; the whole story doesn't show.

~ Andrew Wyeth

array of elements and materials in their work to produce a creative and successful end result. An artist works for a result that expresses their vision in an innovative way, differentiating themselves and their work with a unique voice. While financial goals may need to be an element of the planning process, consider also how to look at a wider range of elements. This can place you in a creative and more dynamic sustainable position. If you broaden your vision and, at the same time, narrow your focus, you can more productively manage your position.

Secondly, artistic efforts are inclusive and balanced in a number of ways. The inclusiveness comes from collaboration with an audience in a performance setting, or with viewers in an exhibit, and with those who commissioned a work in the first place, for example. The planning process is always more successful when including an honest assessment of the depth and breadth of involvement from others. Artists carefully study relationships, arranging and rearranging various elements, to create a moving and powerful work of art. The way artists use the relationships between all elements is critical to the effect. Beauty comes from the way all elements are represented and brought together as a whole.

Unity and variety offer examples of basic elements in the artistic process. In the case of a planning process in any organized group, the overall result must have relational content with all constituents represented and involved in such a way that their ideas and experience are fully utilized. Participation must be consistent and balanced. This requires a community operating together with a commitment to create the desired outcome. Planning processes that are not fully inclusive, particularly those in large organizations, can lack clarity and cause misunderstandings that can take years to overcome. If you allow people within an organization to work on the issues they control and avoid the tendency to try to limit thought processes from a higher position of authority, the result can go well beyond what you could imagine or achieve as an individual or small, exclusive group.

An Engaging Experience

Planning can be an engaging experience in which people who care about the organization can come together to use their imaginations and consider how to build momentum toward the future. Enthusiasm and a sense of enjoyment help create imaginative and useful results. Even with complex or critical issues, being open to a sense of fun can stimulate parts of your brain seldom used in more purely analytical approaches. If you have ever experienced a purely logical and linear planning process, you more than likely understand the limitations imposed by the lack of balance. In being playful or having fun, you can recognize patterns and relationships, and make connections you never noticed before. You can use and adjust your plan to constantly create momentum toward the future. It is a dynamic thing, open and useable, rather than being stuffed in a drawer and forgotten until the next planning session. Both logical and more imaginative thinking processes play a role in understanding and forming organizational goals. Both flow and structure are needed to create momentum.

One of the most memorable moments of Charlotte's experience as a freshman in college was sitting in a music theory class listening to the professor explain the circle of fifths in music with such delight that you could not help but love the structure and what it represented. The circle of fifths represents some of the most fundamental patterns in music; it is essentially a geometrical representation of the relationships between keys, chords, and scales. While every musician uses it to practice scales and learn key signatures, it can also be a boring topic in a class discussion. Yet in this class, the professor explained how in the sixth century B.C. a Greek philosopher named Pythagoras used his discoveries about pitch frequencies in different musical instruments to standardize musical tuning. Excitement built as the teacher explained with pure enjoyment how to read the circle and how it could be used to practice scales, understand key signatures, and easily transpose music. Charlotte said that every member of the class of thirty freshmen sat on the edge of their seat as the professor built momentum around a topic that could under many circumstances be mind-numbing.

Near the end of the hour, he demonstrated the chord progressions that could be created and the harmonic resolution of tension. His energy grew and, finally, at the end of class, he turned away from the board to face the class. With a facial expression of pure joy, a deep breath, and an excited tone he said, "And that's the circle of fifths!" When Charlotte and other members of that class talk with each other about the experience, they all remember the same thing—a feeling of "wow, that's the circle of fifths"—that came about purely from the building excitement of the professor's presentation and the anticipation it created. They were not only fully engaged in the structure of the circle of fifths, but taken in by the structure of the class.

Enjoyment is often thought of as an unnecessary luxury, not to be used in serious situations. Yet, it can transform planning environments, particularly when facing challenging decisions. When used in an appropriate way, fun can create momentum when tackling difficult issues. The perspective and attitudes of everyone involved can shift, and results can be achieved much faster with enjoyment in the process. Artists experience joy and the wonder of aesthetic discovery even when dealing with serious subjects. It is wise and responsible to consider the power of fun.

CONCEPT PRACTICE

The concept of planning and momentum can be adjusted to fit nearly every aspect of your life. It can help you use your time more effectively, influence your work environment, and help your family members achieve their goals. It's likely you have a much greater capacity to achieve your goals than you realize. Planning from an artistic perspective can help you transform limiting habits and create momentum you did not previously consider.

Problem solving capabilities of a person solely depends on his attitude.

~ Anurag Prakash Ray

Quick Tips

Consider your habits to understand your routines and behaviors. Make notes of what you discover.

- Think about the way you see things, whether your attitudes and viewpoints are expansive or limiting. An unfolding and evolving path requires openness to change.
- Consider your emotions, whether they feel predominantly positive or negative. Planning adds power to your thoughts. Determine whether the emotion you contribute to an effort matches your desired outcome.
- Examine how others in your personal and work life influence your attitudes, behaviors, and emotions. Measure your own progress and stay in control of your momentum along the path you choose.

Devise a structural foundation that can help you begin to move in the direction you desire. Consider what you want to accomplish so you can develop a plan that leads you there. Make an effort to understand why you desire a certain result. Consider whether it is an internally focused desire or something encouraged by a particular situation or person. It is important to fully understand these deeper motives and beliefs because they can inspire you to create the momentum you need. Use the practices of artists and carry a notebook or sketchbook to keep track of your thoughts. Spend time in reflective thought to examine and possibly question your intentions. Spending quiet time also helps you truly see, hear, and know without judgment.

The open mind of an artist allows for uncertainty and ambiguity. Images, movement, and sounds in works of art can be understood in more than one way. In fact, most artists know that appreciation and interpretation from multiple perspectives is an important characteristic of their work. Artists set the scene, so to speak, but don't stipulate what another person must see or hear. Participating in the artistic process is incredibly powerful. It is also powerful for the artist—along with other viewers or listeners—to step back and seek inherently personal and satisfying meaning from a work. Artists thrive on this sort of ambiguity that, without distracting, multiplies potential meanings and invites interpretations and various perspectives. Ambiguities in successful works of art emerge from the intuitive and often playful eye or ear of the observer. Experimenting with meaning adds richness to the work as a whole. You can do the same with complexities in your life. Change is a certainty and ambiguity is a part of everyday experience. The artistic process can help you create momentum as you navigate your way.

CONSCIOUSNESS QUERIES

Ambiguity and uncertainty go hand in hand with the creative process of planning.

- Can you let go of trying to control everything?
- Are you willing to change course?
- Are you able to move forward without "all of the information"?
- Do you have confidence in your ability to respond to things that are not in your control?
- Do you use your intuition—listen to your inner voice?

When planning, as you generate ideas, list everything that comes to mind even though some ideas may seem completely unrelated to the current situation. As you begin to focus, make every attempt to create connections between things, whether disparate or not. In the process you will likely discover connections between things you never before considered. In a notebook, jot down ideas, draw images, and consider your feelings about things. Feelings can guide you to greater focus and realizing your goal. Do not list ideas as a logical, linear, numbered set of steps but, rather, a collection of thoughts that, as of yet, have no specific order of importance. The following chart shows the artistic process of planning and momentum in its simplest form.

Planning and Momentum

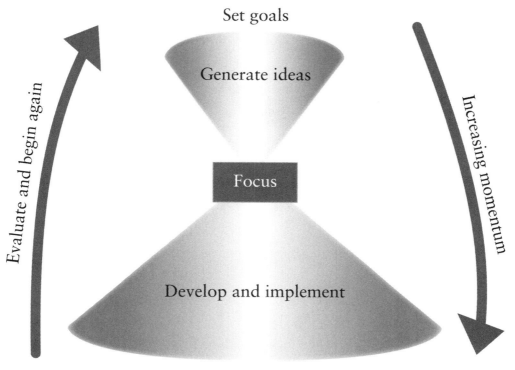

Set goals

Generate ideas

Evaluate and begin again

Increasing momentum

Focus

Develop and implement

Achieve goals

Define the goals you want to achieve and how you will know when you achieve them. Include all constituent elements—people and component parts—in the planning process. Avoid getting completely sidetracked by distractions and irrelevant objectives unrelated to your goals. Consider the resources you need before you get started. Determine a time frame to reach your goal. In an artistic project, the timeline is often determined by the date of an upcoming performance or showing. Allow time to find solutions to any problems that arise. The result should be something useful and fulfills your purpose. The planning process starts over with each new goal.

SUMMARY

The concept of planning is like a journey that takes you to new places, expanding your awareness as you go. As you chart the course from an artistic perspective, you discover a dynamic process, ever unfolding and evolving. Approach the general desire or problem with imagination and integrity. Without an openness to step out of your normal patterns of thinking, you might easily get stuck, not knowing which way to turn, or become distracted by the options.

Planning is the map that sets you on the path and helps you generate momentum to reach your goal. Artists seek out and experiment with a widely diverse collection of ideas to drive their efforts. Momentum builds as they narrow their focus. Along the way, they pay close attention to clues and connections that will move them closer to their goal. The power of the progress toward full realization of their goals is further enhanced by including all basic constituents— component parts, people, and the relationship between them.

While you may not at first notice the underlying structure that creates momentum and realization in a work of art, it is present in at least two ways. First, there is a sense of movement in the design of nearly every work of art, whether visual, aural, physical, or a combination. Your eyes and ears—and at times even your body—sense the momentum, guiding you through an experience in time and/or space. You may not even be consciously aware of the affective movement, just an impression and overall feeling.

While artists create motion in their works to hold your interest and help you see and hear, they also know how to create, build, and maintain momentum in their artistic lives. They make a commitment and are willing to make small and large changes in their approach and work to lead to and build momentum. They understand that momentum doesn't move on endlessly uninhibited by obstacles and adversity. When stopped or slowed, artists create a new way forward and continue until the cycle is complete. The phase continues, and their skill improves with each new beginning.

Understanding the concept of planning and momentum is critical to success in all of your activities. You can gain much by studying the artistic process, both in terms of the use of materials and the discipline of creative practice itself. Momentum comes from disciplined commitment and the consistent willpower to keep showing up. When you experience momentum, you need to keep flowing with the forward motion all the way until it reaches a natural ending. Then you start again. When artists create, they shut out distractions and make a full commitment to their work. Creating momentum requires the kind of focused commitment that allows you to use your full capacity. Artists can't survive in their creative work without that kind of discipline.

Here are some ways you can use the discipline of an artist to plan and move forward in your life and work situations:

- Focus your energy on creating, rather than thinking about what you want to create. That activity creates energy and will produce momentum.
- Move on when the momentum produces results or ends.
- Commit to the discipline needed to create momentum. It requires your whole effort.

Appreciation and enjoyment can provide significant power to the planning process. This approach allows you to think like an artist with an open and flexible mind. Your capacity for connecting disparate things and combining them in ways you never before imagined expands your options. The outcome is more creative and you become even more skilled as you routinely use the planning process to achieve your goals. You can also use this artistic planning process to bring about clarity and a new sense of purpose in others.

Review Questions

- "Strip away the leaves" and explore beneath the surface of your work and personal life experiences. Are you able to see more clearly the underlying structure that supports the situations you experience? Did you plan? Did you include all constituents—people and component parts— in your planning?

> Commitment is an act, not a word.
>
> ~ Jean-Paul Sartre

> The world is wide, and I will not waste my life in friction when it could be turned into momentum.
>
> ~ Frances Willard
> *Journals*

- Consider the paths you take when making decisions about a future goal. Are you open and flexible, exploring all the possibilities for creating momentum? Do you appreciate the journey and find a sense of enjoyment in the process?
- Are you consistently able to narrow your focus and choose a path forward without being sidetracked by distractions and objectives unrelated to your goals?

CONTINUE THE QUEST

Further explore the concept of planning and momentum. Use the suggestions below to consider the unfolding and evolving path of the artistic planning process. Think about how you can create a planning and momentum model that is flexible, fun, and focused. Study planning methods such as:

Mind Mapping—As you research this method, you will find many resources available, but you can begin with this book: Buzan, Tony and Barry Buzan. *The Mind Map Book: How to Use Radiant Thinking to Maximize Your Brain's Untapped Potential.* New York: Plume, 1996.

Dynamic Strategic Planning—Delve into the possibilities of this process with the book: Lawrimore, E. W. "Buck." *Dynamic Strategic Planning: A Powerful Process For Real-World Results.* Lulu.com.

Explore ways artists use structure to create momentum in their work. How might you use the concepts in your life and work environments?

- Go to a museum and study various works of art from a variety of periods. Look for the structural elements that hold a work together. Is it held together in a structural framework with line, with shape, with color?

    Consider how you can experience greater freedom by setting personal structures in your life. How can you move freely within the structure you put in place? What would change?
- Study the floor plans of a new home. How might a plan change if the foundational structure were adjusted? Try to imagine a variety of different outcomes.

If you are an educator, a business or organizational leader, or the head of a family, you can use this floor plan concept along with Martha's experience mentioned earlier in the chapter as models. Consider how you can allow those in your group to have fewer rules and more freedom by giving them a structured environment in which they know expectations and can take ownership on decisions, actions, goals, and ideas for growth. The tough hierarchical organizational structure started to strip Martha of the desire to continue.

- Spend time in nature or looking at photos of different kinds of plants or trees that come from the same family (e.g., pine trees, hostas, lilies, roses, etc.). Can you identify the underlying structure that classifies them in the family grouping?

- Study successful businesses, organizations, or schools where people love to work. Make a list of things you observe that make up their environments. Are there any broad common factors from one to the next?

- Listen to a jazz artist perform a song, starting with the basic melody supported by a harmonic structure. As the piece progresses, listen carefully to hear how the basic melodic and harmonic structure remains, but the sound differs.

Look at productive and joyful individuals. What do they do that allows them to succeed and to enjoy their lives along the way?

- Baroque music uses long phrases, few pauses, rhythmic complexity, and sequences to build momentum. Listen to the way Bach's driving rhythms, regular patterns, steady pulse, and rapid passages in all parts contribute to the overall momentum and affect in his music.

- Study paintings such as *Yellow-Red-Blue* (1925) by Wassily Kandinsky to explore how he used structural elements such as repetition, placement of objects—as well as directional, diagonal, and gestural lines—in many of his paintings to convey an illusion of motion.

CHAPTER 7

ACT, MEASURE, ADAPT:
BUILDING A SENSE OF COMMITMENT

OVERVIEW

RISK AND RITUAL

Creating art of any kind involves an enormous risk. Artists know that if they never take the stage or place the first brushstroke, they never move forward. Yet, taking that first step challenges you to have faith in yourself, to take something from your innermost being and share it with others. Involvement in the artistic process takes courage, commitment, and learning new ways of doing things. Jody (whom you met in Chapter 3) learned this lesson well early in her college life.

Although Jody played music for many years before college, she felt confused in her freshman year as she took the first steps toward the practice room with a course of study she never before considered. As you may recall, her direction changed at the urging of one of her professors, and instead of a typical one instrument performance major, she was now on her way to practice five instruments and was unsure how to begin. In a few short days, her life changed forever. Rather than the flute major route she planned, she was now a woodwind performance major.

When she gained permission to develop this new program, it felt like a tremendous risk. Both excited and terrified, Jody had no idea where this would lead. But there she was, at 4:30 in the afternoon, heading to the practice room with her flute, oboe, clarinet, bassoon, and saxophone. As she entered the small, rectangular, windowless room, she took each instrument out of its case and lined them up. Instrument stands allowed her to sit them upright within easy reach without placing them on their sides, or damaging their keys. She placed her music on the music stand and considered how to begin.

Most comfortable on the flute, she picked it up and began a practice routine:

- Warm-up exercises for tone quality and control of the sound,
- Scales and arpeggios for basic technique,
- Method book exercises designed to improve both her technical and interpretive skills, and
- The detailed process involved in learning the music for her lesson

As she worked on the music, she glanced at the clock. An hour had easily passed. While not unusual (three hours each day was the norm), the other instruments sat there untouched. Jody went through each instrument with the same basic routine. Six hours later, after cleaning and packing up the instruments, she wandered to her dorm room searching for food. She realized she missed dinner in the dining hall altogether!

Over the next few weeks, Jody developed a schedule and routine that worked well and allowed her to make significant progress on each instrument. Her practice sessions were focused. Jody developed a strong sense of relationship with each instrument, constantly evaluating and adapting to match what she heard with what was in her mind's ear. She needed to learn each instrument as if it were the full focus of her expression as an artist: characteristic tone quality, technical mastery, and control of the full range of repertoire.

Jody's experience grew deeper as she performed on recital programs, played in the orchestra and band, in chamber groups, and jazz ensembles, all on different instruments. Her confidence grew and the years of study ultimately led to junior, senior, and master's level capstone recitals on all the instruments. Numerous professional and semi-professional opportunities arose and her performance experiences expanded, allowing her to enjoy expressive and financial rewards well beyond what she ever could have known exclusively as a flutist. Jody's awareness of what took place during those years continues to expand today. Taking a chance, making a genuine commitment, developing a habit of practice, and adjusting along the way can help you in anything you do.

Mastering five instruments broadened her point of view. As a result, she achieved more than she could have ever imagined otherwise. The risk was well worth the effort. Jody's anxiety at the beginning came from the fear of being different, of being ridiculed, and of the potential of artistic failure. She realizes now that the momentum for her success came from these very tensions. Her initial discomfort actually energized her thinking and learning. The anxiety created the energy that motivated her to think in a new way, to change her frame of reference, and adjust to her decisions. It challenged her to think more deeply.

Practice in that tiny room allowed Jody private time to develop a sort of ritual she could rely on. In that place she could focus, and she learned to make the best use of her time with consistent daily practice, allowing her artistic power to surface. She ultimately learned to use this idea of consistent practice in every area of her life. Everyone can learn to use it. But in order to achieve full benefit, you have to have the courage and commitment to enter the artistic process, find your own expressive voice, and connect with the world. Artistic process offers a continuous cycle of new beginnings. It helps you learn to take risks, to make mistakes, to adjust, and to try another time. It can become a means of change and progress. You realize success is not about just getting to the end of something; it is about the commitment to begin again, fully conscious of what you do along the way.

FOREGROUND AND BACKGROUND

Artistic expression is shaped over time. It is chiseled and formed with decisions, lessons, losses, and successes. Learning to express yourself as an artist means you often explore unknowns and face doubts. When you keep at it, you build momentum, and then it is almost impossible to stop. This becomes a constant process of

Begin, be bold and venture to be wise.
~ Horace
Horace: Satires, Epistles and Ars Poetica

I am seeking. I am striving. I am in it with all my heart.

~ Vincent van Gogh
The Letters of Vincent van Gogh

practice, evaluation, and adjustment. The internal push and pull that can come with a decision, like the one Jody made to move in the new direction suggested by her professor, can help you find balance with what is most important at any given moment. Artists actually use this kind of decision-making process to move things in and out of the foreground and background of their works. It helps you place emphasis where you feel it belongs, ultimately leading you on an engaging visual or aural tour.

Everyone is faced with push and pull in their lives, making decisions about what comes forward in any given moment and what falls back as support. Most likely, you often give in to what feels like the safest choice rather than what feels right in a given situation. You can overcome this tendency using the wisdom gained from the artistic process to shape the significance of events. At times, the choice is difficult, but you have the opportunity to express yourself with integrity every moment of every day, just like artists who are deeply connected to expressing themselves without limiting their choices. If artists give in to take the safest route, their expression is never clear, they disconnect from who they are, and their work does not resonate in the same way.

Taking action and adapting along the way is a matter of arranging the parts and using artistic techniques to move elements forward or backward to suggest what is most important or secondary. While it can sometimes become complex with multiple layers, more often than not the eye and ear can easily follow what is placed as primary importance. Perception is important, and multiple layers can add depth, but what is brought to the foreground is certain to influence the outcome.

ARTISTIC INSIGHTS

Some of the techniques used by artists to lead your eyes and ears include:

- Complexity—where there is the most visual or aural activity, there is the perception of greater importance. In your everyday life, the actions you choose in the midst of chaos come to the fore and matter most in the end.

- Contrasts of color or musical timbre—the fullest and most intense colors and timbres demand your attention. You can choose to live your life fully and bring out the brightest and richest aspects of who you are as a human being.
- An unusual or new element—something new in the midst of something familiar. Do not be afraid to bring new things into your life or stand up for what is right in the middle of turmoil and confusion.
- Form—structure can be used to highlight something and bring it forward. A change of routine can lead to important changes of focus and meaning in your life.

CREATIVE SPACE

Artists are open to the world around them. That openness allows them to see, hear, and feel things that may go unnoticed by others. It allows the creative space for observations and ideas to develop with artistic outcomes that are often surprising and unique. Artists get caught up in the material, the idea, the sound, or the feeling and become fully absorbed in the process. Their willingness to enter this authentic creative space puts them in a position to take full advantage of their imaginations.

QUICK TIPS

Creative space is available to anyone:
- Be willing to work beyond boundaries of tradition or what is most familiar.
- Slow down and become absorbed in the process.
- Pay attention and notice that life is constantly presenting you with new information.

Artists not only see things in new ways, but perpetually change the way you see things. They use their imaginations to transform your knowledge and understanding of the world. Once you experience expanded limits of your personal knowledge, whether

I can't understand why people are frightened of new ideas. I'm frightened of the old ones.

~ John Cage
Conversing with Cage

you agree or challenge the learning, life from that point on will never be the same. As the creator of your own life, you can use your imagination, not only to expand your own understanding, but also to influence new possibilities for those in your home, community, and work environments.

As mentioned earlier, my backyard view in Sedona, Arizona had an incredible backdrop of irregularly shaped red rock formations that rose like statues out of the ground. Everyone in the area called the formations by names based on their overall shape. There was a clear view of Bell Rock. Perhaps you can picture it. The view from the house looked west toward Bell Rock, which was illuminated every evening by the setting sun in a brilliant orange and red glow.

Bert and Justine—a delightful retired couple who lived next door—stopped over one evening, and we silently admired the beauty of the colorful display against the red rocks. They lived in that area for some time, and reflected on Bell Rock for many years. Justine suddenly broke the silence with a declaration that Bell Rock looked to her like Bert's nose. As we focused on the actual rock formation, it took a minute to understand. Sure enough, there it was—Bert's nose! We laughed and, as we continued to study Bell Rock, the image of Bert's nose became clearer until, finally, that is all we could see. The head was positioned as if Bert lay on his back staring straight up to the sky. There were slight indentations where his eyes would be, piñon trees formed bushy eyelashes, the nose was quite prominent, the lips shaped by rising and falling outcroppings of rock, and the chin curved perfectly to the neck. There it was—Bert lying on his back watching the sky and the setting sun.

Justine's imagination changed the way we looked at the rock formation forever. When you think about it, new thoughts and ideas permanently change your mind all the time. This sort of imagination can become the source of ideas. Justine used the freedom of mind, the questioning, and the creativity of an artist to see Bell Rock in a new way. Her curiosity and openness to seeing new things launched a new understanding, a new way to look at something she saw every day for many years. Imagination

Every now and then a man's mind is stretched by a new idea or sensation, and never shrinks back to its former dimensions.

~ Oliver Wendell Holmes, Sr.
The Autocrat of the Breakfast Table

initiates everything, and new knowledge and understanding grow from there.

Artists use the creative space of their imaginations to deliberately explore new directions. When you commit yourself to curiosity, to using your imagination, and to expand your own understanding of things, you can transform your own experiences. At the same time, you influence new possibilities for those around you. Just as it does for dancers, singers, painters, and other artists, making an effort to allow creative space in your life and work experiences will produce amazing results and benefits that might have previously been unimaginable.

When you think about Jody's experience of broadening her focus and changing majors, it helps you understand in greater depth the importance of taking the first step. This is true in everything you do, even if you are initially unsure about where it will lead. Once Jody made a commitment, practiced, sought feedback, and reflected on her decision, it gave her greater freedom and the permission to express herself more fully. The artistic process is extremely valuable regardless of your field. You can contribute to your own life and those around you in a way that takes the ordinary and makes it extraordinary. But you cannot remain solely a spectator. Artistic living requires an effort and participation in the process. It requires the willingness to be vulnerable and freely connect your heart and mind and body, and to take the first step to let things unfold. When you do this once, it becomes easier, and you begin to face the future with understanding and awareness.

CONSCIOUSNESS QUERIES

New possibilities, new adventures, and new connections are always within your reach. Initiate something and take the first step forward. It will lead to another and another.

- Are you afraid to consider the first step in creating your dreams? What holds you back?
- Do you use your imagination to explore options and consider possibilities? Are you open to the vulnerability

They always say time changes things, but you actually have to change them yourself.

~ Andy Warhol
The Philosophy of Andy Warhol

We press into the unknown rather than the known. This makes life lovely and lively.

~ Julia Cameron

The beginning is the most important part of any work.

~ Plato

that comes with using what you see in your mind's eye or you hear in your mind's ear?

- If you make a move, do you follow through with practice and ongoing assessment, making changes as you go?

BE BOLD AND BEGIN

Whether creating art, leading an organization, or managing everyday life, you can choose to get started and keep moving like an artist. When you have the courage to begin and keep at it, you will experience the powerful force of momentum. Then it's easier to stay focused, make continuous progress, and find your way through the obstacles and challenges that inevitably turn up as you move forward. The most delightful aspect of this journey is that you never know what life-changing things you might discover along the way.

A former student, who lived her entire childhood in an isolated area of northern Arizona with a population of less than four thousand people, decided she wanted to experience life in other parts of the country. Prior to going to college in Flagstaff, about two hundred miles away from her home, she had never travelled anywhere. Flagstaff seemed like another world altogether. As she explored the diversity of people on campus, the widely varied points of view, and the worlds that came to life through her studies, she committed to moving well out of the Southwest upon graduation.

She applied for positions all over the country in her field of forestry and landed a position in Georgia, more than fifteen hundred miles away. She loved the outdoors, and the strong forestry industry in Georgia seemed a perfect fit. Over the years, she formed a deep commitment to understanding and protecting the environment that came from appreciating two contrasting settings—the multihued desert hills, broad mesas, soaring buttes, and massive mountains of her home and the largest contiguous Ponderosa pine forest in the continental United States near Flagstaff. The broad expanse of forest land in Georgia gave her an impression of the boundless space she experienced in both those environments.

She shared that her love of boundless space started in the art classes she took as a young child and continued through all of her college years. Art was the thread that held her life experiences together. Her lessons in art motivated her to explore the vastness of physical space, along with the space of the canvas. She learned to interpret the scenes she saw in everyday life. She considered countless perspectives as she used the creative space of the canvas in response to her vision. Every setting was an opening to begin anew. She used this consideration for creative space to stretch even further, expanding her understanding of everything she did. It gave her the courage to step into a new culture and create a new life. The wisdom she gained through her arts education gave her the boldness to look beneath the surface for paths she could never consider otherwise.

CONSCIOUSNESS QUERIES

Choose a period of change in your life and take a moment to think about your decisions:

- What new ideas rose to the surface, inspiring you toward a new direction?
- Did you have the courage to take a chance and try it? If so, can you see how it expanded your mind to consider even more possibilities?
- Where can you use this concept of beginning right now in your life, work, or relationships?

> Freedom lies in being bold.
>
> ~ Robert Frost

MOTIVATIONAL STORY— WHATEVER YOU ARE, BE A GOOD ONE

As Joanna (whom you met in Chapter 6) drove the five hundred mile journey from her small hometown in Northern California to attend her first year of college, her excitement about beginning a new experience grew. Her original intention, at the urging of her private violin instructor, was to attend college and pursue her music studies in New York. As you may remember, once she visited, she knew it was not the right move for her at that time. Even though she spent time in cities such as San Francisco and Sacramento, her small town experience took over. Driving in her used 1967 Ford Falcon Futura, she was on the way to her new beginning in southern California. Her parents followed her in their car to be sure she arrived safely and helped transport some of the things she needed to begin her new life. After they arrived and unloaded the cars, Joanna stood and watched her parents drive away to return home. At that moment, from her deepest self, she sensed her life was changed forever. She speaks of it as an odd feeling—a strange mixture of heightened anticipation and fear of the unknown.

While fortunate to have a full scholarship to attend college, she had little money for daily expenses. That was never a consideration in her decision to attend. In her mind, it was the hope of a new beginning that called her to take a chance and explore another way of life. At first, the fear seemed to linger and overpower the sense of enthusiasm for what lay ahead. Once she arrived at the music building for orientation, her courage expanded. In just a short time, she was drawn forward and fully immersed in making music. The compelling power of its pull took precedence over everything else.

Repeatedly over the next few years, Joanna's confidence was shaken with the same sense of anticipation and fear, but she never backed down. Her growing knowledge of the artistic process helped her move through and around obstacles that seemed to show up with a purpose to stand in her way and overpower her commitment. Although not fully conscious of it at the time, the artistic process she learned so well taught her to solve problems creatively with boldness, courage, and focus. Her music practice gave her the tools to carry on and carve a path forward to achieve her goals. In order to create momentum in the music, she learned to confront problems that arose in the artistic process, rather than avoid them. Joanna learned to focus her attention and take action, developing strength that helped her build confidence and endurance.

Courage is being scared to death—but saddling up anyway.

~ John Wayne

When you think about it, for centuries artists have used adversity, breaking down the problems they faced and developing the inner strength to move their work forward. Once they break through the resistance that comes with challenge, their unyielding focus creates an incredible force of forward motion. The friction is threefold: creating momentum, finding balance within the work of art itself, and overcoming internal and external snags that appear when participating in the artistic process.

The snags Joanna faced in her freshman year were largely financial. She did not have the resources to purchase food if she did not make it to the dining hall before it closed at the end of the day. One late afternoon, as she drove back from an orchestral rehearsal about sixty miles away, one of her tires exploded. It was a retread tire and the tread simply fell off as she drove along the freeway. At the first available exit, she found herself in a dangerous part of town. People were loitering in front of abandoned buildings covered in frightening graffiti. Joanna felt the area was not safe for a college woman travelling alone, and certainly not with a car that might stop at any moment. She had no money and the Mobil gas card her parents left her was not accepted at the station she found. After pleading with the station employee, he agreed to put a new tire on her car, and she drove away promising to return the next day with the money. She borrowed it from a friend and they drove back to the station together to repay him. Joanna will never forget his kindness. It was also a good lesson in judgment and appearances.

The instrument she owned was not of high quality. The decision to study music as a major meant she had to borrow university instruments. While generally acceptable, these instruments were not of the level she ultimately needed to succeed. One day, after hearing her perform on a television talent show, a friend told his hometown music store owner about Joanna. He was so drawn to her story that he offered her the opportunity to purchase a high quality professional level violin and bow at a fraction of the cost and with a payment structure that allowed her the freedom to pay as she could. Joanna never met this kind man, yet he helped further her progress, leading to more opportunities to purchase equipment for her performance needs.

Joanna became quite ill in the summer following her freshman year and the doctor sent her home. He told her she was too sick to return to college in the fall. Leveraging her understanding of momentum she had garnered from the artistic process, she took the actions to heal. All along, she never intended to stay home from her third semester of college. She evaluated her progress every day and altered her schedule to get the rest she needed. When the time came, Joanna gained permission to return to campus and begin classes.

Joanna knew from her experiences with the artistic process that your choices can take you where you want to be. The artistic process teaches you to always reach for excellence: evaluate where you are, where you want to be, and your first steps to get there. It gives you the opportunity to identify and create change. She finally found her footing, not only in music performance, but in gaining the financial support she needed. She decided to teach lessons to young children and middle- and high school-aged students on weekends. She also got together with friends and formed a quartet. Besides light classical music, they played standards and pop music and made money performing at events around town. Other paying gigs materialized, as well, allowing her to increase her income and enrich her performance experiences.

QUICK TIPS

The artistic process can help you learn to move out of your comfort zone and broaden your vision. It might be scary, but do it anyway. Here are some suggestions:

- Accept uncertainty.
- Take action. Go for it.
- Challenge yourself.
- Put in the creative effort—practice.
- Replace negative thoughts with more positive ones.
- Change your routines.

Life is a great big canvas, and you should throw all the paint on it you can.

~ Danny Kaye

LESSONS LEARNED

These early college life experiences were only the beginning of learning that, from Joanna's perspective, continues to this day. Through her experiences with the artistic process, she learned that if you are genuine in your intent, make a commitment, and take the risk, you have the opportunity to break down barriers and work beyond boundaries that might otherwise limit you. The constant practice of assessing her progress and making adjustments to persevere opened up unexpected opportunities and experiences she never knew existed.

Artists begin with a goal in mind, which is to create something meaningful that represents their idea, whether a performance, a product, or an object. While some works of art turn out better than imagined, others are plagued with problems or may fail altogether. You learn through the artistic process to use problems or failure as a way to grow and enhance your artistry. While these seeming limitations can be disappointing, Joanna learned how to determine what went wrong, how to fix it, or how to start over to achieve her goals.

Joanna discovered the powerful technique of how to balance the tension between the contrasting experiences of disappointment or fear and the sometimes surprising successes in her journey. Artists constantly balance the dynamics of seemingly contradictory states. The variation form in music is an example of how the artistic process can use the restrictions set by a melody and harmony to create something new altogether. Jazz musicians do this all of the time with improvised solos around a pre-defined harmonic structure. In fact, all artists balance contradictory factors such as the constraints of skill practice—basic techniques, structures, and rules of the art form—with freedom to influence their creative expressions. Joanna found that what at first might appear to be a limitation can, in reality, be what allows you to express yourself fully and help you find new opportunities.

The willingness to step into the unknown, although a path that was often difficult, helped Joanna understand that she has the choice in each moment to either anxiously resist or stay

> The artist is always beginning. Any work of art which is not a beginning, an invention, a discovery, is of little worth.
>
> ~ Ezra Pound

> When things are perfect, that's when you need to worry most.
>
> ~ Drew Barrymore

open and take the steps that lead to the next opportunity. Artists learn from the inside out, tapping into the inner guidance system of the subconscious mind to access a natural but often hidden intelligence. In her freshman year of college, she learned to explore and discover like an artist—to learn new skills and perspectives— and she became fully engaged with the artistic process. These discoveries fascinated her. They helped her bounce back and grab hold of the things that came her way. Joanna learned that once you experience the benefits of the flow of creative space, you never forget it. It continues to enhance your experience for the rest of your life. Even in the midst of struggles, the artistic process helps you learn to generate momentum, change direction, and keep moving.

The artistic process taught Joanna that if you want to achieve a goal, you do not wait until everything is perfect—until everything is just right. You simply begin. There is lightness about simply beginning. Although once you get started, you have to follow through, the beginning is critical. Experience tells you there will be challenges, barriers, and emotions to manage, but the incentive in what lies ahead gives you the power to keep at it. The constant process of practicing, assessing, and correcting leads you forward. You discover that something earned after a struggle is often much more rewarding than one which is easy and immediately clear. Artists manipulate the relationship of elements—such as structure, size, texture, shape, and position— to enhance or redefine possibilities and convey deeper meaning. The contrasting opposites are synthesized, coming together as one unique and complex whole.

QUICK TIPS

You can learn to use the skills of an artist:
- Make a commitment to begin.
- Focus, create space, and clear away distractions.
- Eliminate or work around any obstacles or challenges that appear to be in your way.
- Use your heart—live your life from the inside out.

When my daughter was about seven years old, she asked me one day what I did at work. I told her I worked at the college—that my job was to teach people how to draw. She stared at me, incredulous, and said, "You mean they forget?

~ Howard Ikemoto
The Art of Remembering

Artists have sole control of taking their artistic expressions in the direction they want. True artists begin a work of art from an honest and authentic place, from a place that inspires them to express themselves fully. They create art for a reason and strive to be the best they can be.

DEEPENING PERSPECTIVES OF COMMITMENT

CREATIVE CONFIDENCE

Artists often experience dramatic and varying waves of confidence swings. Some days, things go well and you feel strong and productive. Other days, you may question your abilities or feel weak and insignificant. That is not so different from what everyone experiences in nearly all aspects of their daily lives. Everyone experiences disappointments in life. You might have had to perform in certain ways to achieve the approval of others, perhaps even feeling at times you were not quite good enough. More than likely you experienced cruel words and hurtful behaviors coming at you from others. In spite of the fluctuating emotions of certainty and insecurity, successful artists take charge and find a way past the feelings of doubt and fear, transforming them into confidence and courage. The more you experience the swing from fear to faith in yourself, the more you have the capacity to face challenges, persevere in trying times, and remain strong when confronted with difficulties and disappointments. You transform obstacles to opportunities and create new beginnings.

ARTISTIC INSIGHTS

- Successful artists learn to let go of the stories they created about themselves that came from past difficulties and failures.
- They let go of the stories from others about their personal worth or the merit of their work.
- They use every experience they have, whether positive or negative, to build their confidence.

Always be a first-rate version of yourself, instead of a second-rate version of somebody else.

~ Judy Garland
Business Etiquette for the Nineties: Your Ticket to Career Success

If you hear a voice within you say "you cannot paint," then by all means paint, and that voice will be silenced.

~ Vincent van Gogh

- As they open to the challenges and opportunities of obstacles and failures, they are empowered by the strength that comes from working through the fear of starting again.
- They let go of the insecurity of comparisons.
- They keep showing up, no matter what, willing to take risks, to be open, and to be themselves.

Time and again, artists have used the artistic process to conquer their fears and overcome obstacles. They risked showing up amidst struggles, failure, and the negative opinions of others.

- Although Vincent van Gogh sold only one painting when he was still alive, he produced nearly 900 paintings and more than 1,100 watercolors, drawings, and sketches over the course of his decade-long career.
- It has been said that Beethoven's music teacher told him he was a hopeless composer.
- Fred Astaire is said to have received a dismissive studio evaluation claiming he could dance a little, but could not act.
- Famous opera singer Enrico Caruso is said to have been told by a teacher that he had no voice at all and he could not sing.
- Anna Marie Robertson Moses—known as Grandma Moses—taught herself to paint when she was 78.

There are many more stories of similar experiences of the some of the greatest artists in history. They worked through the angst and fear of the unknown. They prepared themselves. They practiced and adjusted, and they made a fresh start. They were proactive and took control, fully focused and aware.

Learning in the arts helps you find ways to do the things that need to get done. Life for most people is busy, with constant sound and visual stimulation. You might work on a project, skip to another, and another, never completing one until it becomes urgent. Often at that point you discover it is too late to do it well

You can, you should, and if you're brave enough to start, you will.

~ Stephen King
On Writing: A Memoir of the Craft

or to get it done at all. Even if you are good at taking on several things at a time, your ability to concentrate is likely diminished and you may yearn for experiences that are truly meaningful.

CONSCIOUSNESS QUERIES

- Do you feel in charge of your work or activity, or do you feel confused?
- Do you pay attention to the meaningfulness of what you are doing?
- Do you start your work or activity with an end in mind, constantly evaluating and adjusting along the way?

BALANCE BETWEEN THE CREATIVE AND CRITICAL

Artists find the balance between the creative and critical when forming their work. The artistic process requires a balance of imagination and evaluation, with creative as well as critical thinking. While many planning models are used inflexibly, the artistic process allows for creative space and flow. Yet, in order to reach a goal, the process involves more than simply imagining things. Artists take action that often involves focused research. They test their ideas and make necessary adjustments, and they generate the energy to achieve their goals. One of the greatest benefits is that artists fully connect with their innermost selves during the process. Their heart-mind connection is essential.

Sam, now 45, is a seasoned world traveler and the co-founder of his own video production business. But it took a lot of hard work and some strategic financial and work–life balancing for him to get where he is now.

To pay off the sizable college debt he incurred in his late teens and twenties, Sam took on four jobs, working out of his apartment as a freelance video editor, seasonal work in pool maintenance, restaurant host, and seasonal work in construction. He worked between eighty-five and one hundred hours a week for two years. He was familiar with a schedule of long, grueling days as a film and television production major in college, but he was now determined to find balance between his financial obligations and his income.

A few months into the plan he developed, Sam's mother became ill and, with no siblings or other relations to chip in, he felt obligated to find time to offer the care she needed. He negotiated schedules, moved back home and served as caregiver while his mother recuperated from her illness. Even with this added responsibility, Sam had earned more than double what he owed his creditors by the end of the second year, but there was no freedom or creativity in his life.

As his mother improved, he was able to make creative choices about his life. He quit his jobs, sold his furniture that was still sitting in his apartment, and travelled the world for several months planning the next phase of his life. He visited friends in the video and television industry and, rather than spend the rest of his life working for someone else, he decided to form his own company. When he returned home, he put everything in place to create his own video production business.

Sam's business is now thriving. He manages to run the business remotely from various locations as he travels around the world gathering ideas and nurturing his creative capabilities. He visits his mother and hired someone to help her when he is gone. He meets his staff in person when needed. Sam not only reached the income–expense balance he sought, but achieved a work–life balance as well. He would have it no other way.

Balance is central to artistic expression. Artists—painters, sculptors, designers, composers, photographers, writers, directors, choreographers, film makers, dancers, musicians, conductors—balance compositional elements in ways that impact the overall feeling of a completed work of art. When creating or performing, artists use both imaginative and analytical thinking as they work with their judgment, make associations, and determine how to direct viewers' or listeners' eyes or ears or both. They use composition to set the stage—to determine how visual or aural lines, colors, textures, shape, values, position, and weight will lead to important areas that hold attention and guide the eye and/or ear to another part of the work.

Learning about the concept of balance through the creative and critical thinking of artistic expression helps you recognize that there is more than one way to achieve it in everything you do. Everyone deals with the need to balance various aspects of things in nearly every moment of every day. Whether you think about it or not, balance is a gauge by which you weigh things that affect every aspect of your life. In a work of art, the elements can be manipulated to create a sense of symmetry or asymmetry that supports the overall essence of the artistic expression. Depending on how each element is used, each moment or part is perceived as strong or weak in relation to the whole and gives you a sense of stability and movement through seeing or feeling or both. The elements work together to produce an overall sense of harmony. You, too, can learn to create this overall sense of harmony in everything you do through a willingness to take risks, a commitment to try again, and focused practice. This sort of effort helps you measure your progress and adapt to the challenges that emerge along the way.

The principle of balance is in everything you do. The distribution of various internal and external elements in family life, personal relationships, teaching environments, leadership, or work is central to your existence as a human being. When you experiment with symmetry and asymmetry, you can experience how to plan and create your life or work experience in its entirety. Whether the paths are the same, crooked, or disproportionate in relationship with different weights, creative tension occurs where they meet. At this meeting point, they are separate and held together as one because, even though they might be of different weight values, if done with the principles of artistic expression, they have the feeling of balance.

MAKING THE MOST OF YOUR CREATIVE VOICE

In order to get the full benefit of the artistic process, you need to review your strengths and talents regularly, and learn how to

What I dream of is an art of balance.

~ Henri Matisse
Notes of a Painter

A career path is rarely a path at all. A more interesting life is usually a more crooked, winding path of missteps, luck and vigorous work. It is almost always a clumsy balance between the things you try to make happen and the things that happen to you.

~ Tom Freston
Commencement Speech at Emerson College

use them in everything you do. No matter what the project, you have to take the first step, understanding right from the start how you can use your strengths to contribute to the process. Once on the path, stay on it. If you are part of a team, be certain you contribute to the fullest extent using your strengths, while recognizing your vulnerabilities and weaknesses.

One of the most challenging aspects of the artistic process is maintaining your creative integrity. In a difficult situation you may be tempted to allow your effort to be watered down or marginalized. You may remember feeling this way in various planning efforts you were involved with in the past. Every time you simply take a direction based on the judgment of someone else—neglecting to check in with your own instincts—you lose your unique creative voice. The result can be ineffective and disappointing. After a few of these situations, you begin to realize you have to change the process in order to succeed, even if it means taking a risk. Judgment from others often comes as a result of your idea landing outside the lines, so to speak—imaginative and inspired, but violating certain standard procedures. It is imperative that you evaluate and use your strengths to achieve the desired result.

This does not mean that the input of others is not important. Flexibility is important in any team process, but the vision for the desired outcome needs to be kept in mind and not hijacked by one person, whether well-meaning or not. When balanced, the efforts of a team can be extremely effective and inspiring. It is important, however, for everyone to trust the creative process in a teamwork environment. A true team is not pushed to come to a certain conclusion, but rather the end evolves, with everyone fully engaged with a mutual understanding of the goal the entire time. Projects seized by an individual, leaving everyone else in the dark, are not balanced and most often lead to disappointing results that are unsupported.

You must use your creative voice like an artist—to create or express something meaningful. Artistic expression helps artists understand a deep knowing within. At the same time, artists engage others with the significance of that knowledge. The knowledge is not something they can articulate with the same essence and power in any other way. Mary remembers viewing of a production of *Vieux Carré* by Tennessee Williams that helped strengthen her awareness that, day after day, you create your life in the same way artists or performers express themselves through art. Every moment in your personal and work life is filled with seeing, feeling, and sensing—each moment understood through your strengths, weaknesses, values, and life experiences. In the film—and later musical—*Billy Elliot*, Billy discovered the possibilities of being fully alive, awake, and aware through his body in dancing. He had no other way to express the deep connection with his heart, mind, and spirit, and relate his feelings to the wider world.

Artists intend to make something—they use their imagination, they mix and remix, they focus, and they take action. Each moment in your relationships, work, and daily lives gives you the opportunity to do the same—to use your thoughts, words, and values to take action and combine things in new ways, and bring forth something new to your experience that didn't exist before. Artists have a desire to express themselves to the fullest in a way that takes precedence over everything else.

Artists of all kinds work persistently in their art form to develop their skills. They continually seek ways to grow and evolve in the full expression of themselves. While every artist strives for excellence, they also know they are constantly refining and evolving. They become absorbed in the process. Everyone can grow and evolve like this. It just requires you to listen deeply to your own creative voice and change your perceptions and interpretations of your life experiences.

Much of the time you may unconsciously go about your daily life experiences without expressing yourself with artistry, not consciously choosing a path, creatively shaping and reshaping your understandings, or expanding your artistic awareness. As Mary reflected on the *Vieux Carré* production, she realized that—much like the work of an artist—your outer world is a reflection of your inner world. The play, set in a dilapidated building in the New Orleans French Quarter, speaks of seeing, hearing,

That inner voice has both gentleness and clarity. So to get to authenticity, you really keep going down to the bone, to the honesty, and the inevitability of something.

~ Meredith Monk
*Authentic Voice:
An Interview with
Meredith Monk*

Don't let the noise of others' opinions drown out your own inner voice.

~ Steve Jobs
*Stanford Commencement
Address*

It is how we choose what we do, and how we approach it, that will determine whether the sum of our days adds up to a formless blur, or to something resembling a work of art.

~ Mihály Csikszentmihályi
Finding Flow

feeling, and learning. Every character, and those around them, experiences a reflection of their inner world in each moment. Just like an artist, you have choices: you can decide what you do and how you make sense of the things around you, and you do get to choose to take action. When you consider Billy's choices in *Billy Elliot*, it is the stubborn persistence of creative expression that clearly wins out in the midst of painful family struggles and the depressing and ruthless environment brought about by the British mining industry.

ACCOUNTABILITY AND CHANGING PERSPECTIVE

The artistic process provides an opportunity to work within structures and manage them with some flexibility. While holding one another accountable in a team effort is important, the empowerment aspect of the artistic process gives you permission to be flexible and change your perspective as you move forward. Openness to changing perspectives is critical in any environment.

The changing perspective of light caught Robert's attention on his daily walk to work in Boston each fall. His route past the buildings, fountains, sculptures, trees, flowers, ground covers, and planters in the city attracted his attention in a new and unusual way. It had to do with the way the sunlight was changing at that time of year. He experienced a different feeling at each location along the path every day as the light affected various colors and surfaces, and thus the sensation of each moment of his walk. During one week, in particular, he noticed a difference each day in each location depending on the intensity and angle of the light. As the week went on, he realized this awareness is what artists do every day. They often create their work based on the sensation they experience—what they perceive—rather than an exact descriptive manner or what some might consider to be real.

Monet comes to mind as an example of an artist—an Impressionist painter—who shared his perceptions of things as he saw them at the moment. Since he spent a lot of time painting in the open air, he became extremely sensitive to the fact that when light changed, his whole perception of the subject changed. He presented different aspects of things according to the changing light, time of day, and his viewpoint as the artist. His willingness to explore and experience the same site many times, recording how he perceived the change that came about as a result of the light and shadows depending on the time of day, was extraordinary. In some cases, it took long periods of time to complete a series of these paintings. He dedicated the second half of his career to several series paintings capturing his perception of the changes caused by light in several subjects: *Rouen Cathedral, Water Lilies, Poplars, Haystacks, Houses of Parliament,* and *Morning on the Seine.*

Robert's walk took on a rhythm created by the feeling of the changing perspectives along the way. The shifting rhythm of movement on the walk made him think about how everyone could use this artistic process of perspective and perception to think about changes in everyday life and work. Seeing and understanding more deeply what you experience can allow you to explore the things that occur, opening your mind to new possibilities, helping you know that things can and will change from moment to moment, each day and year. In order to understand yourself, other people, and the world around you, shine a light on various aspects of your experiences. This can help you change and adapt your perspectives. The artistic process can help you blend adaptability and discipline with commitment and passion to sustain your efforts.

> You must look within for value, but must look beyond for perspective.
>
> ~ Denis Waitley

CONCEPT PRACTICE

You can use this concept of building a sense of commitment in a way that has a positive impact on everything you do. Whether designing a process for a personal goal, a family event, beginning an entrepreneurial venture, or developing a full-fledged business or organizational plan, the power of using the artistic process can help you begin, keep going, and grow all along the way. Whatever you have accomplished up until now is only a small part of what is truly achievable using the artistic process.

You gain strength, courage, and confidence by every experience in which you really stop to look fear in the face. You must do the thing which you think you cannot do.

~ Eleanor Roosevelt
You Learn by Living

The artistic process is a broad set of guidelines used in an art form. It combines both the rules and procedures of a system with the flexible variables of your creative voice. The rules and procedures simply lay the groundwork for the process. They are not hard and fast rules that hold you hostage, stifling your ability to express your ideas.

CONSCIOUSNESS QUERIES

- Are you willing to take the first steps and begin?
- Are you ready to put things in the background that are not important to the project at the moment?
- Are you fully committed to the project?
- Are you willing to engage others who are impacted or involved, with integrity?
- Are you open to adjusting your thinking and adapt to changes as new insights are discovered along the way?

If fear is in your way, focus fully on your goal. See yourself as successful at the end of the process. Your fear can actually provoke the confidence if you do not possess it in the first place. It can create just enough tension to get you moving, helping you take the first step. Once you focus and momentum builds, ideas flow. If the artistic process is new to you, you may doubt your ability to use it to achieve your goal. Perhaps you are afraid of failing so you try to control things without allowing the flow of the artistic process to unfold. Whatever the reason, you must take the action needed to get started.

Artists know that the artistic process requires you to keep at it—to constantly create and maintain momentum. While most difficult when you first begin—because there is no sense of progress or forward motion—once you get started and persist, you can build momentum. That can keep you going. Artists work on their art every day and keep working until they use up every bit of their creative energy. That kind of focus will give you the confidence to begin and keep moving to reach your goal.

Once you focus on your goal and establish a clear idea of what you want to achieve, take the time to gather everything you need. This is important because it prepares you for the process. Whether you need data, research, documents, or physical things like the musical instruments Jody lined up when she practiced, have everything you need at your fingertips. Establish a path to achieve your goal, and set up a physical and imaginative creative space free from distractions. Push everything else into the background. If irrelevant disruptions pop up as you move toward your goal, push them aside. Do not let distractions sidetrack you.

Consider your progress and work through problems as they arise. Some ideas work, others do not, and it does not matter. Evaluate your decisions, revise, and make adjustments as you move forward. Each day, use what you learned the day before and build on the knowledge you gain throughout the process, assessing the results of your effort to inform your next project.

You can use this same process whether working on a personal goal or a plan that involves others. The more people involved, the more complex it becomes, but this process can be used as a guide to keep you on track and reach your goal with a committed, cohesive team.

SUMMARY

Every time an artist begins a new work or prepares for a performance, the world is wide open. The excitement about that moment is invigorating. Past creative experiences inform an artist's work but do not dictate the outcome of what they create at the moment. In authentic process, there is a full commitment to create, to let go of everything prior, and to focus without distraction. Artists know there will be challenges to overcome but that the performance or work of art—and what they discover along the way—is well worth it. It may take an hour, a day, a week, a month, or a year to complete, but the effort is fully concentrated on the fresh start. Beginning a new choreographed work, musical composition, painting, sculpture, or preparing for a music or theater performance is much like beginning a new year. This fresh start focuses on that moment, using everything you have gained along the way, to move toward the future.

Paul Gauguin and other painters became known in the late 1880s for a style of art called "Synthetism," in which the important thing was how an image is remembered, not so much how it really looked. The feeling the artist experiences about the subject creates the work. The techniques and elements of the art form are synthesized with the major idea or feeling of the artist about the theme of the work. This helped Gauguin expand beyond what seemed to him as confining, superficial, and unmindful of individual thoughts and ideas. These artists sought a new way of expressing themselves that did not limit their experience and expression. The artistic process allows for that sort of flexibility.

Every moment is a fresh beginning.

~ T. S. Eliot
The Cocktail Party

There is something hopeful about beginning a new project or plan. Artists know that the beginning of a work or performance is the most important step. It gives you the feeling of renewal and of being able to begin anew. Yet you can tap into that special feeling and atmosphere any time to motivate yourself to take action using the artistic process. You can create a beautiful masterpiece—a plan, an outcome, a product—that is aligned with your dreams and values. If you lose your sense of excitement about moving forward, maybe you are missing the willingness to take the first step and create a path toward your goal.

Give yourself permission to risk, including the possibility of failure. If you experience yourself at a standstill, look for another solution, and yet another, if necessary, until the way becomes clear. Artists do not drown in the changes that take place as their work takes shape. They recognize it, test it, and move with it. Part of the excitement in the process is discovering the unexpected. Without a process that invites you to measure your progress, grow from your observations, and apply new knowledge, you may miss truly creative opportunities.

The artistic process is one of learning, growth, and discovery. When you work with others in realizing a goal, it deepens your understanding of shared experience. At the same time it expands your awareness and appreciation for new opportunities that come your way. It does not eliminate your own individual thinking, but expands your ability to imagine what others see beneath the surface of thought. Engrossing themselves deeply in the artistic process helps artists slow down. They act, measure, and adapt, which allows creativity to flourish.

REVIEW QUESTIONS

- Think about how you make decisions. Do you use the artistic process of acting, measuring, and adapting? Do you stick with things the way they are, fearful of taking the first step? Do you try to force or control the path toward a goal, not allowing creative opportunities to emerge?

> Without delay I began work, without hesitation and all of a fever.
>
> ~ Paul Gauguin
> *Noa Noa:*
> *The Tahitian Journal*

> Start where you are, use what you have, do what you can.
>
> ~ Arthur Ashe

> Barn's burnt down—now I can see the moon.
>
> ~ Mizuta Masahide
> *Barns burnt down*

- Consider your response to obstacles and failures. Do you work through problems, making adjustments and gaining new knowledge to inform your next move? Are you able to move beyond disappointments and grow from experiences? Do you evaluate your decisions to determine their integrity?
- Think about what should be in the foreground and what should be in the background. Do you allow your progress to be sidetracked by irrelevant things that pop up? Are you able to push distractions to the background to deal with later, if necessary? Do you establish physical and imaginative creative space that allows ideas to emerge?

CONTINUE THE QUEST

Explore this concept using some of the suggestions below. Develop your own sense of the artistic process and how you can use it to achieve the goals in your experiences. Work to get past fear, evaluate your decisions and progress, and make changes to keep yourself on track toward your goals.

- Explore the options for establishing physical and imaginative creative space in your personal and work life. Examine how various artists do their work and how their work evolves. Look online at the unique creative space used by Simon Beck. His enormous works of snow art created by walking across the terrain in snow shoes came from openness to both physical and imaginative space. He climbs further up the mountain when finished to photograph the immense patterns—patterns that are often short-lived installations because the winds blow them away. After each snowfall, Beck designs and redesigns his incredible patterns on the same site. He sometimes spends nine or ten hours at a time making the patterned tracks. He produces meticulous patterns that have different effects when viewed from various vantage points in the changing light throughout the day.

- Read about your favorite artists—vary the genre—and explore why they do what they do and what it means to them to create as both a daily routine and a lifelong passion.
- Watch the YouTube video, *New Beginnings*, a 2013 New York City Ballet performance filmed at sunrise on the 57th floor of 4 World Trade Center in lower Manhattan: https://www.youtube.com/watch?v=3zMCxmdkcRY. It is a moving performance of Christopher Wheeldon's *After the Rain* and a testament to new beginnings and a fresh start.
- Listen to "I Can See Clearly Now" by Jonny Nash. It was recorded and released by Jonny Nash in 1972. Listen to the original recording at https://www.youtube.com/watch?v=FscIgtDJFXg. It is a song of hope and courage in overcoming the challenges of the obstacles and adversity we often face in life.
- Listen to and read about Beethoven's *Symphony No. 3 in E-flat major*. A YouTube recording with Herbert von Karajan conducting the Berlin Philharmonic is available at https://www.youtube.com/watch?v=YObQ6bP0eDQ.

  The symphony was written after Beethoven learned of his advancing deafness. Although he agonized over his fate, Beethoven was determined to go on composing in the midst of this tremendous challenge. He did not allow the impending loss to impact his momentum. He worked through the challenge and began work on *Symphony No. 3*. The work was the beginning of a new creative period for him and ultimately led to the compositional style of the Romantic period. An article and interview about the symphony are available online at http://www.npr.org/templates/story/story.php?storyId=5456722.

CHAPTER 8

FILL YOUR CUP:
THE PRACTICE AND DISCIPLINE
OF LIFELONG LEARNING

OVERVIEW

THINKING AND FEELING

So much information fills everyday life that considering anything new can feel overwhelming. You just do not have any room. By getting rid of information you don't need at the moment, along with values and beliefs that no longer serve you, you can move forward, learning and growing as you go.

ARTISTIC INSIGHTS

- Artists learn to develop an environment that promotes openness to new ideas.
- They create a sort of open network—made up of their minds, bodies, and depth of awareness—that allows them to make known the uniqueness of who they are as creative human beings.
- This process allows them to move forward without seeing the world through a filter stuffed with beliefs, opinions, and past experiences.
- This frees them to see and hear more clearly.
- Artists learn how to create and manage contrasts, and balance them in a way that expresses their ideas with a special kind of beauty.
- Artists breathe freely to gain access to their innermost thoughts and emotions.

- Artists take different routes and find the pathways that lead them to achieve higher goals.

The ongoing self-motivated pursuit of knowledge that can take place in both your personal and professional worlds is an important part of the artistic process. Learning takes place in a wide range of situations throughout life. While it is important to study the wisdom of others, you must think through and ponder ideas for yourself. Taking time for yourself and valuing the daily interactions with others and the world around you can help you begin to look at your life as art.

BREATHE!

The way you breathe can have a significant impact your ability to think through ideas. Breathing can influence your ability to open to your innermost thoughts and manage your physical and emotional well-being. It can give you the room you need to explore your thoughts and dreams. As a woodwind performer, Jody learned the importance of the breath and proper breathing from an early age. It may sound funny because breathing is something that happens automatically, but this was an important part of Jody's training and performance. Deep diaphragmatic breathing and control over the amount of air being expelled became natural and enhanced her ability to focus.

As a young flutist, Jody went to her lesson each week prepared to play a sustained pitch for ninety seconds. She had to play this sustained pitch at the beginning of every lesson before she could move on to the music. If she failed, her instructor asked her to try repeatedly until she reached the ninety seconds. She learned how the breath worked, and that knowledge and skill helped her play more difficult passages in the music, control phrases requiring delicate dynamic control, and produce a warmer, more resonant tone. The influence and strength of heightened awareness that came through her breathing eventually informed her artistic work as a woodwind performer and conductor, and later as a higher education administrator. It helped give her the space to open up and examine situations, making room around them to gain perspective.

Performing artists also learn to use breath to create silence. The silence allows the music, words, or action to breathe. It gives the performer and the audience a chance to absorb what happened or what is coming. The silence is an important part of the sound or action. Visual artists use white space in the same way. The white space essentially creates breathing room for the image or design. Think of it this way: breath is fundamental to life. When done in certain ways, breathing gives you the effective mental state for high levels of creativity and heightened awareness. Images, words, and ideas are greatly enriched with proper breathing.

Understanding the power of the breath can help dancers experience more energy to explore a greater expressive range. It helps them move past mere technique to higher levels of artistic expression. Actors enjoy the same experience as they become great artists. In fact, movement for everyone begins with the breath. It is easy to take breathing for granted, but you can learn to use your breath and breathing more consciously in everything you do—thinking, speaking, and moving. It can expand your awareness and creativity.

Great art comes about through increased awareness, vision, deep understandings, and wonder. Your breath connects you to these elements. In fact, the Latin root of the words "respiration" and "inspiration"—*spirare*—means "to breathe." If you feel uninspired, then no breath has been put into what you are doing and that leaves you feeling unenthusiastic and indifferent. With a focus on your breath and breathing, you can learn to listen to your inner voice and enthusiastically share your unique expression with the world in new ways. You will be more productive, have more energy and enthusiasm, and can enhance the creativity of your life and work.

> He lives most life whoever breathes most air.
>
> ~ Elizabeth Barrett Browning
> *Love*

> Listen, are you breathing just a little and calling it a life?
>
> ~ Mary Oliver
> *West Wind*

QUICK TIPS

Consider the following common uses of the word "breath." Think about how you use breath in your life.

- The director breathed new life into the play.
- Working with that conductor was a breath of fresh air.
- The actor breathed confidence into the role.
- Remember to pause and take a breath.
- That experience left her breathless.
- Her attitude breathed new life into the institution.
- Artists breathe life into stone.

The role of the breath, silence, and space in an artistic sense came to mind when I was attending a semi-staged production of Mozart's *The Magic Flute* (which was a delightful experience). It is no wonder that this opera has captivated audiences for more than two hundred years. It was particularly enjoyable to experience it in an intimate setting with performers, orchestra, and action so close that it felt as if everyone there were part of the production. You could see and feel the breathing of the characters and almost hear the thoughts that came from their inner voices.

While *The Magic Flute's* overarching story speaks to the many tests you face as you move through life, the real interpretive magic comes through reflection, awareness, and ever-deeper personal understanding of who you are as a human being. That experience does not necessarily happen in the notes or dialog, but rather through the stillness that can be found in each character's innermost thoughts and feelings.

Beyond the technique of space and silence in works of art, this concept is also reflective of the artistic process itself. In silence, many things grow and flourish, including awareness of everything outside yourself as well as everything within. While performing artists spend hours expertly playing or singing the notes in music, they spend a lifetime perfecting the pauses between notes. That is where the true artistry resides. They focus and concentrate, going

The music is not in the notes, but in the silence between.

~ Wolfgang Amadeus Mozart
A Life in Letters

into their minds and hearts to become ever more aware of all the nuances to be found in that quiet place.

QUICK TIPS

It is amazing how powerful silence, stillness, and deep breathing can be. Here are some of the benefits:

- Ideas, insights, and creative answers come more easily.
- Silence, stillness, and deep breathing can give you more energy and help you get things done.
- You can become more focused and aware of everything happening around you.
- Silence, stillness, and deep breathing can help you know yourself better.

The world is a noisy place. If you explore the concept of deep breathing and the silences between words and sentences, you can begin to see and feel the quiet beauty of the environments where you live and work. Mozart builds anticipation through his compositional technique to create dramatic pause, building tension and holding back resolutions. The pauses prolong the tension of the preceding buildup of tension creating a dynamic, charged silence. Silence is part of what gives the music such beauty and life.

CONSCIOUSNESS QUERIES

- How do you allow breath, silence, and space in your life?
- Do you turn on the radio every time you get in your car?
- Does the television or music play in the background every moment at home?
- Do you sit at your computer or stare at your cell phone every free moment?

Music and silence combine strongly because music is done with silence, and silence is full of music.

~ Marcel Marceau

Mozart's music is so pure and beautiful that I see it as a reflection of the inner beauty of the universe.

~ Albert Einstein
  Der Private Albert Einstein

GAINING CLARITY

One day during Jody's first year teaching in higher education, she noticed she took deep breaths with a controlled exhalation, similar to what she used as a wind performer. It was not something she did purposely. It just seemed natural. After exploring these occurrences a little further—noting when they happened and what she was doing at the time—she did some research to better understand them. The more she explored, the more she understood; Jody soon realized the deep breathing she learned as a performer was for her an instinctive and effortless release. Jody has a lot of energy and she worked long, hard days. The breathing helped get more oxygen to her brain. It felt great and cleared her mind. When you work hard and become deeply engaged with something, your breathing can become shallow. After her insights, Jody started using big deep breaths on purpose, not waiting for them to just appear. That practice helped her accomplish much more in a shorter time, and with less stress.

Deep diaphragmatic breathing is a remarkable way to help you gain better control of everything you do. In her first year of full-time college teaching, it helped Jody focus more flexibly and effortlessly on her goals. She felt invigorated and refreshed. Jody experimented with it to discover ways to help her students overcome stage fright. They became more skilled at controlling their breathing, especially right before they went on stage, both to manage stage fright and to maintain the edge that came from anticipation and excitement. This prepared them to perform with a unique and powerful artistic voice.

The breath helps you experience inner stillness similar to the silence in music or the white space in a painting. You eventually learn you do not have to consciously control your breathing every minute. When you practice breathing this way, it becomes more natural and, as your awareness builds, you begin to notice you can respond naturally to tension and resistance. You learn to balance the contrasts in your environment and see greater beauty in the things around you.

Every day brings a chance for you to draw in a breath, kick off your shoes, and step out and dance…

~ Oprah Winfrey

BALANCING CONTRASTS

The deep breathing Jody practiced in her daily work helped her balance the contrasts—the push and pull—of everyday life. You often experience contrast in a work of art or performance by perceiving the elements in relationship with one another. Different elements work together in a way that creates interest and variety. The contrast can sometimes come from elements used in direct opposition to one another, yet they balance beautifully. In fact, the beauty often comes from the deliberate use of opposites in a way that they offset one another and create a sense of balance. Through her breathing experiments, Jody found the ability to balance the contrasting elements of tension and stress in her new work environment with ease. The resulting balance enriched her experience.

Breath, the stillness of silence, and white space are just a few of the ways artists can create and balance contrasts. In a performance, the performer uses the elements in the composition to bring out certain things and hold others back. Artists can distribute various elements, such as color, texture, value, rhythm, and shape, to create a sense of perceived weights that offset one another. The tension is similar to what most everyone experiences every day and makes things whole and beautiful. The natural deep breathing provided the contrast and wholeness for Jody.

A performance of Benjamin Britten's opera *The Rape of Lucretia* made me think about the role of contrast in creating and performing art. One theme of the opera—the sense of the dualities of masculine and feminine—as well as the elements used to portray the conflicting and complex moral metaphors creates the tension. Artists learn to understand and use the duality of opposites, such as the theme of masculine and feminine in this opera. The mixing of contrasts create a sense of push and pull throughout the entire opera. Yet, in the end, the various aspects work together as a whole.

The dualities of masculine and feminine not only have an impact on your life as an individual, but also the collaborative work with others in relationships, family, and work settings. If

I experience a period of frightening clarity in those moments when nature is so beautiful. I am no longer sure of myself, and the paintings appear as in a dream.

~ Vincent van Gogh
Conversations with van Gogh

All existence seemed to be based on duality, on contrast.

~ Hermann Hesse
Narcissus and Goldmund

In Benjamin Britten's the *Rape of Lucretia,* a Roman general's wife is driven to despair and suicide after being raped by a prince. The push and pull of the contrasting concepts of masculine and feminine work together beautifully and create the wholeness in the work.

~ Philip Brett
Grove Book of Operas

you think like an artist to balance the contrasting elements of your life, you can stimulate your thinking and deeper understanding of living and leading in the midst of present-day realities. When you understand the differences and the power of these contrasting elements and how to manage them, you will be better able to balance them and create more powerfully from that fullness.

CONSCIOUSNESS QUERIES

An artist learns to balance the distribution of creative elements within a work of art. You can learn to do the same thing in life and work environments.

- Do you ever find yourself wanting to withdraw from others and become silent?
- Do you get easily irritated?
- Do you want to get even?
- Do you ever become inflexible and cruel?
- Do you feel insecure and vulnerable?

When you breathe deeply and find balance, it allows you to connect with people from inner strength. With balance, you can deal peacefully with your environment and the people in it. You can feel more fulfilled. You are centered and flexible.

In addition to the opera by Britten, many other depictions of the story of Lucretia have been created by visual artists. Albrecht Dürer's painting of Lucretia shows the moment before she took her own life. Power struggle, strength, and honor fill this moment in the story and demonstrate the dynamics of seemingly contradictory tendencies of control and freedom. This is done in a way that produces enduring artistic results. Everyone faces the same challenge in life and work: to develop the ability to use the contrasting aspects at the most productive moments.

Imbalances in the world today are evidenced by the anxiety, fear, and state of chronic stress that many people experience every day. You can contribute a great deal to your own life, your work environments, and the lives of others by developing the strength to balance, bringing together contrasts within yourself

Balance is beautiful.

~ Miyoko Ohno

I try to contrast; life today is full of contrast.... We have to change.

~ Gianni Versace

and in every aspect of your experience. As a work of art evolves, so does the artist. Your overall well-being is often influenced by the paths you choose during this evolution.

THE PATHWAYS

A pathway, in the artistic sense, is often created by qualities of line. The line is one of the most fascinating and essential elements of artistic expression. The powerful emotional impact that can come from what may seem like a simple line is widely varied, ranging from feelings of calm or stability to excitement or anger.

ARTISTIC INSIGHTS

Artists can create emotional impact in their works by exploring the visual and aural qualities of line:
- Lines can be short, long, straight, curved, thick, thin, horizontal, vertical, diagonal, zigzagged, combined, or implied.
- Every line is a sort of pathway that connects two points.
- A line can even be a path made by a moving point in a choreographed dance, staged drama, or melodic line.

There are several aspects that can be used to explore the impact of line, but line direction has the potential for the greatest expressive power. Here are a few examples:
- Horizontal lines create the feeling of expanded space or time—a sense of peacefulness, quiet, tranquility, or serenity.
- Vertical lines seem to defy gravity and create a feeling of stability and strength. They draw your attention upward.
- Diagonal lines create a sense of instability and restlessness—the feeling of activity and movement.
- Zigzag lines create a sense of energy, life, and excitement.

A line is a dot that went for a walk.

~ Paul Klee

- Curved lines create the feeling of gracefulness, softness, and balance. They express the impression of flexibility and movement. Spirals and wavy lines are more complex versions of a curved line.

While the nature of these lines can change depending on other design elements—and there are endless combinations—the expressive aspects can lead you to a deeper understanding of the power of pathways in your own life. You can develop awareness through the artistic process and understand line in daily life. Personal goals are not necessarily achieved in a straight line.

CONSCIOUSNESS QUERIES

- Can you imagine setting a goal to lose weight and you go straight to your target without any zigzags or curves along the way?
- Have you ever thought that the only way to get what you wanted was to take a certain path, only to discover that a different kind of path actually gave you greater opportunities and richer experiences?
- Look at the interior design of your office and home, the design of buildings on your street and in your town, and the lines of your clothing. What feeling do you experience in each of these environments or when wearing the clothing?
- Can you imagine the impact of a different line in these cases: a more vertical space, clothing with horizontal stripes, a curved pathway rather than the shortest route?

Lines can be thick or thin, long or short, solid or dashed, clear-edged or fuzzy. You can learn to be more aware of the feeling and impact of line in reaching your goals, in accomplishing tasks, in creating stimulating or relaxing environments, and in moving throughout your day. Be open to taking a different path. You never know what you might discover along the way.

Line is a rich metaphor for the artist. It denotes not only boundary, edge or contour, but is an agent of location, energy and growth. It is literally movement and change— life itself.

~ Lance Esplund
Modern Painters

Straight lines go too quickly to appreciate the pleasures of the journey. They rush straight to their target and then die in the very moment of their triumph without having thought, loved, suffered or enjoyed themselves.

~ Rene Crevel

MOTIVATIONAL STORY—WALKING AND WONDER

WALKING

While at a conference in southern Florida, Maya and her colleagues had an opportunity to stroll through the Morikami Museum and Japanese Gardens. As they walked through the well-manicured pathways, the first thing that came to mind was the skillfulness required to create such a masterpiece. Maya was immediately taken by the stunning use of space—not emptiness, but space with the sense and feel of dimension. The spaces were designed to allow those walking through to be creative, and to experience emotion and movement from their own perspective. Not only was the quality of space and silence evident in the overall design, but it was also present in every one of the exquisitely crafted garden rooms, from the smallest detail of each individual plant, to well-placed art, rocks, benches, and water elements.

Open space shapes the values and spirit of Japanese design. In fact, all great artists use space as an important element in their art making. Artists have the ability to create without filling every space—visual and time legroom, so to speak. This aspect of the artistic process is one of the most important factors of effective creative expression. It shows respect for the artist's audience, by allowing the viewer or listener to become a part of the work of art, free from the sense of being closed to a certain perspective.

Certainly there is room for more space and silence in the complex world we experience every day. Think about your conversations, your living and working environment, and the presence of digitized sound in nearly everything you do. Silence and space give way for everything to take on deeper meaning. Beyond gardens, design, art, and music, space and silence can also be used in the design of your life. The right amount of space and silence in daily life can have a profound impact on the way you think, on your relationships, and on the actions you take.

Space allows balance and permits you to focus on what is most important. It gives you a feeling of peace that cannot be achieved with the overcrowding that almost everyone experiences on a daily basis. The breathing room built in to the design of the

It's not just a question of conquering a summit previously unknown, but of tracing, step by step, a new pathway to it.

~ Gustav Mahler

I always listen to what I can leave out.

~ Miles Davis

Space is the breath of art.

~ Frank Lloyd Wright

Morikami Gardens has tremendous power. The experience gave Maya an important reminder of the value of those artistic qualities in art, as well as how space and silence add a special quality to life. The heightened awareness gives you an opportunity to explore and wonder.

WONDER

Artists explore and wonder as a basic part of their creative work. Much more than a skill or a line of work, artistic expression is an imaginative, inspired, and innovative way of communicating and living life. Artistic expression offers ways of portraying beauty in disparate and wide-ranging areas, from the inconceivable or outrageous to the exceptionally uplifting or awe-inspiring. Wonder and insight are as crucial to all art forms as creativity and imagination.

Wonder is a beginning—an opening—to notice and engage with everything around you. Artists engage with the world and the materials and elements of their art forms, making connections that many people do not ever consider. Walking through the Morikami Museum and Japanese Gardens was such an experience for Maya and her colleagues, out in the open—in nature.

The walk through the garden gave them an opportunity to see and hear and know in greater depth. Through the process of attentiveness and contemplation, artists gain deeper understanding of the world around them. They often suddenly see a new way to express something in this more reflective environment. What they discover might be simple or complex, but it is almost always unexpected and can offer a new awareness—a sudden realization or inspiration.

The effort to see and hear and feel things in greater depth appears throughout history. Cubism, an artistic movement of the early twentieth century, explored objects by depicting things from a wide variety of viewpoints simultaneously. Artists who created these works deliberately took things apart to see them in new ways. People and landscapes were represented as combinations

Without wonder and insight, acting is just a trade. With it, it becomes creation.

~ Bette Davis

A week ago it was the mountains I thought the most wonderful, and today it's the plains. I guess it's the feeling of bigness in both that carries me away.

~ Georgia O'Keeffe

The invariable mark of wisdom is to see the miraculous in the common.

~ Ralph Waldo Emerson
The Prose Works of Ralph Waldo Emerson

of geometric shapes, often showing multiple viewpoints of a particular image. Looking at things in new ways and taking things apart to see what is inside requires openness and allows space for wonder and insight. Wonder and insight together can help everyone think about new ways of seeing things and approaching everyday life. Think of wonder and insight as a team that can spark creativity and help you create your life just as an artist creates a masterpiece.

QUICK TIPS

Here are some ideas to open to wonder and insight in your life:
- Live your life with passion whether in grief or in great joy.
- Pay attention—look, listen, and reflect—with all your senses.
- Be open to answers to questions or solutions to problems that come to mind suddenly without warning. Pay attention and make notes.
- Take time every day for silence, solitude, and reflection.
- Make time to think deeply about the solutions and ideas that come to mind.
- Read "Miracles" (a poem by Walt Whitman).

Whether an artist or not, it is important each of us to allow for openness and wonder every day. Although written for children, there is a great deal of wisdom in Dr. Seuss's simple quote about wonder.

> Think and wonder, wonder and think.
>
> ~ Dr. Seuss (Theodore Geisel)

LESSONS LEARNED

SURRENDER

The garden walk reminded Maya to make special note of the openness and beauty in nature. It helped her rediscover and surrender to the benefits of space and silence she had found in performing music many years before. Artists spend hours in this kind of openness that frees their minds from being in complete control.

A couple of years ago, while on vacation in Princeville on the island of Kauai, Maya watched as people gathered every evening to see the sunset. It was a spectacular sight and everyone sat there in silence, allowing space for nature to display its splendor. People prepared and set up lawn chairs well in advance so they could watch the brilliant display of colors as the sun went down and appeared to disappear into the ocean. The experience stimulated all of the senses. Just like the garden walk, the space filled with sounds and sensations of nature. At the cliff overlooking the ocean, the experience offered spectacular colors, the fragrance of saltwater in the air, the sound of moving water and flight of birds, and the peaceful feel of a gentle breeze. Everyone's intention each evening appeared the same—to witness the event and experience the quiet awareness of what they found in that space. Such awareness opens your world and gives you permission to dream.

PERMISSION TO DREAM

Maya wondered on her walk how often people remember to dream. The world is so busy, it seems like you need some sort of special approval to take that kind of time. Yet, the knowledge and heightened awareness you gain from dreaming can inspire you. It can give you the courage to live a life true to yourself rather than the life others expect of you. Every year as Maya watches *The Nutcracker*, it occurs to her that it would be extremely valuable if everyone could give themselves permission to dream a little more often, not restricted by when the calendar tells them it is acceptable. Imagination, dreaming, and visualizing are important qualities and skills artists and performers learn to use, and they use them every day. This gives them the vision and awareness to create their art. Imagination allows artists to explore thoughts of things that are not necessarily real or present in their environments. What they dream or imagine comes from the space and silence within.

You see things; and you say 'Why?' But I dream things that never were; and I say, 'Why not?

~ George Bernard Shaw
Back to Methuselah

QUICK TIPS

Imagining and dreaming help you:
- Put your memory to good use.
- Consider and create different scenarios.
- Use your knowledge in new ways.
- Create a new vision for the way you manage your life.
- Challenge the status quo, push boundaries, and move forward.

Dreaming helps you create a reality for tomorrow from what may seem impossible today. During the walk, Maya remembered how space and silence can unlock your imaginative power. While *The Nutcracker* ballet captures the imaginative mind and spirit of a child's dreams, and the garden walk creates space in one's innermost being, from an artistic point of view, one does not have to be a child to enjoy a little fun and dreaming. Along the garden path, Maya remembered how we can create joy and magic in our own personal worlds regardless of age.

It may not be the toys, animals, snow, dolls, and angels of *The Nutcracker* that you imagine and dream to magically transform your life but, whatever it is, a little imagination and play can help your days be much more fulfilling, interesting, and productive. You will become motivated and experience greater enjoyment in everything you do.

FINDING FUN IN EVERYDAY LIFE

At one point along the walk, Maya and her friends came across the koi fish with their distinctive red, orange, and white markings. The koi gathered in a feeding area along with a huge assortment of turtles. Maya had never seen so many turtles in one place. Everyone who gathered there had fun watching the antics of these characters as they dove and rose to the surface, almost in a greeting to those who lingered. A little further along, the plant life cleared and the group of friends had fun posing for pictures alongside a massive Buddha sculpture that lounged on the ground.

I saw the angel in the marble and carved until I set him free.

~ Michelangelo

Everything you can imagine is real.

~ Pablo Picasso

There is no single way to interpret the experience of the garden. While inspiring and peaceful, the experience also allowed the group of friends to laugh a little and discover the magic of the garden spaces. The walk reminded Maya of the mindset she had used in her performance experiences—exploring, experimenting, and opening to a perspective of discovery. It is easy to forget this kind of enjoyment in everyday life and work.

A more playful state of mind allows you to make connections you would not normally make, and it helps you see things from a different perspective. Participating in daily experiences this way heightens your mood, makes you laugh more often, and allows you to engage with the world in a new way. With a playful mindset, some things work and some do not, and it does not matter. As a performing musician, if something did not work at all, Maya broke things down and practiced until she found the way to success. A playful mindset helped. You might think, "Playful? Are you kidding me? This is serious." Yet, a playful approach can bring out the highest mental, creative, emotional, and sometimes physical functioning you can experience. You can build this approach through practice. Along the walk, Maya remembered the fun of making music and why it pulled her to share it with others. She ultimately found the same joy in creativity as an arts educator.

One evening, leaving a Boston Pops Concert, Clara found two pedicabs on Massachusetts Avenue in front of Symphony Hall ready to transport members of the audience to their destination. Yes, pedicabs—not taxi cabs. Clara's response was immediate—pedal-powered transportation; what fun. She enjoyed the balmy and beautiful evening—a perfect end to a night at the Pops. Clara's spontaneous ride added a new dimension to enjoying the evening. As an adult with a playful mindset, you can hold your focus and move through the creative process without being hijacked by the past or distracted by other things in your life.

We don't stop playing because we grow old; we grow old because we stop playing.

~ George Bernard Shaw

Just keep taking chances and having fun.

~ Garth Brooks

CONSCIOUSNESS QUERIES

- How do you find fun in your world?
- Do you experiment and try new things?
- Do you use your knowledge and experiences to explore different ways of expressing something?
- Do you maintain a playful mindset with the various things that pop up in your environment?

DEEPENING PERSPECTIVES OF LIFELONG LEARNING

LEARNING AND LETTING GO

The artistic process is a continual succession of events, letting go of old learning and making way for new. Each new bit of knowledge deepens and broadens your understanding. All along the way, as you grow, you let go of things that no longer serve you—previous learning that is no longer relevant is replaced by a higher level of awareness and skill. Artists of all kinds strive to express themselves in ways that can stimulate thought and new ideas. They do all they can to create something that offers meaning and value to the world.

The best compliment you can give an artist is that you felt their work held meaning and value for you. They work hard at what they do, spending long hours, day after day, to achieve their goals. Their art is an extension of who they are as human beings. Artists constantly search internally and externally, sensing things in their world, making note of them, and exploring. They open to new ideas allowing, responding, and leading the way. This involves changing your thought process from an attitude of control to one of evaluating the knowledge and determining how it can best be used.

Arts teachers are particularly vulnerable to long hours. While they strive for meaning in their artistic endeavors, their focus is on creating meaning and value in the lives of their students. They return to classes every day, speaking with passion about their discipline. They teach with energy and listen with empathy.

> The very essence of playfulness is an openness to anything that may happen, the feeling that whatever happens, it's okay... you're either free to play, or you're not.
>
> ~ John Cleese
> *Lecture on Creativity*

231

Besides the knowledge of expressing themselves through the elements of their art form, they must also learn how to share their knowledge in a way that students can understand. If that sort of communication is not part of their experience, they might struggle a little, learning it as they go. It requires them to let go of assumptions and open space for expression of a different kind.

Communication is much more than just words. It is also the body language you use and the way you say something. Just as it is in acting or performing on an instrument, nuance is critical to express the full meaning. Changes in tone of the voice, the pitch, loudness, emphasis, and the speed of the words all have expressive impact, influencing the way students understand. Besides all of the other pressures on education, a constant learning process is needed to keep pace with the changes that seem to occur every day. In order to avoid complete exhaustion and burn-out, arts teachers have to make choices about what to keep and what to give up to move forward, sustaining the joy of what they do.

WHOSE LESSON IS THIS?

Both artists and arts teachers give from their hearts. When Joanna first taught music lessons as a young college student, she opened her heart to share her love of music with young students. She was shocked at how much she learned. Joanna found that the true test of whether she really understood what she was doing as a performer was when she tried to teach it to someone else. Her understanding of this observation positively influences everything she does. Artists who make a commitment to teach others learn that the more they are able to communicate successfully, the more they know themselves and the more consequential their art. As they teach their art form, they use the self-reflective aspects of their arts experiences to become effective communicators, good listeners, and excellent observers. Everyone needs to learn to use these tools, whether interacting with a friend, a coworker, or a child, at home, at work, or at the grocery store.

Joanna once asked Sherry, a gifted high school clarinetist, to consider taking private lessons from one of the teachers in the area. Sherry hung her head and said in a shy, soft voice, "I can't do that. I had one lesson with Dan. He kept telling me to look at my embouchure in the mirror. I had no idea where to look and no idea what an embouchure even was." If you are not familiar with the particulars of wind playing, the embouchure is the position and use of the lips, tongue, and teeth in playing. Even if she had known where to look, she would not have known what to do with it. Dan truly cared about Sherry's progress, but it was obvious he did not communicate in a way that could help her improve her playing, and he was not fully aware of her dilemma. They both made some incorrect assumptions.

- Dan assumed Sherry knew what the word "embouchure" meant.
- Since she was looking in the mirror, he assumed she was trying to do what he asked.
- He assumed she simply was not capable of doing what he asked.
- Sherry assumed she would appear ignorant or disrespectful if she asked what she was looking for in the mirror.
- Sherry was afraid to tell him she did not understand what to do.

Situations like this frustrate both parties. After several conversations with colleagues, Dan became aware of what caused the problem. Once he realized the issue, he adapted quickly by connecting to the same effort he used as a clarinetist himself—reflecting, opening to new knowledge, practicing, and using it to continue to grow. He was on his way to higher awareness and new communication skills that ultimately helped him achieve greater success. He was excited and motivated to try his new learning in all of his teaching situations. When you pay attention to what you learn, it can bring you great joy for who you are and what you do.

ARTISTIC INSIGHTS

Artists continually participate in a process—learning and letting go—that informs their knowledge and awareness.

- Artists are self-motivated.
- They are fully committed to pursuing more knowledge and understanding.
- They use conscious self-reflection to expand their ability to communicate artistically.
- As they create or perform their art, they strive to make meaning.
- In artistic collaboration or performance, they set themselves aside to truly be with others in attentive creative cooperation.

BRING JOY TO WHAT YOU DO

One of the most important aspects of artistic expression is passion: the desire to create something meaningful and share it with the world. When you consider passion from an artist's point of view, it is important to note the strength of her or his desire. It takes them on a journey to and through their ideas. They get inside their thoughts and dreams to research them, and learn from them. From my own experience, I know this is not something you just decide to have. It takes effort and grows out of the creative process; artistic expression is a result of that process.

Artists can radiate a dynamic enthusiasm from what they do and discover that draws you in and keeps you there, held firm by its magnetic power. Audiences and art lovers are pulled in whether they are aware of it or not. Artists make an effort to create the space for their dreams and visions to be realized. The compelling influence of their discovery grabs hold of them and gives them the energy to keep going, learning, creating, and sharing. It gives them energy to set continually higher goals.

Change is the end result of all true learning.

~ Leo Buscaglia

We must act out passion before we can feel it.

~ Jean-Paul Sartre

234

CONSCIOUSNESS QUERIES

Many people go through life without truly thinking. Consider your experiences.

- What really matters?
- Why do I do the things I do?
- What is important to me?

Artistic passion gives you the energy to move toward your potential and purpose. Exploring inside things with depth and bringing the findings out into the world makes a life of wholeness possible. Just as in art, the elements do not compete with one another whether they are contrasting or not; they work together to create a whole. You enjoy self-confidence that is not possible otherwise.

Consider your response when you see or hear great works of art. You do not just decide to experience sensation. It comes about through openness and space—a process of engagement not easily explained. In a sense, you do not take hold of this kind of feeling; rather it grabs hold of you. It may even catch you by surprise.

- Artists think deeply about topics and subject matter outside the arts when creating. How can you become more engaged in this way?
- Artists often combine subjects and disparate elements and create something new. How can you create this synthesis and live your art?
- Artists understand the connection of their art making to other people, communities, and the world at large. How can you have this awareness and understand these connections when creating your life as art?

Works of art are objects and occurrences to be prized and appreciated—each one special and unique. While their creation requires skill, it comes from understanding and awareness. A sense of creative consciousness supports their existence. What if you applied this same artistic principle to your life? Passion helps

> There is no passion to be found playing small—in settling for a life that is less than the one you are capable of living.
>
> ~ Nelson Mandela

you live your art right now rather than chasing a dream that may or may not arrive in the future. You can learn to have passion for many things—getting inside them and exploring—learning and letting go.

MOVING AUTHENTICALLY

Several years ago Alexis attended a Boston Early Music Festival performance of Handel's opera *Almira*. She did not know it when she purchased the ticket, but the opera is four hours long with two intermissions. Alexis said she cannot ever remember sitting for four hours and having time fly by so quickly. The performers made you feel as if you took part in the action. The sets, staging, costumes, and lighting added a real sense of the place, time period, and moods without you ever noticing their presence. These seamless technical aspects expanded the dramatic context in ways that truly enhanced the emotional affect for the audience. The performance lived up to the reputation of opera as one of the most collaborative of all art forms.

Many people think of opera as simply a certain way of singing, but that is a misunderstanding. Opera is a full theatrical achievement, and even the singing has style differences depending on the historical era and theme. As Alexis sat near the top of the mezzanine of the Cutler Majestic Theater she said that, at first glance, the performers seemed miles away, but when the opera began she was immediately drawn in and held captive by the spectacle. As she reflects on it now, she wonders why it was so powerful. It was, after all, written by a very young composer—Handel was only nineteen at the time—and there must be a reason it had not previously been staged in this country. Yet, here it was in full scale production, still fresh after two hundred years because it deals with timeless and universal human emotions. Even the playfulness of the comical character, Tabarco, held emotional content that kept her engaged.

Opera performers are singers, actors, dancers, and linguists. Besides the high quality of the singing, these artists held Alexis's undivided attention through their acting, using every means of communication available, expressing their characters with honest and powerful body language. Actors communicate emotions—that is what moves you.

Actors stir your passions and grab hold of your attention by moving authentically—not pretending, but being. If you were to watch without sound, you would see the way they use their bodies in the expression of sadness or anger or light-hearted mischievousness. They create something real out of various movements and gestures and—along with the relevant singing and vocal nuance—connect you to an authentic human being. They use every means of communication in a congruent manner, commanding your emotional response. You are taken into the drama.

QUICK TIPS

Try this in your work, relationships, and everyday life.
- Communicate with honesty, energy, and expressiveness—truly feeling what you try to convey.
- Pay attention—check to be sure your body language, gestures, words, and tone of voice match your intention when communicating.
- Practice and try again.

A commitment to this attentiveness you gain from the artistic process will help you communicate and connect to those you meet and work with in a meaningful way. You can make as much of an impact as an opera performer in your various roles in life by using every means at your disposal to express yourself dynamically and authentically.

MEANINGFULNESS

One benefit of using the artistic process as a means and model for lifelong learning is the intrinsic reward of meaningfulness—of really making a difference. A sense of self-respect, responsibility, and accomplishment can come through participation in the

Our passions are, in truth, like the phoenix. When the old one burns away, the new one rises out of its ashes at once.

~ Johann von Goethe
The Maxims and Reflections of Goethe

237

artistic process. Thousands of artists and arts educators do the same things day after day:

- They practice.
- They evaluate and restructure.
- As they create and perform their art, they often struggle, build on strengths, and face their weaknesses.
- They regularly yield to new ways and change their methods.
- They succeed and they fail. And they try again.
- They share their learning growth with others.

As Alexis stands back and looks at the growth in her own artistic life, the first thing she notices is the increasing ability to do things she could not do before. It was life altering when she realized the collection of those experiences from a larger perspective. Observing and evaluating changing patterns of action, thought, and habitual behavior teach you that sometimes you have to unlearn in order to learn. The more closely Alexis explores the benefits of her experience with the artistic process, the more she sees the influence and understanding of patterns of learning and their contribution to gaining greater understanding. Patterns are powerful:

- They each tend to be a problem and a solution all wrapped up together. You gain sophistication and precision by understanding patterns.
- In the arts, patterns create a sense of momentum. Patterns help you grasp a sense of movement and meaning. Movement and meaning motivate artists to become more aware of their processes.
- Patterns help develop higher-order thinking skills like problem-finding, evaluation, analysis, and synthesis.
- Patterns develop and use personal strengths in meaningful ways and help you better understand difficult concepts.

The artistic process can help you deal with the same issue time and again at an increasingly higher level. When you understand where you are in the process, you experience a higher degree of creativity and motivation. The beauty in this understanding can be expanded to your experiences in daily life and work, and you enjoy an evolutionary process of learning and growing. Life, just like the artistic process, does not move forward in a straight line. You seem to pass the same point over and over again but from a different perspective each time.

Fear of failure can lead to self-imposed inhibitions that prevent you from moving forward in the face of life's experiences. Artists and performers experiment with various ways of creating motion, moving forward. They expect that some will not work. They practice. This is the process of learning and creating the art. These experiences help artists treat challenges as experiments and help them move forward, invigorated with new ideas and understanding. You can use this thought process in daily life and work so that challenges and disappointments do not stop you in your tracks, but rather help you act on what you discover to create meaning for yourself and those in your environment.

CONCEPT PRACTICE

Artists create every day. Artistic expression is a way of life that leads them to practice and expand their personal understanding and abilities. When they use the artistic process as a means of teaching or working with others, they enjoy a synergistic effort and can accomplish more than they might experience on their own. Becoming an accomplished and knowledgeable thinking artist takes practice.

Practice in an artistic sense is not mindless; it is practice that is deliberate and focused with clear goals and objectives. When artists practice, they break down their skill into clearly defined elements and work intently on an element they want to improve the most. They learn to analyze new information, evaluate and process it, and apply it in their art, teaching, or in their own life

What I'm concerned about is the people who don't dwell on the meaninglessness of their lives, or the meaningfulness of it—who just pursue mindless entertainment.

~ Michael K. Hooker

Without continual growth and progress, such words as improvement, achievement, and success have no meaning.

~ Benjamin Franklin

We learn by practice. Whether it means to learn to dance by practicing dancing or to learn to live by practicing living, the principles are the same.

~ Martha Graham
The Routledge Dance Studies Reader: I Am a Dancer

Art does not solve problems but makes us aware of their existence. It opens our eyes to see and our brain to imagine.

~ Magdalena
   Abakanowicz

situations. They solve problems and challenges along the way. Practice through the artistic process requires a connected heart and mind, tapping fully into your inner awareness as a human being to bring something meaningful to the world.

You can learn to practice with the focus of an artist, enhance your understanding of your world, and learn even more by sharing that knowledge with others. In practice, an artist identifies problems and devises a routine that changes those problems into assets.

QUICK TIPS

Use the problem identification and lifelong practice skills of an artist in everyday life.

- Identify something in your own life experience that needs a solution.
- Be grateful for the awareness of the problem.
- Practice a new way of being in relation to the problem—a new way of communicating, a new way of organizing, a new way of thinking.
- Evaluate your progress as you practice and adjust along the way.
- Identify new problems that arise as you experience each day and devise a deliberate practice.
- Be open to ongoing practice for a lifetime of learning and sharing with others.

Don't only practice your art, but force your way into its secrets; art deserves that, for it and knowledge can raise man to the Divine.

~ Ludwig van Beethoven
   Letter to Emilie

Artists learn to work with what they have at hand, they look for growth in every experience, and they try to use everything at their disposal to achieve their goals. Once challenges and obstacles come to their attention, they have the information they need to devise a planned and purposeful practice that strengthens the area. They work with a concerted effort in the studio, in performance, or in teaching to put many things together to create art, experiences, and opportunities to practice and grow and learn.

Fill Your Cup

You can use this same process whether working on a personal or collective goal. The effort of a group adds complexity but the results can be even more rewarding when everyone can connect with the artistic process. The connection of everyone to their own internal awareness, along with having the utmost respect for one another as thinking, feeling human beings, is critical and can lead to extraordinary results not realized otherwise. Working as an artist can sometimes feel isolating. While artists need some solitude in order to create, many also spend time in collaboration with others to accomplish their goals. Some forms of art actually require a collaborative experience to bring the works to life.

Whether you work individually or in a collaborative environment, the artistic process of learning and letting go can transform your life and work. First, you need to be willing to practice your life as art in the sense of a commitment to lifetime learning. If you do not use the continual process of emptying and filling your cup, meaning is elusive and there is most often nothing of value to share with others.

SUMMARY

One of the most important aspects of the artistic process is enjoying some solitude in the midst of a noisy world. Growing and learning through the artistic process can be life-changing. It can enhance your creativity and the quality of your life experiences. Creating as an artist requires openness to space and silence that you may not explore otherwise. Breathing, thinking, and feeling from the inside out are powerful tools for everyone, connecting you to remarkable inspirations and opportunity.

You might think the space you find in solitude is boring or a reminder of all your negative thoughts and experiences. But once you find the space and silence of true inner wisdom, you learn it is not a place filled with words of discouragement or a list of failings. In fact, there are no words at all. It is instead a place of feeling. The more you find it, the more you find yourself in a space that feels natural and you can grow and create from that stillness.

Vivian experienced the result of that feeling—seeing and hearing through all her senses—as she took an art walk through a number of artists' studios in Scottsdale, Arizona. The art works were inspired by the natural beauty of the surrounding Sonoran Desert. Some people think of the desert as desolate, harsh, and restrictive, but many artists find their inspiration in this environment. In the stillness of their explorations, they seemed to move past the stretches of sunbaked sand, scorpions, rattlesnakes, extreme temperatures, javelina, thorny plant life, Gila monsters, circling buzzards, and bobcats. Vivian noted the diversity of their artistic work, filled with wonder and insight. While some artists saw and created from the starkness, others based their art on the amazing array of colors and shapes. The constraints of the desert environment became extraordinary sculptures, paintings, and pieces of jewelry in the hands of the artist. The works used a wide variety of materials—stone, acrylic on canvas, watercolor, metals, and all sorts of natural objects—to draw viewers in to look more closely and to consider the indescribable spirit of the desert.

As Vivian walked among these extraordinary works of art, she thought about the depth of understanding for what at first seemed to be challenging, adverse, or harsh conditions. In many ways, everyone has an opportunity like this to see beyond the razor sharp and jagged edges in daily life. You can make a distinction between the physicality of where you stand and the way you frame the picture in your mind's eye. There is an inherent value judgment associated with what you see.

The beauty of the desert as seen through the eyes of artists reminds us that sometimes the greatest discoveries are made by exploring inner space, the creative consciousness that can be found in the cracks and crevices of your belief system. The artistic process has everything to do with how you perceive your world. It invites you to see beyond what is visible to see things in a new light—to move authentically through experiences and create something meaningful. The next time you see a desert, try to make a point of seeing beyond what appears most visible. Dream a little—have fun.

When you open from the inside out, you create space for growth. When you explore that space with intention and mine it for meaning, you can let go of certain beliefs and perceptions, along with words and images from others in your world. You can dream and enjoy the experience. It gives you a chance to discover new things, uncover imaginative ideas, and expand your understanding. When you embrace what you discover and let go of things that no longer fit in that new awareness, you can grow and learn like an artist—or as an artist.

The desert and the ocean are realms of desolation on the surface.... Dare to breach the surface...

~ Vera Nazarian

The question is not what you look at that matters, it's what you see.

~ Henry David Thoreau
Journal

I have always loved the desert. One sits down on a desert sand dune, sees nothing, hears nothing. Yet through the silence something throbs, and gleams....

~ Antoine de Saint-Exupéry
The Little Prince

REVIEW QUESTIONS

- How do you find answers in your experiences? Do you take time for yourself, breathe deeply, and explore the feeling of space and silence? Do you wait until you have a serious problem to solve, or do you commit to practice every day?
- Do you allow yourself to find a little magic in everyday life? Give yourself permission to dream? How often do you take time to explore the wonder of nature?
- How often do you examine your intentions to find the meaningfulness of what you create? Do you choose to move authentically, letting things go that no longer serve you, making choices in line with a true sense of your inner self?

CONTINUE THE QUEST

Explore the concept of filling your cup. Use the ideas below to think about authenticity and creating from within. Consider how you can embrace new understandings and beliefs and let go of old ones that no longer serve you. You can experience the joy of the practice and discipline of lifelong learning:

- Study deep breathing methods found in the techniques of yoga and mindfulness. These methods can also help you discover the silence and space to create from a truly original and inspired place.
- Take quiet walks in nature or sit on the beach—see and hear from your heart.
- Take time to enjoy the magic in things like *The Nutcracker* ballet or the imaginary characters in a Disney film. Observe your child or grandchildren playing by themselves and make note of the magic of play through their eyes.
- Talk to your pet. Take your dog for a walk.
- Read about wonder in the world and the insights of artists that come forward in their works of art.

Practice this concept with a focus on letting go of things that no longer serve you to make way for new understandings and beliefs. Open to your imaginative ideas and allow them to come forward.

Awareness for Life
Creating a Masterpiece

When you listen to Beethoven's *Ninth Symphony*, gaze at Michelangelo's *Pietà* or da Vinci's *Mona Lisa*, hear Leonard Bernstein's music in a production of *West Side Story*, or read the works of William Shakespeare, you may well be left in a state of wonder and amazement. Each and every day artists wake up to their works of art; they consider where they left things the day before and open themselves to discover yet again another aspect of their expression as an artist. They chip away at their creations, some days making more progress than others. A single work of art may take ten minutes, ten days, or ten years or more to complete. Each single masterpiece takes a lifetime, and each one that follows builds on experiences of the one before, setting up an ongoing sequence of extraordinary and powerful creative expressions.

Great artists are highly motivated to express their visions and share them with others through the medium of their art form. They look past the starkness and chaos of random raw materials, prescribed structures, and artistic elements to bring out something fresh. The potential of what is possible is hidden deeply, and their full commitment to finding and sharing it is a driving force in their efforts. Some of the crucial elements to the artist's success lie in fundamental approaches everyone can learn to use in their daily life.

Quick Tips

You have choices as you make your journey. Masterpieces come from authenticity and a trust in the artistic process. You can choose to take this path to ever-evolving awareness and understanding.

> Respect the masterpiece. It is true reverence to man. There is no quality so great, none so much needed now.
>
> ~ Frank Lloyd Wright

> Every block of stone has a statue inside it and it is the task of the sculptor to discover it.
>
> ~ Michelangelo

- Great artists are committed to share their vision with the world. You see or hear the remarkable result—the masterpiece—but you rarely see an artist's actual struggle that might occur each day: the weariness, the fading energy, or the darkness of dampened spirits that artists experience from time to time as they work with passion and commitment to communicate what they see and hear.

- If something is not working, artists keep at it until it feels right, or they start all over again, remaining open to an unexpected route. They do not give up or feel they have to control every detail. The powerful pull of passion toward full expression continuously fuels their efforts.

- Great artists are lifelong learners, always open to explore, grow, and evolve into something new, better than the day before.

- Resilience is an essential aspect of their success. Committed artists bounce back, knowing that things do not always happen overnight and that they owe it to their vision to keep at it until it feels right.

- Successful artists understand how to seek out other people who are supportive. They limit or eliminate their time and emotional involvement with those who are negative.

- Artistic expression is the essence of their day-to-day lives.

Learning never exhausts the mind.

~ Leonardo da Vinci

In your daily life, you probably make mistakes or experience things that do not work out the way you expected. As an artist of your life experience, you can create a masterpiece by using aspects of the artistic process. You can focus on solutions and learn continuously from one experience to the next, enjoying stunning success as you build your life. Each day, experience, success, or failure allows you the opportunity to make new connections between ideas or thoughts, to be objective, and to choose motivation in order to create something truly special to share with the world. You can choose to become a great artist, leader, teacher, parent, friend, manager, or life partner.

Discontent seems to be everywhere these days. Even some artists lose their love for what they do. Many live or work in an environment over which they appear to have no control. Leaders sometimes make decisions based on a personal desire to get ahead rather than something that truly benefits everyone involved. It is easy to forget the artistic process when your focus is placed elsewhere. Years of building belief systems that do not align with the principles of the artistic process cannot be erased in an instant. But when you begin to see the productive benefits of thinking and feeling with the connected heart and mind you gain through *Arts Awareness*, and you willingly open to risk a new way, you will find the remarkable ability to create a masterpiece for yourself and those around you.

SUCCESS AND SATISFACTION

When you hear the countless regional, national, and international news stories, it becomes clearer every day that this age is unlike anything we have ever experienced. It was my desire from the outset of this book to design a set of concepts from the artistic process to help you navigate what feels like the unstable ground of constant change in modern life. The stresses, information overload, and distraction of constant connection to technology today can steal time, slow momentum, and cause frustration and fatigue. Using the artistic process as explored through *Arts Awareness* will help you learn how to do things with the concepts and tools artists use to express themselves and create their art. *Arts Awareness* will serve as a resource to continue to learn and think with. The concepts will help you find meaning and beauty in everyday experiences. *Arts Awareness* can have a positive impact on your future and the futures of those you love and, at the same time, expand possibilities for those you lead, manage, or teach.

Through the seven creative concepts presented in *Arts Awareness*, everyone has the capacity to shape their experiences, forge meaningful relationships, and move flexibly through the world with success and satisfaction. Use the concepts of *Arts*

In the long run, we shape our lives, and we shape ourselves. The process never ends until we die. And the choices we make are ultimately our responsibility.

~ Eleanor Roosevelt
You Learn by Living

Awareness to achieve more than you thought possible and move forward through the twists and turns of your life with grace and ease. As you prepare to expand your understanding of the value of the arts, refer often to the seven concepts:

- Learn to use the patterns that come from your unique array of internal and external experiences to build and sustain momentum in everything you do.
- Manage the challenge or expressivity of each moment and achieve greater success by maintaining a balanced perspective in relation to the bigger picture.
- Unlock your desires by learning to make a passionate effort; explore what you do with openness and curiosity.
- Manage tension points and releases and move more easily beyond difficult circumstances while fully enjoying the easier moments.
- Produce meaningful results and achievements through the beauty and freedom of structure.
- Take the risk of a first step to reveal new possibilities, new adventures, and new connections that are always within your reach.
- Open from the inside out and allow imaginative ideas to come forward with a constant process of learning and letting go to make way for new understandings and beliefs.

A LEAP IN THE DARK

Move authentically, find meaning, and trust yourself. Nothing is a given, yet you can choose how to make your way. The processes outlined in *Arts Awareness* can help you step into the world of unpredictability without a clear picture of the outcome. Great artists do their work in this sort of environment. They do not force a clear picture of the end result. While they may set restrictions and principles, the boundaries they put in place are not so strong that they limit flow or their ability to move in new, more inspired directions. They trust themselves and the artistic process.

As a significant modern artist, Pablo Picasso's art form was well ahead its time, and the works he created still influence artists today. So, much of his art depended on his ability to trust his intuition, not knowing what might or could come next. He said, "All children are artists. The problem is how to remain an artist once he grows up." Children play with abandon. There are no constraints or limits. Picasso's originality came from taking a chance with this sense of childlike abandon.

Dancer and choreographer Agnes de Mille experienced a rather uncertain journey through the twentieth-century American theater and ballet world, but she ultimately developed a long and successful career by blending classical and modern dance. Her willingness to trust herself and take a chance led her to make significant contributions to dance and the American theater. She made innovative use of natural motions and folk dance forms like tap and square dancing in her choreography, contributing significantly to the development of the narrative aspect of dance in ballet and theater. She was able to show the emotions and thoughts and decisions of the characters through movement in a way that had never been seen before. In 1943, de Mille's choreography of the dances for *Oklahoma!* not only added to the dramatic atmosphere of the work but also, for the first time in American theatrical history, was instrumental in advancing the plot. The entire musical theater concept of dream ballet is thought to have originated in her choreography. When questioned about her decision to use American folkdance instead of ballet in her choreography, de Mille said she had to do what she could do, and she didn't feel skilled in ballet. She found her artistic voice, and it was with that kind of authenticity that she made a stronger connection between herself and others. People joined in and moved with her to expand the language of dance.

> The artist never entirely knows. We guess. We may be wrong, but we take leap after leap in the dark.
>
> ~ Agnes de Mille

> You don't make art, you find it.
>
> ~ Pablo Picasso

> Don't think about making art, just get it done. Let everyone else decide if it's good or bad, whether they love it or hate it. While they are deciding, make even more art.
>
> ~ Andy Warhol

LET'S DANCE

Continue to play with the ideas, write in the margins, and explore the spaces to discover the truth inside the seven concepts.

Your understandings will grow and evolve over time, with ever-deepening awareness. Consider sharing the experiences and expand on them with your family, coworkers, students, and business partners. The information shared in this book comes from personal experience, observations, reflections, and study of thousands of artists, educators, and students over the years. As a result, they have all in some way contributed to this new learning paradigm that promotes creative consciousness in everyday life.

I believe there is a deep body of knowledge in arts learning that we have not even begun to tap, and it is time we do something about it. The artistic process is a way of knowing and acting. Philosopher Alan Watts said, "The only way to make sense out of change is to plunge into it, move with it, and join the dance." Let's dance.

POSTSCRIPT—PATHWAY TO POWER

The internet adventures and reading excursions listed below can be a means to inspire you and help you further explore your creative potential to imagine possibilities and create momentum toward your goals.

Internet Adventures:

Gabrielle Roth's *5 Rhythms* is a dynamic movement practice intended to ignite creativity, connection, and community. (http://www.5rhythms.com/gabrielle-roths-5rhythms/)

Louie Schwartzberg: *Nature. Beauty. Gratitude*, filmed June 2011 at TEDxSF
The video features the stunning time-lapse photography of Louie Schwartzberg whose work is meant to celebrate life, revealing connections, universal rhythms, patterns and beauty. (https://www.ted.com/talks/louie_schwartzberg_nature_beauty_gratitude?language=en)

Quixotic Fusion: *Dancing with light*, filmed February 2012 at TED2012.
Quixotic is an ensemble of artists from various disciplines including aerial acrobatics, dance, fashion, film, music and visual f-x. The group goes beyond the limits of any specific art form, challenging traditional perceptions and creating a total sensory experience. (https://www.ted.com/talks/quixotic_fusion_dancing_with_light?language=en)

Uri Alon: *Why truly innovative science demands a leap into the unknown*, filmed June 2013 at TEDGlobal 2013. While studying for his PhD in physics, Uri Alon was also learning to be an improvisation theater actor. The improvisation theater practice of staying creative inside a stuck place helped him move beyond the scientific research methods of a direct line from question to answer to something more creative. (http://www.ted.com/talks/

uri_alon_why_truly_innovative_science_demands_a_leap_into_the_unknown?language=en)

Eric Whitacre: *Virtual Choir Live*, filmed February 2013 at TED2013.

In this video, composer and conductor Eric Whitacre creates a virtual choir performance that includes singers from around the world who Skype in to join an onstage choir for a performance of his composition, *Cloudburst*. (http://www.ted.com/talks/eric_whitacre_virtual_choir_live?language=en)

Reading Excursions:

Shore, Bill. *The Cathedral Within: Transforming Your Life by Giving Something Back*. New York: Random House, 2001.

Bateson, Mary Catherine. *Composing a Life*. New York: Grove Press, 1989.

Palmer, Parker. *The Courage to Teach*. San Francisco: Jossey-Bass, 1998.

Csikszentmihályi, Mihály. *Creativity: Flow and the Psychology of Discovery and Invention*. New York: HarperCollins, 1997.

Goleman, Daniel, Paul Kaufman, and Michael Ray. *The Creative Spirit: Companion to the PBS Television Series*. New York: Penguin Books, 1992.

Hale, Robert Beverly and Jacob Collins. *Drawing Lessons from the Great Masters*. New York: Watson-Guptill, 1989.

Robinson, Ken and Lou Aronica. *The Element: How Finding Your Passion Changes Everything*. New York: Penguin Books, 2009.

Csikszentmihályi, Mihály. *Flow: The Psychology of Optimal Experience*. New York: HarperCollins, 2008.

Brown, John L. and Cerylle A. Moffett. *The Hero's Journey: How Educators Can Transform Schools and Improve Learning*. Alexandria, VA: Association for Supervision and Curriculum Development, 1999.

Campbell, Joseph. *The Hero's Journey: Joseph Campbell on His Life and Work*. The Collected Works of Joseph Campbell, edited by Phil Cosineau. San Francisco: New World Library, 2014.

Bach, Richard. *Jonathan Livingston Seagull*. Reissue edition. New York: Scribner, 2014.

Barenboim, Daniel. *A Life in Music*. New York: Arcade Publishing, 2003.

Marcic, Dorothy. *Managing with the Wisdom of Love*. San Francisco: Jossey-Bass, 1997.

Vaill, Peter B. *Managing as a Performing Art*. San Francisco: Jossey-Bass, 1989.

Frankl, Victor. *Man's Search for Meaning*. Boston: Beacon Press, 2006.

Buckingham, Marcus and Donald O. Clifton. *Now, Discover Your Strengths*. New York: Free Press, 2001.

Rath, Tom. *Strengths Finder 2.0*. New York: Gallup Press, 2007.

Coyle, Daniel. *Talent Code*. New York: Bantam, 2009.

Pink, Daniel. *A Whole New Mind*. New York, Riverhead Books, 2006.

Sources of Quotations

"About." Deep Listening Institute, accessed August 5, 2015. http://deeplistening.org/site/content/about

"About." Pauline Oliveros, accessed August 8, 2015. http://paulineoliveros.us/about.html

Alcott, Louisa May. *Little Women*. New York: Bantam, 1983.

Andersen, Hans Christian. "The Butterfly." *The Complete Hans Christian Andersen Fairy Tales*. Edited by Lily Owens. New York: Gramercy Books, Avenel Edition, 1981.

Austin, James H. *Chase, Chance, and Creativity. The Lucky Art of Novelty*. Cambridge, MA: MIT Press, 2003.

Barenboim, Daniel. *A Life in Music*. New York: Charles Scribner, 1992.

Beethoven, Ludwig van. "The Letters of Ludwig van Beethoven." CCXCV to Emilie M. at H. Toplitz, July17, 1812. Accessed August 6, 2015. http://archive.org/stream/beethovensletter01beet/beethovensletter01beet_djvu.txt

Blum, David. *Casals and the Art of Interpretation*. Los Angeles: University of California Press, 1977.

Bohm, David. "Nature as Creativity: An interview with Rene Weber." *ReVision*, 5, (1982): 35–40.

Brett, Philip. "Benjamin Britten." *Grove Book of Operas*. Second edition. Edited by Stanley Sadie and Laura Marcy. Oxford: Oxford University Press, 2009.

Browne, Brené. "Listening to Shame." TED2012. March 2012. Accessed August 4, 2015. http://www.ted.com/talks/brene_brown_listening_to_shame/transcript?language=en

Browning, Elizabeth Barrett. *Love*. Poetry Foundation. Accessed August 6, 2015. http://www.poetryfoundation.org/poem/180650#poem

Buckingham, Marcus. *Now, Discover Your Strengths*. New York: The Free Press, 2001.

Burke, Edmund. *The Writings and Speeches of Edmund Burke*. Volume VI. Edited by P. J. Marshall and Paul Langford. Oxford: Oxford University Press, 1991.

Cameron, Julia. *The Artist's Way*. New York: G. Putman's Sons, 1992.

Carter, Alexandra and Janet O'Shea, eds. *The Routledge Dance Studies Reader*. Second edition. New York: Routledge, 2010.

Carter, Claire. "We're Going to be Friends for Life." *The Times-News*, January 16, 1994. Accessed August 8, 2015. https://news.google.com/newspapers?nid=1665&dat=19940116&id=Mh0aAAAAIBAJ&sjid=RSUEAAAAIBAJ&pg=4945,3848037&hl=en

Chandler, Raymond. *Selected Letters of Raymond Chandler*. Edited by Frank MacShane. New York: Columbia University Press, 1981.

Cleese, John. *Lecture on Creativity*. Genius.com. Accessed August 5, 2015. http://genius.com/John-cleese-lecture-on-creativity-annotated

Coyle, Daniel. *The Talent Code: Greatness Isn't Born. It's Grown. Here's How*. New York: Bantam Books, 2009.

Cromie, William J. "Ig Nobel Prizes are Laughable." *The Harvard University Gazette*. October 10, 1966. Accessed August 9, 2015. http://news.harvard.edu/gazette/1996/10.10/IgNobelPrizesar.html

Csikszentmihályi, Mihály. *Finding Flow: The Psychology of Engagement with Everyday Life*. Reprint edition. New York: Basic Books, 1998.

Csikszentmihályi, Mihály. *Flow: The Psychology of Optimal Experience*. New York: HarperCollins, 2008.

Csikszentmihályi, Mihály. "The Creative Personality." *Psychology Today*. Last reviewed on June 13, 2011. Accessed August 8, 2015. https://www.psychologytoday.com/articles/199607/the-creative-personality

Dawson, Julie. "How Art Works." *How Stuff Works Entertainment*. Accessed August 5, 2015. http://entertainment.howstuffworks.com/arts/artwork/art.htm

de Saint-Exupéry, Antoine. *The Little Prince*. Translated by Richard Howard. New York: Mariner Books, 2000.

Eisenhower, Dwight D. "Remarks at the National Defense Executive Reserve Conference." November 14, 1957. Online by Gerhard Peters and John T. Woolley, *The American Presidency Project*. Accessed August 8, 2015. http://www.presidency.ucsb.edu/ws/?pid=10951

Edwards, Tyron. *The New Dictionary of Thoughts: A Cyclopedia of Quotations from the Best Authors of the World, Both Ancient and Modern, Alphabetically Arranged by Subjects*. Rev. and enl. edition, India: The Standard Book Company, 1961.

Ed Wood, Dir. Tim Burton, Touchstone Pictures, 1994, Film.

Einstein, Albert. "Quotes." Quoted in P.A. Bucky, *Der Private Albert Einstein*, 276. Accessed August 8, 2015. http://einstein.biz/quotes.php

Eliot, George. *Middlemarch*. United Kingdom: Wordsworth Editions, 1998.

Eliot, T. S. *The Cocktail Party*. Florida: Harcourt Brace & Company, 1950.

Ellis, Havelock. *Affirmations*. Ulan Press, 2012.

Emerson, Ralph Waldo. *The Complete Prose Works of Ralph Waldo Emerson*. Whitefish, MT: Kessinger Publishing, 2010.

Esplund, Lance. "Abstraction and Nature." *Modern Painters*, Autumn 2001. Accessed August 8, 2015. http://triciawright.com/artistInfo/triciawr/thumb/519.pdf

Fitzgerald, Ella. "Quotes by Ella Fitzgerald." Accessed August 5, 2015. http://www.ellafitzgerald.com/about/quote.html

Franklin, Benjamin. *Wit and Wisdom from Poor Richard's Almanack*. Mineola, NY: Dover Publications, 1999.

Friedman, S. Morgan. "Etymologically Speaking." Accessed August 8, 2015. http://www.westegg.com/etymology/#freedom

Frost, Robert. *The Poetry of Robert Frost: The Collected Poems*. Edited by Edward Connery Lathem. New York: Henry Holt and Company, 1969.

Gibran, Kahlil. *The Prophet*. New York: Alfred A. Knopf, 1923.

Gauguin, Paul. *Noa Noa: The Tahitian Journal*. New York: Dover Publications, 1985.

Gell-Mann, Murray. *The Quark and the Jaguar: Adventures in the Simple and the Complex*. Henry Holt, 1994.

Green, Barry. *The Mastery of Music: Ten Pathways to True Artistry*. New York: Three Rivers Press, 2005.

Goethe, Johann von. *Wilhelm Meister's Apprenticeship: Johann Wolfgang von Goethe*. Edited by Eric A. Blackall. *Goethe: The Collected Works, Vol. 9*. Princeton: Princeton University Press, 1917, 1995.

Graham, Martha. "The American Dance." *The Modern Dance*. Edited by Merle Armitage and Virginia Stewart. New York: Dance Horizons, 1970.

Hansen, Mark Victor, Barbara Nichols and Patty Hansen. *Out of the Blue: Delight Comes into Our Lives*. New York: HarperCollins, 1997.

Heathcote, Charles William. "Franklin's Contributions to the American Revolution as a Diplomat in France." Excerpted from a summary of an address delivered in the Washington Memorial Chapel, February 22, 1956. Accessed August 7, 2015. http://www.ushistory.org/valleyforge/history/franklin.html

Hegel, Georg Wilhelm Friedrich. *Lectures on the Philosophy of World History*. Cambridge Studies in the History and Theory of Politics. Translated by Hugh Barr Nisbet. Great Britain: Cambridge University Press, 1981.

Hesse, Hermann. *Narcissus and Goldmund*. Translated by Ursule Molinaro. New York: Bantam Books, 1984.

Holmes, Oliver Wendell. *The Autocrat of the Breakfast Table*. United Kingdom: Echo Library, 2006.

Holmes, Oliver Wendell. *The Poet at the Breakfast Table*. Colorado Springs, CO: CreateSpace Independent Publishing Platform, 2014.

Hoyle, Elbert and John Hubbard. *In the Spotlight: Personal Experiences of Elbert Hubbard on the American Stage Leather*. Buffalo: The Roycrafters, 1917.

Hughes, Dennis. "Interview with Daniel Goleman." *Share Guide Holistic Health Magazine*. Accessed August 5, 2015. http://www.shareguide.com/Goleman.html

Introducing Haiku Poets and Topics . . . WKD. "Mizuta Masahide." Translated by Lucien Stryk and Takashi Ikemoti. Accessed August 9, 2015. http://wkdhaikutopics.blogspot.com/2006/03/mizuta-masahide.html

Jobs, Steve. "Stanford Commencement Address." Stanford Commencement, Stanford, California. June 12, 2005. Accessed August 5, 2015. http://news.stanford.edu/news/2005/june15/jobs-061505.html

Jones, Michael. "The Long and Wind(l)ing Road—An Interview with Terri Windling." *The Green Man Review: The Roots and Branches of Arts and Culture*. Accessed August 5, 2015. http://www.greenmanreview.com/book/interview_windling.html

Kennedy, John F. "University of North Dakota Address by President John F. Kennedy." Resources Week Convocation. University Fieldhouse, Grand Forks, North Dakota. September 25, 1963. Accessed August 5, 2015. http://library.und.edu/digital/john-f-kennedy-archive/delivered.php

Kennedy, Lou. *Business Etiquette for the Nineties: Your Ticket to Career Success*. South Carolina: Palmetto Publishing, 1992.

King, B. B. *The Charlotte Observer*. October 5, 1997.

King, Stephen. *On Writing: A Memoir of the Craft*. Tenth edition. New York: Scribner, 2010.

Klickstein, Gerald. *The Musician's Way: A Guide to Practice, Performance, and Wellness*. Oxford: Oxford University Press, 2009.

Kostelanetz, Richard. *Conversing with Cage*. Third edition, New York: Limelight Editions, 1988.

Lennon, John. "Imagine." 1971. Song Lyrics.

Marsalis, Wynton and Selwyn Seyfu Hinds. *To a Young Jazz Musician: Letters from the Road*. Reprint edition. New York: Random House Trade Paperbacks, 2005.

Marceau, Marcel. "Speaking out from behind the mask of mime." Interview by Richard Z. Chesnoff. *U. S. News & World Report*, February 23, 1987.

Maslow, Abraham H. *Motivation and Personality*. Third edition. Edited by Robert Frager, et al., London: Longman Publishing Group, 1987.

Masters, Ryan. "The Art of Remembering: Howard Ikemoto teaches artists how to be young again." *Monterey County Weekly*. November 11, 2004. Accessed August 9, 2015. http://www.montereycountyweekly.com/news/local_news/howard-ikemoto-teaches-artists-how-to-be-young-again/article_57e9b56c-40f5-5dae-ac19-706775492c6e.html

Matisse, Henri. *Notes of a Painter*. 1908. Accessed August 9, 2015. http://www.austincc.edu/noel/writings/matisse%20-%20notes%20of%20a%20painter.pdf

Meet the Robinsons. Dir. Steve Anderson, Walt Disney Pictures, 2007. Film closing credits.

Menashe, Samuel. *New and Selected Poems*. Edited by Christopher Ricks. New York: Library of America, 2005.

Mills, Nancy. "5 Minutes With ... William Shatner." *New York Daily News*. August 30, 2005, Accessed August 5, 2015, http://www.nydailynews.com/archives/nydn-features/5-minutes-william-shatner-article-1.588821

Mingus, Charles. "Creativity." *Mainliner Magazine*, July 1927, 25.

Monk, Meredith. "Authentic Voice: An Interview with Meredith Monk." *Mountain Record: The Zen Practitioner's Journal; Dharma Communications*, Summer (2004): 54-58.

Moses, Anna Mary Robertson. *Grandma Moses: My Life's History*. Edited by Otto Kallir. New York: Harper & Brothers, 1952.

Mozart, Wolfgang Amadeus. *A Life in Letters*. Edited by Cliff Eisen. Translated by Stewart Spencer. London: Penguin Classics, 2006.

Oliver, Mary. *West Wind: Prose and Prose Poems*, New York: Houghton Mifflin, Company, 1997.

Osborn, Ronald E. "Thoughts on the Business of Life." *Forbes*. March 1945.

"Passion." Merriam-Webster.com. Accessed August 5, 2015. http://www.merriam-webster.com/dictionary/passion

Patterson, Rob. "For Herbie Hancock, Music Is More than Notes." *MusicWorld*, May 19, 2004. Accessed August 8, 2015. http://www.bmi.com/news/entry/20040520herbie_hancock_for_herbie_hancock_music_is_more_than_notes

Pausch, Randy. *The Last Lecture Hardcover*. Jeffrey Zaslow, Contributor. New York: Hyperion, 2008.

Peirce, Bradford K. *Trials of an Inventor: Life and Discoveries of Charles Goodyear*. South Carolina: Nabu Press, 2011.

Pessoa, Fernando. "Odes Ricardo Reis." Translated by Edouard Roditi. *Poetry Magazine*, October, 1955. Accessed August 8, 2005. http://www.poetryfoundation.org/poetrymagazine/toc/516

Pink, Daniel. *A Whole New Mind: Why Right-Brainers Will Rule the Future*. New York: Riverhead Books, 2006.

Plato. *The Republic*. Book II. Translated by Benjamin Jowett. Accessed August 9, 2015. http://classics.mit.edu/Plato/republic.3.ii.html

Ransom, Ralph. *Steps on the Stairway*. Hollywood, FL: Frederick Fell Pub, 1981.

Rath, Tom. *Strengths Finder 2.0*. New York: Gallup Press, 2007.

Roosevelt, Eleanor. *You Learn by Living: Eleven Keys for a More Fulfilling Life*. New York: Harper & Row, Publishers, Inc., 1960.

Rose, Gilbert J. "The Power of Implicit Motion: It Goes Straight Through." *American Imago*, Spring (2003): 116-121, accessed August 5, 2015. https://muse.jhu.edu/login?-auth=0&type=summary&url=/journals/american_imago/v060/60.1rose_g.html

Roskill, Mark. *Letters of Vincent van Gogh*. Reprint edition. New York: Touchstone, 2008.

Rowling, J. K. *Harry Potter and the Goblet of Fire*. New York: Scholastic Press, 2000.

Shakespeare, William. *Troilus and Cressida*. New York: Digireads.com, 2009.

Shambora, Jessica. "Tom Freston's commencement speech at Emerson College." *Fortune*. May 27, 2009. Accessed August 5, 2015. http://fortune.com/2009/05/27/tom-frestons-commencement-speech-at-emerson-college

Shaw, George Bernard. *Back to Methuselah: In the Beginning*. Complete Plays and Prefaces, Vol. II. New York: Dodd, Mead & Company, 1963.

Star Trek: The Next Generation, Executive Producer Gene Roddenberry, Paramount Domestic Television, 1987–1994. American science fiction television series.

Streep, Meryl. "The Ken Burns Interview." *USA Weekend. com*. 1 Dec. 2002.

Swift, Jonathan and Walter Scott. *The Works of Jonathan Swift: Miscellanies, by Mr. Pope, Dr. Arbuthnot, Mr. Gay, &c. Prose Miscellanies by Swift and Sheridan*, Ulan Press, 2012. Primary source edition. Reproduction of a book published before 1923.

Thoreau, Henry David. "Journal." August 5, 1851. The Walden Woods Project. Accessed August 7, 2015. https://www.walden.org/Library/Quotations/Observation

Vallas, Léon. *Claude Debussy. His Life and Works*. Oxford: Oxford University Press, 1933.

Van Gogh, Vincent and Simon Parke. *Conversations with Van Gogh*. United Kingdom: White Crow Books, 2010.

Warhol, Andy. *The Philosophy of Andy Warhol*. San Diego, CA: Harvest Books, 1977.

Watts, Alan. *The Essence of Alan Watts*. Berkeley: Celestial Arts, 1977.

Weber, Renee. *Dialogues with Scientists and Sages: the Search for Unity*. London: Routledge, 1986.

Wheatley, Margaret J. *Finding Our Way: Leadership for an Uncertain Time*. San Francisco: Berrett-Koehler Publishers, 2007. Kindle edition.

Wilder, Thornton. *The Cabala and the Woman of Andros.* New York: Harper Perennial Modern Classics, 2014. Kindle edition.

Willard, Frances E. "Journal Transcriptions." Transcribed by Carolyn DeSwarte Gifford. Accessed August 5, 2015. http://willard.archivestree.com

Winfrey, Oprah. "What Oprah Knows for Sure About Living in the Moment." *O. The Oprah Magazine.* May, 2002. Accessed August 5, 2015. http://www.oprah.com/spirit/What-Oprah-Knows-for-Sure-About-Living-in-the-Moment

Remaining quotations are from unidentified sources.

About the Author

Dr. Patricia Hoy is a writer, speaker, educator, artist, and forward-thinking activist who works on issues in education, leadership, and the arts. Her widely varied work links the learning that can be gained through the artistic process to successful living, working, teaching, and leading in twenty-first century society.

Dr. Hoy travels throughout the country speaking, consulting, and offering in-services, workshops, professional development, and conference sessions about the many lessons to be learned through the practice and processes of artistic expression. Prior to her *Arts Awareness* work, Dr. Hoy spent more than thirty years in a variety of performance, conducting, and arts education administrative roles, including her work as the Director of Bands at Northern Arizona University, Director of the School of Music at the University of Memphis, and Vice President for Academic Affairs at The Boston Conservatory.

She has served as a guest conductor with professional and semi-professional orchestras as well as college and high school regional and all-state bands in more than thirty states. As an active performer on flute, oboe, clarinet, bassoon, and saxophone, her freelance work history includes performances in orchestral, chamber, solo, jazz, and pop settings.

Dr. Hoy is a recipient of the Tau Beta Sigma Outstanding Service to Music Award in recognition of her national contribution to music and music education and the O. M. Hartsell Excellence in Teaching Music Award presented by the Arizona Music Educators Association. She was honored by her colleagues in 1996 by being elected into the membership of the American Bandmasters Association. While at Northern Arizona University, she was awarded the Faculty Artist Award from the Northern Arizona University Chapter of the Phi Kappa Phi Honor Society. Her wind and chamber recordings of music by African American composers are heard on broadcasts throughout the United States, Canada, and England.

Dr. Hoy holds the Bachelor and Master of Music degrees in woodwind performance from the University of Redlands and a Doctor of Musical Arts degree in orchestral conducting with a minor in bassoon performance from the University of Arizona.

Author note: I invite you to visit my website—www.artsawareness. com—to join in the *Arts Awareness* conversation on my blog posts, Facebook, or Twitter. The future of the site includes podcasts and videos as well as invitations to webinars and teleseminars to explore more deeply the concepts of *Arts Awareness*. If you have an *Arts Awareness* story to tell, I would love to hear about your experiences. You can reach me at *patricia@artsawareness.com*.

Arts Awareness at a Glance

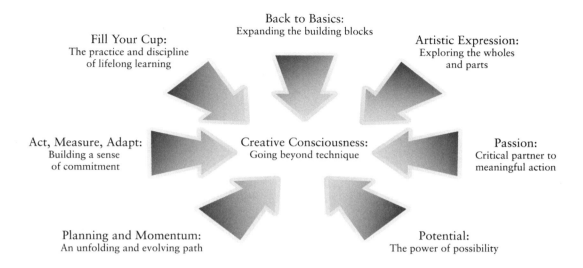

Back to Basics:
Expanding the building blocks

Fill Your Cup:
The practice and discipline
of lifelong learning

Artistic Expression:
Exploring the wholes
and parts

Act, Measure, Adapt:
Building a sense
of commitment

Creative Consciousness:
Going beyond technique

Passion:
Critical partner to
meaningful action

Planning and Momentum:
An unfolding and evolving path

Potential:
The power of possibility